Canada Among Nations 2014

· ·

Canada Among Nations 2014

CRISIS AND REFORM
Canada and the International Financial System

Edited by Rohinton Medhora and Dane Rowlands

Published by the Centre for International Governance Innovation
in partnership with the Norman Paterson School of International Affairs,
Carleton University

ISBN 978-1-928096-00-9 (paper)
ISBN 978-1-928096-01-6 (ebook)

The Centre for International Governance Innovation and Carleton University gratefully acknowledge and thank the International Development Research Centre for its financial support of this publication.

Published by the Centre for International Governance Innovation in partnership with the Norman Paterson School of International Affairs, Carleton University.

Printed and bound in Canada.

Cover and page design by Steve Cross.

Centre for International Governance Innovation
67 Erb Street West
Waterloo, ON Canada N2L 6C2

www.cigionline.org

Contents

● ●

Preface

Rohinton Medhora and Dane Rowlands

• • • • • • • • • • • • • • • • • • • •

This is the 28th edition of the Canada Among Nations series. While the series was conceived and developed at the Norman Paterson School of International Affairs (NPSIA) at Carleton University, it has, over the years, been produced in partnership with other Canadian institutions. This edition is the result of a continuing partnership between NPSIA and the Centre for International Governance Innovation (CIGI), which was first forged for the 2005 edition. This partnership has been enhanced with the generous support of the International Development Research Centre (IDRC). This is the second of three years in which NPSIA, CIGI and the IDRC have worked together on the series, and we all look forward to a productive and innovative collaboration.

From among the many worthy candidate topics for this year's volume of Canada Among Nations, we settled relatively easily on an examination of Canada and the global financial crisis. This choice inevitably reflects the bias of the series co-editors, both of us being economists with an interest in international finance. Since the crisis and associated recession represent the largest decline in global economic activity since the Great Depression of the 1930s and continues to be the prevailing focal point for recent international economic diplomacy, we felt it merited attention in a series dedicated to Canadian international policy. The complication is that the duration and the varied rate at which the crisis appears to be receding from different countries make it difficult to balance the desire for both immediacy and perspective. With the ripples of the crisis still reverberating in many parts of the world (particularly in the euro zone) and with new manifestations of the crisis emerging elsewhere (for example, in some previously unscathed emerging markets), some might argue that this volume is too early. Canada, however, despite remaining vulnerable to the economic anemia and continued financial instability in its key partners, appears to have switched from crisis mode to desultory recovery. While risks remain that the accumulated debts of other countries and the unwinding of their extraordinary monetary measures could yet generate new shocks for a fragile global economy, postponing further our examination of Canada and the crisis risks a response from relatively cosseted Canadians of "Crisis? What crisis?"

Canada Among Nations was established to explore different topics in order to shed light on how Canada's foreign policies are formed, how Canada is affected by world events and they, in turn, by developments here, and to strengthen Canada's research community around a particular theme. We at NPSIA and CIGI, with the IDRC's generous support, look forward to working together in coming years to continue this tradition.

Foreword

Tiff Macklem

●　●　●　●　●　●　●　●　●　●　●　●　●　●　●　●　●　●　●

Canada's financial sector employs about 700,000 people or roughly five percent of Canadian workers. Last year, it generated activity of more than CDN$100 billion or about seven percent of our GDP. These are big numbers, but the contribution of the financial system to Canada's economic growth and prosperity is in fact much larger. More important than its direct contribution is its role as an *enabler* of growth and stability in the rest of the economy. Every day, the financial system channels savings to productive investments, helps households and businesses manage a myriad of risks, and settles billions of transactions to buy and sell goods, services and assets. Many of these credit flows, risks and transactions cross international borders, so it is not only our own financial system that concerns Canadians, but indeed the global financial system.

The global financial system has also helped propel global economic integration, with enormous benefits to Canadians and citizens the world over. Despite frequent shocks to the system, it has facilitated a remarkable postwar expansion in advanced economies and ushered in a new era of rapid economic growth in newly integrated emerging market economies.

But, as the financial crisis that erupted in late 2007 reminded us, the global financial system can also be a source of instability, with devastating consequences. In an integrated world economy, all economies suffer when the financial system of a major country falters. The International Monetary Fund estimates that 30 million people lost their jobs worldwide in the wake of the global financial crisis that began in the United States. That's almost the entire population of Canada. Trust in the global financial system has been undermined, and many are questioning the wisdom of economic integration. The anemic global recovery has done little to dispel these misgivings. In Canada, we weathered the storm better than most. Our financial system proved to be resilient, but the collapse in global trade hit us hard. Our exports plummeted by 21 percent, and today, more than five years after the crisis, they remain below their pre-recession peak.

Reforming financial services and rebuilding trust in the global financial system are essential if we are to return to strong, stable and sustainable growth.

The core message in this volume is that Canada has an important role to play in that process. This excellent collection chronicles the evolution of the global financial system, from the founding of the Bretton Woods institutions following World War II, through to the 2007–2009 global financial crisis and beyond. It reviews and assesses Canada's priorities and influence in shaping the global financial system, and looks ahead to Canada's role in a post-crisis and increasingly multipolar world. The central theme that emerges is that as a mid-sized economic power that relies heavily on an open global trade and financial system, Canada has long invested heavily in promoting a sound global financial system with clear rules and responsibilities for all players. This has been particularly true in the wake of the global financial crisis.

As the chapters by Eric Helleiner and James A. Haley bring to life, Canadian policy makers played a prominent role in the design and formation of the Bretton Woods institutions, and have worked to strengthen these consensus-based institutions and their system of rules and responsibilities. The Group of Twenty (G20) was created in the late 1990s and, as Barry Carin outlines, Canada played an instrumental role in its birth. Tony Porter highlights that Canada's leadership also extends to key financial standard setters and international financial institutions, including the Basel Committee on Banking Supervision, the International Organization of Securities Commissions, the Bank for International Settlements, the Financial Stability Forum and the newly formed Financial Stability Board (FSB).

The 2007–2009 financial crisis increased the demand for Canadian thinking at the global table. The question that I have been asked more than any other in capitals around the world during recent years is: how is it that no banks failed or had to be rescued in Canada? Canada is right next door to the United

States and its financial markets are the most integrated with the US financial system, yet in the wake of the Lehman failure, it was UK and European banks that failed or had to be rescued. The chapters by Eric Santor and Lawrence Schembri, David Longworth, Louis Pauly and Randall Germain argue that the resilience of the Canadian financial system reflects a combination of factors, including the lessons learned from our own earlier failures, higher financial regulatory standards, more rigorous supervision on the ground and better coordination across our financial authorities.

These chapters, together with the contribution by Domenico Lombardi and Pierre Siklos, review the important role Canada has played in the sweeping financial reform agenda launched by the G20 at the London summit in April 2009 and assigned to the FSB. This has included importing Canadian thinking into the Basel capital standards and introducing a Canadian-style leverage cap; Julie Dickson's leadership of the FSB initiative to strengthen supervisory practices around the world; my own chairmanship of a new FSB peer review process to transparently assess the adoption of and adherence to the new standards; Mark Carney's chairmanship of the FSB; and the Canada-India co-chairmanship of the G20 "Framework for Strong, Sustainable and Balanced Growth." Canada has had a prominent place at the global table in recent years.

Other chapters in this volume draw the links to trade (John Curtis), development (Roy Culpeper) and the European Monetary Union (Juliet Johnson), and also reflect on what has been accomplished and where we go from here. These are more difficult questions. Together, the chapters in this volume provide a comprehensive analysis of what went wrong, what worked, what's been fixed and where the jury is still out. They also candidly assess where Canada has made a difference and where it has missed opportunities.

There can be no doubt that the crisis was the catalyst for a tremendous burst of reform to the global financial system; Canada has had a significant influence on this reform, and much has been accomplished. Banks are safer, crisis management has been strengthened and the plumbing of the financial system has been reinforced.

Still, some Canadian humility is required. There is much work to be done to fully implement the reforms that have been agreed. In many global banks it is more than the capital and liquidity rules that must change — a shift in culture is required to return the focus of banking to serving clients in support of the real economy. Financial fragmentation must be avoided if we are to reap the benefits of economic integration. And continued vigilance will be needed on the part of supervisors and central banks to identify and mitigate new systemic vulnerabilities as they emerge.

There are also some bigger issues. The inflexibility of the international monetary system remains a problem and the governance of the global financial system is a patchwork. As James Boughton writes in the final summary chapter, "There is no institution with a mandate to oversee, much less guide, the [international financial system]." At the same time, there is a risk that Canada's influence could wane. As Boughton highlights, with the urgency of the crisis fading and now large emerging market economies taking a bigger seat at the global table, it is going to be more difficult for Canada to make its voice heard.

Fortunately, this volume concludes with a range of suggestions on what Canada can do to remain an influential player in the design of the global financial system. The stakes are high. This volume leaves us all better prepared.

Acronyms

· ·

ABCP	asset-backed commercial paper
AIG	American International Group
AMF	Autorité des marchés financiers
APEC	Asia-Pacific Economic Cooperation
BCBS	Basel Committee on Banking Supervision
BIS	Bank for International Settlements
BoC	Bank of Canada
BoE	Bank of England
bps	basis points
BRICS	Brazil, Russia, India, China and South Africa
CACs	collective action clauses
CBA	Canadian Bankers' Association
CC	conditional commitment
CCB	Canadian Commercial Bank
CCF	Cooperative Commonwealth Federation
CCPs	central counterparties
CDFAI	Canadian Defence and Foreign Affairs Institute
CDIC	Canadian Deposit Insurance Corporation
CDN	Canadian
CDN-SIB	Canadian systemically important bank
CDOR	Canadian Dealer Offered Rate
CDOR-OIS	Canadian Dealer Offered Rate-overnight indexed swap
CGFS	Committee on the Global Financial Crisis
CIGI	Centre for International Governance Innovation
CMHC	Canada Mortgage and Housing Corporation
COD	cash on delivery
CPI	consumer price index
CPSS	Committee on Payment and Settlements Systems
EC	European Commission

ECB	European Central Bank
EDP	excessive debt procedure
EMDCs	emerging market and developing countries
EMEs	emerging market economies
ESFS	European System of Financial Supervision
ESM	European Stability Mechanism
FDI	foreign direct investment
FISC	Financial Institutions Supervisory Committee
FLS	Funding for Lending Scheme
FOMC	Federal Open Market Committee
FSAP	Financial Sector Assessment Program
FSB	Financial Stability Board
FSF	Financial Stability Forum
FSOC	Financial Stability Oversight Council
G5	Group of Five
G7	Group of Seven
G8	Group of Eight
G10	Group of Ten
G20	Group of Twenty
G22	Group of Twenty-Two
G24	Group of Twenty-Four
GATT	General Agreement on Tariffs and Trade
G-SIB	global systemically important bank
GVC	global value chain
HIPC	Heavily Indebted Poor Country
IASB	International Accounting Standards Board
IASC	International Accounting Standards Committee
IBRD	International Bank for Reconstruction and Development
IDRC	International Development Research Centre
IFS	international financial system
IMF	International Monetary Fund
IMFC	International Monetary and Financial Committee
IOSCO	International Organization of Securities Commissions
LTROs	long-term refinancing operations
MAP	Mutual Assessment Process (G20)
MDGs	Millennium Development Goals (UN)
MDRI	Multilateral Debt Reduction Initiative
MIP	Macroeconomic Imbalance Procedure
NPSIA	Norman Paterson School of International Affairs
ODA	official development assistance
OECD	Organisation for Economic Co-operation and Development
OIGB	Office of the Inspector General of Banks

OIS	overnight indexed swap
OMT	Outright Monetary Transactions
OSC	Ontario Securities Commission
OSFI	Office of the Superintendent of Financial Institutions
OTC	over-the-counter
PRA	Purchase and Resale Agreement
QE	quantitative easing
RIIA	Royal Institute of International Affairs
SCSI	Standing Committee on Standards Implementation (FSB)
SDRM	Sovereign Debt Restructuring Mechanism
SGP	Stability and Growth Pact
SIB	systemically important bank
SRM	single resolution mechanism
SSBs	standard-setting bodies
SSM	single supervisory mechanism
TPRM	Trade Policy Review Mechanism
VaR	value at risk
WTO	World Trade Organization
ZLB	zero lower bound

Introduction

Rohinton Medhora and Dane Rowlands

• • • • • • • • • • • • • • • • • • •

MOTIVATION

The period from 1985 until near the end of 2008 has been referred to by some economists as the "Great Moderation," in reference to the marked reduction in economic volatility in key global economies such as the United States. Some analysts went so far as to wonder whether central banks and finance departments in most major industrial countries had found the key to economic stability, and now possessed the tools needed to tame the business cycle into the distant future. Like some classical Greek tragedy, that hubris came to an abrupt and humiliating end by the close of 2008. Global output growth of over five percent in 2007 slowed and became a decline of over one percent in 2009 (International Monetary Fund [IMF] 2009). Advanced economies fared even worse, with their output declining by 3.4 percent. When blame for the crisis came to be assigned, much of it was placed at the door of financial markets.

The most frequently cited trigger for the crisis was the popping of the US housing market bubble in 2006, which then set in motion a chain of shocks that were transmitted around the world by the international financial system (IFS). What had been seen as worrying but minor and isolated domestic problems in different parts of the world, became catastrophes as financial systems became paralyzed with paranoia about counterparty risks and the real values of financial assets. Inevitably, these financial sector difficulties had real sector implications, as liquidity in the market dried up and buyers were incapable of financing purchases, firms were left bereft of working capital to pay employees and suppliers, and investment opportunities were left dormant for want of capital. For many, the main villain was the financial system, and it was the IFS that transmitted the disease, even to countries that had declined to partake in the excesses of financial innovation.

International finance is a big part of the economic lives of Canadians, even if we don't always have much direct contact with it. The Bank for International Settlements (BIS) estimates that turnover in the global foreign exchange market reached US$5.3 trillion per day in 2013, a 35 percent increase over the 2010 level of US$4 trillion per day (BIS 2013). This rapid growth of international transactions hit a peak at 72 percent from 2004–2007 in the lead up to the global financial crisis exchanges (ibid.). Over the main crisis period of 2007–2010, this three-year growth slowed markedly, but was still at 19 percent. The financial system's expansion seems inexorable, even in the face of dramatic crisis.

In contrast to the more freewheeling nature of the financial systems in many other wealthy countries, Canada was seen as a bit of a financial backwater. A cozy oligopoly of banks anchored a stable if uninspired system, where financial innovation was slow and profits assured by high transaction fees on a captive market. Prior to the crisis, there was pressure on the banks and bank regulators to modernize the system faster in areas such as mortgage finance. Canada was seen as having erred too much on the side of stability at the cost of efficiency. Fast-forward to the post-crisis era and the Canadian system is seen as worthy of emulation, while its alternatives attract opprobrium. But the perceived optimal trade-off between stability and efficiency in financial regulation is a pendulum that swings with the times, and the crisis has set off yet another round in this long-standing debate about the financial system.

THE FINANCIAL SYSTEM AND SCOPE OF THIS VOLUME

A key role of the financial system is to mediate between savings and investment. This quite simple description means that "financial markets facilitate such central economic actions as producing and trading, earning and spending, saving and investing, accumulating and retiring, transferring and bequeathing" (Friedman 1987). These functions are just as true today as they were when the subject was first treated by classical economists over two centuries ago. Indeed, financial development is correctly seen as integral to the larger process of economic development. However, as financial systems have grown and become more complex and connected, they have gone beyond neutral mediation and enablers of growing economies to sources of disturbance to them.

The wide array of sometimes quite opaque assets generated by financial innovation has confounded national authorities even in advanced countries, where capacities and regulatory structures are well developed. Many of these financial innovations and their economic consequences — good and bad — occur even in the absence of national borders. Finance has become complicated in most countries, even without the international context.

With globalization, however, finance has become exponentially more difficult to control. The movement of capital has outpaced the capabilities of domestic regulators to monitor and manage their own savings and investment systems, and the presence of international financial linkages offer opportunities for firms to circumvent domestic regulations and arbitrage across competing national rules. The development of these extra-national financial activities and linkages has proceeded far faster than the evolution of an international capacity to regulate capital at the global level. This dichotomy between the need for institutional capacity at the global level and the inability of the state-based system to deliver such governance is common in all areas of international affairs, but it is, perhaps, most pronounced in the hyperactive and instantaneous field of global finance.

The speed of innovation and the complexity of financial instruments have left regulators, and many others, at a loss as to how to evaluate the trade-off between the risk and efficiency of new financial products. Thus it was that the act of bundling mortgages of varied quality into seemingly self-standing financial instruments in the United States was first seen as an ingenious new financial instrument, and only later recognized as a key trigger and transmission mechanism of global crisis. There are dozens of other fractured links that brought the global financial chain to the breaking point in 2008, from an incomplete monetary union in Europe to the over-accumulation of foreign exchange reserves in China. In the end, the net result is that financial systems have gone well beyond the classical ideal role of a neutral and efficient mechanism for allocating savings to productive investment activities, liquidity provision and risk mitigation, and have emerged as a major source of national and international economic instability.

Any examination of the financial crisis encounters the additional problem of scope. Even a focus on Canada requires choosing one of many specific, but ultimately fairly narrow, perspectives that others might regard as unbalanced, even misguided. Our chosen emphasis is on understanding the evolution of the IFS that transmitted the crisis around the world, and the Canadian policy response and role within that system. As many notable commentators such as Carmen Reinhart and Kenneth Rogoff (2009) have observed, the virulence of this particular recession arises primarily from the accompanying financial crisis that rendered many domestic and international financial markets incapable of playing their core roles of liquidity provision and financial intermediation. Our chosen focus on history and interconnectedness, however, comes at the cost of having to subordinate other important dimensions of the crisis.

The three key omissions that we recognize as editors of this volume, and that the contributors correctly raised during our discussions, but did not have as part of their specific chapter mandates, are: the real economic and social implications of the crisis for Canadians; the other areas of public policy response (notably fiscal stimulus); and an integration of the details of some of the other real-economy dimensions of the crisis' origins and transmission (specifically trade and investment flows). To provide appropriate context and offer some penance for these omissions, these items are briefly reviewed here.

Canadians felt the pain of the economic and social dislocation caused by the crisis. In terms of the accompanying recession, quarterly Canadian GDP (income-based) fell from its pre-crisis high of CDN$1.682 trillion in the third quarter of 2008 to a low of CDN$1.545 trillion in the second quarter of 2009, a decline of around eight percent; output did not return to pre-crisis levels until the fourth quarter of 2010 (Statistics Canada 2014a). Mirroring these output numbers, unemployment rose from 5.9 percent at the beginning of 2008 to 8.7 percent by August 2009, slowly declining thereafter to its current level of around seven percent towards the end of 2013 (Statistics Canada 2014b). The percentage of the unemployed out of work for more than a year almost doubled from 7.1 percent in 2008 to 13.5 percent in 2011 (Organisation for Economic Co-operation and Development [OECD] 2014). The poverty rate (percentage of the total population with disposable income that is 50 percent below the median disposable income level) increased from 11.3 percent in 2007 to 12.3 percent in 2009, representing almost 340,000 more Canadians below the defined poverty line (ibid.). While the comparisons of economic and social statistics often show that Canada did relatively better and suffered relatively less than its Group of Seven (G7) partners and many or most OECD countries, the fact that the crisis had serious, even tragic, consequences for many Canadians cannot be ignored. The authors of the chapters in this book are clearly aware of this important and wider social context, but were constrained to focus on their more narrowly defined tasks of examining the financial policy implications of the crisis.

While the volume focuses on finance, we must also acknowledge that the public policy response went beyond the domestic and international dimensions of monetary policy and financial supervision. We made the decision not to address these responses directly because most were undertaken largely within the context of purely domestic policy frameworks, and with only minimal international spillovers and coordination. For example, the Canadian government's discretionary and automatic fiscal expansion in response to the crisis certainly contributed to our stronger aggregate economic performance relative to many other wealthy nations. Canada's structural fiscal surplus moved from 1.1 percent of GDP in 2007 to a deficit of 0.8 percent the following year and, ultimately, to a maximum deficit of 3.3 percent of GDP in 2010 (IMF 2013). The cumulative magnitude of Canada's associated fiscal expansion over the five years after the crisis (2008–2013), relative to what it would have been had the 2007 structural surplus been continued, amounted to 19.7 percent of GDP. This was the third-largest expansion of the G7 countries, exceeded only by Japan (28.5 percent) and the United States (20.2 percent). By contrast, Italy had a contractionary fiscal position over the 2008–2013 period relative to their 2007 balance, amounting to a total of 4.5 percent of their GDP. Therefore, the Canadian government had a fairly robust fiscal expansion following the crisis, despite having a perceived relatively shallower recession.[1] In theory, the Canadian government's fiscal policy could have been affected by the international attempts to coordinate an expansion, as was

---

1   It should be noted that the magnitude of the fiscal expansion and the recession are, of course, not independent, since the fiscal response could be seen as having caused a relatively shallower recession. It is difficult to identify the counterfactual of what the recession would have looked like in the absence of the fiscal and other policy responses.

the case with discussions within the Group of Twenty (G20), but in the end, these decisions primarily reflect domestic policy-making processes designed to address domestic economic priorities. There was no international attempt to introduce any formal regulatory or organizational framework to coordinate fiscal responses in the same manner as there was for financial regulation or even monetary policy. With no real international regime or formal framework for fiscal discussions, there was really no critical international dimension to Canada's policies in this regard. Similarly, while there were some discussions about social protection, these were typically parallel to the crisis response rather than integral to it, and despite its earlier origins in the same discussions that created the Bretton Woods system (see chapter 1), such discussions were largely a response to the anticipated and impending expiry of the United Nations Millennium Development Goals initiative. Hence, from the perspective of international policy, it did not seem that much attention needed to be lavished on these additional responses to the crisis.

Finally, our contributors were not asked to dwell on the origins of the crisis. These debates do inevitably emerge in some of the chapters, and the links between the financial sector and the international economy do get some specific attention (see chapter 9). While much of the blame for the crisis has been attributed to some combination of "financial excess" (however defined) and inadequate regulation, the pre-crisis debate about potential economic risks focused on imbalances in external accounts, conflicting exchange rate regimes and unsustainable debt. There are, thus, dimensions of the crisis debate that encompass a wider set of connections and linkages beyond the financial sector. These links are clearly seen in the standard measures of international imbalances. For example, in the third quarter of 2008, Canada had a current account surplus of just over CDN$5 billion. By the next quarter, this balance had switched dramatically to a CDN$10 billion deficit. That deficit has persisted ever since, reaching a high of over CDN$18 billion in the third quarter of 2010, remaining until now (third quarter 2013) at over CDN$16 billion (Statistics Canada 2014c). More broadly, many observers saw the pre-crisis US current account deficit (which had reached six percent of GDP in 2007, twice the typical threshold of three percent for avoiding a payments crisis) as unsustainable and at critical levels. Whether these imbalances arose from pathologies in either the current account or its obverse, the capital account, or whether they arose from more fundamental and deeper domestic economic imbalances, is an important question, but one we do not seek to answer in this volume.

Our policy focus has instead guided us toward how this crisis has affected the policy responses to the problem of how to manage an international financial and monetary system. The typical starting point for such a discussion is the post-World War II system created at the Bretton Woods conference, where illustrious experts and public officials wrestled with the same sorts of policy questions that arise in this volume: who should provide surveillance of the global system and how should they do so; how will we apportion the burden of adjustment when imbalances emerge; what is the proper framework for determining exchange rates; how should we constrain or shape domestic monetary and financial rules to support a stable international system; and how much domestic sovereignty should be given up for the common good? Calls for a "new Bretton Woods," a phrase that emerges in several chapters in this volume and was a recurrent theme at our authors' workshop, is effectively a recognition that the current post-Bretton Woods system has failed to deliver international stability, and thus there is the need to revisit the same fundamental conundrums and attempt once again to solve them with a new, improved comprehensive and integrated system. By implication, piecemeal and incremental reform is unlikely to be adequate, and certainly not in the absence of acknowledging and resolving the core tensions at the heart of any such system.

THE CHAPTERS

It is, therefore, at Bretton Woods that this volume starts, with an overview of the fundamental elements of international financial policy cooperation being provided in the first two chapters by Eric Helleiner and James A. Haley, respectively. In many ways, this broader conception of the core tensions within the IFS frames the more detailed analyses about the subsequent evolution of the related institutional arrangements (chapters by Barry Carin and Tony Porter, as well as Haley), its links to trade (the chapter by John M. Curtis), the operations of monetary authorities (chapters by Eric Santor and Lawrence Schembri, and Domenico Lombardi and Pierre Siklos) and financial regulators (the chapter by David Longworth). The remaining chapters examine these matters from the perspective of other country groups

(Juliet Johnson and Roy Culpeper) or address even broader questions about national sovereignty (Louis W. Pauly) and the overall balance between the indulgence and restraint of the interests of private capital (Randall Germain). Their arguments are reviewed in more detail below.

A common theme for all chapters, however, is a focus on Canadian policy responses to the crisis. How did Canada's integration with the global economy cause it to respond to a crisis that was largely created outside its borders? What lessons did Canada learn from others? To what extent were its policy responses shaped by its obligations to the international system and its partner countries, and in coordination with them? Did Canada provide new ideas and examples of best practice to the world stage? Was Canada able to leverage its limited power in support of its own domestic interests? To what extent do Canada's interests coincide with those of the global community and international system? These are the challenges we posed to our authors.

A principal objective of this volume is to situate contemporary discussions of Canada and the IFS in a historical context. The logical place to start is the Bretton Woods conference, held over three weeks in July 1944. In the opening chapter to this book, Eric Helleiner signals the leading role that the Canadian negotiators took at the conference, particularly in three areas that might have formed the contours of a stable and effective postwar economic order — "inclusive multilateralism"; support for capital controls and, more broadly, international macroeconomic cooperation; and social protection worldwide. It is striking how resonant these themes are to current debates in the field.

The conference resulted in the creation of two and a half institutions — the International Bank for Reconstruction and Development, the IMF, and the General Agreement on Tariffs and Trade — that together were meant to underpin a liberal postwar economic order. In practice, the system has been more stovepiped than the founding fathers might have anticipated, with the IMF the clear lead in all matters related to international money, finance and macroeconomics. Chapters 2, 3 and 4 (by James A. Haley, Barry Carin and Tony Porter) treat three aspects of the evolution of the global financial system and Canada's role in it.

James A. Haley provides an account of the key debates in the IMF that, in his words, are meant to "complete the work of Bretton Woods." Incidentally, like Eric Helleiner, he too shows that the quality and breadth of proposals put on the table at Bretton Woods were high and wide indeed, almost belying the narrower bandwidth of such discussion subsequently. A series of debt crises starting with Mexico in 1994 once again highlighted the age-old question of the balance between adjustment in creditor and in debtor nations under fixed and flexible exchange rates. A parallel challenge was the nature and pace of capital account liberalization. A third connected stream was the orderly resolution of sovereign debt, surveillance more broadly and the minimization of moral hazard. Canada has worked with the IMF on all of these questions, and particularly on the basic one of IMF governance, for the credibility and effectiveness of the IMF depends on it.

Canada's role — indeed seminal role — in the broader governance issues of the international monetary system is described by Barry Carin through the lens of the G20. Born in crisis (first at the economic ministers' level in 1999, and then at the leaders' level in 2008) and by necessity structured in an ad hoc manner, this group continues to see itself as the "management board" of the global economy. The obvious trade-off here — between balanced representation and effectiveness — has yet to be addressed, particularly as there is growing disappointment about the concrete impacts of the G20's deliberations. Carin suggests a series of these discussions in which Canada is well placed to take the lead, mainly to keep the focus on economic management, add longer-term problems, such as climate change, within this context and strengthen the quality of analysis on which the leaders deliberate.

The development of the Financial Stability Board (FSB) (née Financial Stability Forum [FSF]) has tracked that of the G20, and Tony Porter covers its evolution. Just as former Prime Minister Paul Martin did in the G20, Canada has had an outsized role in the FSF/FSB with Mark Carney, Tiff Macklem and Julie Dickson. They, in turn, have no doubt had "wind on their backs" by the widespread recognition that Canada's banks have received for their resilience and probity in the face of financial distress all around them. Still, Porter notes, "For a country Canada's size, it is unusual to have this number of regulators with this level of recognition." Clearly, here is a case where policies and the persons who steward them are mutually strengthening. But Porter ends on an appropriate note of caution in two regards — the still fractured nature of securities regulation in the Canadian federation and the sideswipes from such developments as the implementation of the Volcker rule in the United States.

This theme continues in subsequent chapters. David Longworth (chapter 5) reiterates the exceptionally active nature of Canada in the financial regulation arena, due to both its policies and its people. Five elements of a "Canadian model" in financial regulation might be discerned from his exposition: exceeding minimum international standards (for example, in capital adequacy); creating an environment that fosters cooperation among domestic regulators; avoiding a legalistic, confrontational regulatory regime, and instead relying on principles and guidance; using mortgage insurance rules to buttress macroprudential policies; and more broadly, viewing supervision as an "art." He, too, ends on a cautionary note, observing that countries, such as Australia, Canada and Sweden that weathered the crisis, have ongoing credit and housing booms that might still "end badly." Properly, there is no claim that the Canadian model can or should be exported, as is, to other countries.

Eric Santor and Lawrence Schembri (chapter 6) relate Canada's response to the crisis and lessons learned from it, from the perspective of serving officials at the Bank of Canada (BoC). Two important lessons, one domestic and the other international, are derived from their experience. The first is that since the economic consequences of the crisis are high and persistent, financial stability is now given the same prominence as monetary policy is in central banking. Second, thanks to financial integration, global cooperation must be privileged. The FSB is held up as a salient example. They also recognize the limits of central banking actions in dealing with all of the outcomes of the crisis, notably on the real and microeconomic side. Global recovery, as opposed to global crisis management, requires "appropriately timed fiscal consolidation in the advanced economies," structural reform in the euro zone and East Asia, and greater exchange rate flexibility in emerging market countries with current account surpluses.

Domenico Lombardi and Pierre Siklos (chapter 7) also centre their contribution to this volume on the role of the central bank, but focus on what has come to be termed the unconventional part of central bank policies. The starting point for unconventional action is agility, a "recognition that monetary policy strategies are not timeless." Although, on account of having weathered the crisis better than many other countries, Canada's central bank did not have to resort to unconventional policies, it did establish principles to create — and procedures to operate — extended liquidity facilities. These, coupled with the pre-existing ability to target specific market segments (such as housing), bode well for whatever a future crisis might bring.

All chapters in this volume explicitly or implicitly buy into Louis W. Pauly's (chapter 8) dictum that integrated markets require integrated oversight. Put another way, countries must cede autonomy in dealing with matters of money and finance to existing and emerging supranational bodies. How much autonomy, and when and why depends on the country and the state of the multilateral organizations themselves. While the role of the FSB is defined and strengthened, and the IMF continues its quest to reform its own governance and enhance its purview to include the impact of countries' monetary and financial policies nationally and (crucially) beyond, Canadians will "buy insurance just in case." This insurance is in the form of the domestic power of all of the national institutions that stood Canada in such good stead these past few years — notably the BoC, the Office of the Superintendent of Financial Institutions and the federal Department of Finance. There isn't a better indicator of Canada within the global financial system than this — extraordinarily active multilaterally to create the right global structures, yet just as prudent domestically to ensure that stability remains a hallmark of policy.

The principals at the Bretton Woods conference foresaw the links between trade and finance, but they did so in a world that was not as integrated as it is currently, and consequently, their analytical tools did not stand the test of time. In this world, international capital movements essentially accommodated domestic savings-investment imbalances, which in turn manifest themselves through trade imbalances. In reality, there are several channels that connect international trade and finance. To be sure, capital flows are triggered by domestic savings-investment imbalances. But with integrated capital markets and constant financial innovation, capital flows are multiples of the value of trade flows and trigger short-run exchange rate volatility as well as lock in persistently misaligned exchange rates. Moreover, financial sector fragility has consequences on the availability of finance for trade. These and the related questions of real financial linkages and side effects are covered in the chapters by John M. Curtis (chapter 9), Juliet Johnson (chapter 10) and Roy Culpeper (chapter 11).

Curtis notes that the institutional links between the IMF and the World Trade Organization (WTO) are pro forma, and have not resulted in any meaningful appreciation of the consequences of monetary policies on trade at the IMF or the obverse at the WTO. Picking up on the point made by several authors in this volume about the intellectual leadership that Canada has shown in the financial regulation arena, he notes that Canada has considerable credibility intellectually in the trade-finance nexus of issues as well. The pioneering work of Harold Innis and W. A. Mackintosh on "staples" anticipated the literature on the "resource curse." Robert Mundell is recognized for his seminal contributions to our understanding of open economy macroeconomics and optimum currency areas. The list must also include Richard Lipsey (theory of the second best), and James Brander and Barbara Spencer (strategic trade policy). While Curtis does not point to a unique way forward, the first step in seeking it is mapping the connections in this complex set of issues. He ends his chapter on a more pragmatic note — the way ahead might lie in assessing the role of the US dollar in the global economy, and the incentives and disincentives that the United States faces in revisiting the status quo.

Nowhere else has the complex web of issues related to the current financial crisis gone more awry — and predictably so — than in the euro zone. Indeed, in this region, the crisis is not simply financial, but increasingly social and political. Juliet Johnson outlines what went wrong under the label of four challenges: lack of adherence to the fiscal compact that underlay the monetary union; the "original sin" nature of the limits to the role of the common central bank; inadequate financial sector oversight nationally and regionally; and disparate growth models, particularly between the northern and southern members. Canada is not directly involved in the euro-zone situation nor is it among those most affected by events there. But it inserted itself into the global debate on this issue in three ways: by vocal support for the European Central Bank's foray into unconventional monetary policies; by overtly supporting the non-European candidate Augustin Carstens, rather than France's Christine Lagarde to head the IMF in June 2011; and by joining the United States in not contributing to the European stabilization fund cobbled together by the IMF. The latter two are particularly telling, not just for their substance, but also the forthrightness with which Canada expressed its views, vis-à-vis a region considered a traditional ally and intellectual soulmate of Canada. Johnson's prognosis for what remains a messy situation: the union "staggers on."

The narrative about the current financial crisis is — correctly — mostly about advanced economies, mainly the United States and Western Europe. This is where the roots of the crisis lie, and this is where its consequences are felt the most. In this narrative, developing countries and particularly the emerging economies escaped the worst of the crisis, either because they were on hyper growth paths and/or had achieved structural transformations that made them more resilient to exogenous events. Roy Culpeper puts this group's performance in context. No country has been immune from the crisis. Growth rates have slowed appreciably everywhere in the developing and emerging worlds. And currency volatility or misalignment, already high in many countries, has only increased in late 2013 and early 2014 on account of the announced tapering by the US Federal Reserve. What has looked like resilience in developing countries might be damaging, nationally and globally, in the long run. The list here would include holding abnormally high levels of currency reserves (so-called self-insurance), a reliance on domestic savings, investments and markets, and forays into commodity derivatives. While the association of Canada with the development enterprise is a long and honourable one and should be seen on its own merits, Canada's active role to make the IMF more inclusive and effective, and create a more stable international financial architecture holds additional benefits for developing and emerging economies.

A second narrative about the current financial crisis is that liberalization and economic integration has reached a limit. While national finance grew, but was fettered by national regulatory institutions and policies through most of the post-World War II era, global finance grew unabated because of the absence of parallel institutions and regulations internationally. The consequences of an unfettered global financial system were felt, starting with the implosions in the United States and Western Europe in 2008, and continue to be felt today. As a result, nationally, governments have implemented new measures to oversee and control their financial players, and they continue to work to do the same internationally as well. Randall Germain (chapter 12; emphasis in original) fleshes out this thesis and largely agrees with it — "we have turned a corner towards what might be identified as an increasingly *deliberalized* and somewhat *deglobalized* global political economy." But the conclusion is a nuanced one. The forces whose interest lies in financial globalization are powerful and rich; the vast amounts of liquidity pumped into the system during the monetary stimulus years will lend only more strength to them. In Canada, where banks have historically readily traded heavier regulation for a captive domestic market, the turn away from innovation towards stability is only more of the same.

In his concluding essay to the volume, James M. Boughton reminds us of the web of international institutions tasked with governing the IFS, and the rules and norms under which each operates — "to call this structure a 'non-system' is clearly a misnomer, and yet it would be just as wrong to pretend that it is a complete and integrated system." Building on the theme recurrent throughout the volume about Canada punching above its weight, he reminds us that Canada might have played an even larger role in all of this (if, for example, one or more of its three candidates to run the IMF had ever been properly promoted by the Canadian authorities and selected to do the job). It is precisely the gap between the needs of the current day to encourage and regulate a global financial system and the imperfection of current propositions such as the G20 and International Monetary and Financial Committee that provides Canada with the opportunity to continue to play its outsized role in the future.

Financial sector development and regulation is a work in progress within individual states at the national level, and collectively at the global level. The instruments the global community has to manage these complex national and international systems are varied, potentially powerful, but also imperfect and almost certainly hold consequences — good and bad — not yet foreseen. Canada, the dispassionate player with capabilities that belie its size, can continue to play a powerful role in these developments, even as Canadians continue to face the consequences of the actions of their government, business people and those in other countries. Here, as in so much else, Canada is indeed among nations.

Acknowledgements

We would like to thank Carol Bonnett for managing this project and ensuring the design and production of this book in a timely manner; Vivian Moser for her careful editing and proofreading; and Lauren Amundsen for organizing the authors' meeting in Waterloo in December 2013. Rory Morrison, Bente Molenaar Neufeld and Lisa Scheltema provided assistance for Carleton's participation. We also thank Samantha St. Amand of the

Centre for International Governance Innovation (CIGI) for excellent research assistance. We are grateful for the financial support of Carleton University, CIGI and the International Development Research Centre. Last, but certainly not least, we thank all the contributors to this volume, and the external reviewers, for all their hard work in meeting our tight deadlines and ensuring the delivery of manuscripts of high quality.

WORKS CITED

BIS. 2013. "Triennial Central Bank Survey." September. www.bis.org/publ/rpfx13fx.pdf.

Friedman, Benjamin M. 1987. "Capital, Credit and Money Markets." In *The New Palgrave: A Dictionary of Economics.*

IMF. 2009. *World Economic Outlook.* Washington, DC: IMF.

————. 2013. *World Economic Outlook.* Washington, DC: IMF. October.

OECD. 2014. "Country Statistical Profiles: Canada." OECD database. http://stats.oecd.org/.

Reinhart, Carmen and Kenneth Rogoff. 2009. *This Time is Different: Eight Centuries of Financial Folly.* Princeton, NJ: Princeton University Press.

Statistics Canada. 2014a. "Table 380-0063: Gross Domestic Product, Income-based." www5.statcan.gc.ca/cansim/a26?lang=eng&retrLang=eng&id=3800063&paSer=&pattern=&stByVal=1&p1=1&p2=1&tabMode=dataTable&csid=.

————. 2014b. "Table 282-0087: Labour Force Survey Estimates (LFS), by Sex and Age Group, Seasonally Adjusted and Unadjusted." www5.statcan.gc.ca/cansim/a26?lang=eng&retrLang=eng&id=2820087&paSer=&pattern=&stByVal=1&p1=1&p2=1&tabMode=dataTable&csid=.

————. 2014c. "Table 376-0103: Balance of International Payments, Current Account and Capital Account." www5.statcan.gc.ca/cansim/a26?lang=eng&retrLang=eng&id=3760103&paSer=&pattern=&stByVal=1&p1=1&p2=1&tabMode=dataTable&csid=.

1

Inclusiveness and Creativity at the Creation: Canada and the Bretton Woods Negotiations

Eric Helleiner

● ● ● ● ● ● ● ● ● ● ● ● ● ● ● ● ● ●

The Bretton Woods conference of 1944 is often a touchstone for those seeking to redesign global financial governance in the wake of international financial crises. Drawing lessons from the Great Depression, the Bretton Woods architects developed a comprehensive design of a new international financial order for the postwar world. The innovative and ambitious nature of their vision and its enduring influence has served as an inspiration for reformers ever since.

It is sometimes forgotten that Canadian officials played an important role in the Bretton Woods negotiations alongside more famous US and British policy makers such as Harry Dexter White and John Maynard Keynes. Canadian policy makers were particularly supportive of three aspects of the Bretton Woods vision that have often been neglected: its inclusive multilateralism; its support for capital controls and international cooperation to bolster their effectiveness; and its prioritization of social protection worldwide. This chapter argues that these aspects of Bretton Woods deserve to be remembered today because of their relevance to contemporary international policy debates in the wake of the 2008 global financial crisis.

THE IMPORTANCE OF INCLUSIVE MULTILATERALISM

The 2008 crisis has prompted initiatives to bolster more inclusive forms of global financial governance than existed before the crisis. As the crisis intensified in the fall of 2008, the Group of Seven (G7) was quickly shoved aside by the more widely constituted Group of Twenty (G20) forum that had first been created at the level of financial officials in 1999. Meeting now at the leaders' level for the first time, the G20 then replaced the G7-dominated Financial Stability Forum with the G20-dominated Financial Stability Board (FSB) in April 2009. Important international standard-setting bodies (SSBs), such as the Basel Committee, also widened their membership in 2009 to include all G20 countries.

These reforms have been important in widening the governing clubs of global finance. But a large number of countries remain unrepresented in the G20, the FSB and key SSBs, and their exclusion generates resentments. A more legitimate form of global financial governance would be centred around institutions with more universal membership in which all countries can participate. The International Monetary Fund (IMF) and World Bank have such universal membership, but their significance is often overshadowed by the other more network-based governance clubs.

The universality of the Bretton Woods institutions reflects the strong commitment of the 1944 conference to inclusive multilateralism. Indeed, the Bretton Woods negotiations pioneered the application of this concept to global financial governance. Before those discussions, the only official multilateral financial institution in existence was the Bank for International Settlements, a narrowly constituted body established in 1930, with the central banks of only six countries (Belgium, Britain, France, Germany, Italy and Japan) as founding members. By contrast, the Bretton Woods agreements established two public international financial institutions at the core of global financial governance whose membership was open to all the United Nations and "Associated Nations" (the latter referred to countries that had broken diplomatic relations with the Axis powers during World War II, but had not formally joined the United Nations).

US President Franklin Roosevelt's administration was particularly committed to this vision of inclusive public multilateralism, even in the face of vociferous opposition from the New York financial community. The bankers preferred a "key currency" approach to postwar stabilization involving the extension of a bilateral loan to Britain to restore sterling's convertibility, rather than the establishment of multilateral financial institutions. In rejecting that approach, US Treasury Secretary Henry Morgenthau made the following case: "I doubt that the 42 other United and Associated Nations, who have been fighting and working with us during the war, would take kindly to what might be regarded as dictatorship of the world's finances by two countries.... The fact is that the problems considered at Bretton Woods are international problems, common to all countries, that can be dealt with only through broad international cooperation" (Morgenthau 1945, 192).

This support for inclusive multilateralism was apparent in the very first US drafts of the Bretton Woods proposals, developed by Harry Dexter White in early 1942, which called special attention to the needs of smaller countries:

> It is true that rich and powerful countries can for long periods
> safely and easily ignore the interests of poorer or weaker
> neighbors or competitors, but by doing so they only imperil the
> future and reduce the potential of their own level of prosperity.
> The lesson that must be learned is that prosperous neighbors
> are the best neighbors; that a higher standard of living in one
> country begets higher standards in others, and that a high level
> of trade and business is most easily attained when generously
> and widely shared. (quoted in Helleiner 2014, 103)

US officials were also strongly committed to "*procedural* multilateralism," in which all the United and Associated Nations would have an opportunity to contribute to the design of the postwar international financial order (Toye and Toye 2004, 18; emphasis in original). This point needs to be emphasized because much of the secondary literature portrays the Bretton Woods agreements as a product of bilateral Anglo-American negotiations in which the views of smaller and poorer countries were ignored. It is true that Keynes initially proposed that Britain and the United States design the postwar international financial order by themselves, with other countries invited to join only after the rules had been set. But White and other US officials consistently rejected this idea on the grounds that it would be seen as an Anglo-American "gang-up" (Helleiner 2014, 108). As White told one Canadian official in April 1943, he strongly believed "all the brains were not concentrated in two great powers and that many of the smaller countries might have an important contribution to a discussion of the type" (W. C. Clark summarizing White's comments in Wardhaugh 2010, 242).

After White's initial drafts of the Fund were released publicly in the spring of 1943, Morgenthau invited all 43 United and Associated Nations to come to Washington to comment on them. After a three-day, multilateral session involving 18 countries in June, the influential US State Department official Adolfe Berle privately applauded that "the significance of the meeting was not what it said, but that it was the first more or less democratic procedure for dealing with this sort of thing" (Helleiner 2014, 130-31). After further consultations over the next year, Morgenthau invited the same 43 countries to the Bretton Woods conference in July 1944. The transcripts of the famous conference reveal the active participation of many of these countries in the deliberations.

Canadian officials were very strong supporters of Bretton Woods' inclusive multilateralism. In addition to sharing the ideals of US policy makers, Canadian policy makers worried that the alternative key currency plan would undermine Canadian interests. Not only would it leave Canada and other smaller powers without much of a voice in international financial affairs, but it might also force them "to become monetary satellites of one or other 'key' currency" (Helleiner 2006, 78). Because Canada's economic interests were "equally divided" between the United States and Britain at the time, the scenario of becoming a monetary satellite of just one of these key currencies was one that Canadian policy makers sought to avoid at all costs (Wardhaugh 2010, 239). And, more generally, as an open export-oriented economy, Canada would derive particular benefits from the growth of multilateral trade.

In a high-profile article published in *Foreign Affairs* during the month of the Bretton Woods conference, one of the key Canadian delegates, the Bank of Canada's (BoC's) Louis Rasminsky, forcefully critiqued the key currency for ignoring the interests of smaller countries. As he put it, "it is difficult to see where smaller countries fit it. I have the uneasy feeling that the 'key currency' approach is the monetary counterpart of the Great Power doctrine of international organization generally" (quoted in Helleiner 2006, 79). Other Canadian policy makers, including the powerful W. C. Clark in the Department of Finance, strongly endorsed Rasminsky's views, arguing that the multilateral vision outlined by the Bretton Woods proposals was necessary as a foundation for broader postwar international economic and political cooperation (ibid.). In an explicit effort to encourage a reconciliation of Keynes' and White's plans, Rasminsky and other Canadian officials developed and published a formal plan in July 1943 that integrated ideas from each. The Canadian government then sent a delegation to the Bretton Woods conference that was larger than that of all countries — except the United States, Britain and China — and its members contributed actively to the discussions.[1]

The inclusiveness of the Bretton Woods negotiations is often overlooked today. In advance of the first G20 leaders' meeting in November 2008, leading politicians such as Gordon Brown called for a "new Bretton Woods" (Kirkup and Waterfield 2008). These policy makers seem to have forgotten that the original Bretton Woods conference — formally named the "United Nations Monetary and Financial Conference" — embraced a more representative kind of multilateralism than the G20 leaders' forum. Indeed, many of the policy makers were rather dismissive of smaller countries' efforts to give the United Nations more of a leadership role in the post-2008 global financial reform discussions.

It is the critics of the exclusivity of the G20 — rather than its supporters — that have the more legitimate claim to invoke the Bretton Woods precedent. Canadian officials have not been particularly prominent among these critics. To be sure, they have continued to support the universal Bretton Woods institutions and to play an active role within them, but they have also lobbied hard to gain entry to, and then happily participated in, the more exclusive core clubs of global finance such as the G7, G20, FSB and SSBs. While Canadian officials have sometimes been advocates for the widening of the membership of these clubs, they no longer display quite the same enthusiasm that they showed in the early 1940s for the more fully inclusive vision of Bretton Woods.

CAPITAL CONTROLS AND INTERNATIONAL COOPERATION

After the crisis of 2008, the IMF underwent a process of reconsidering the merits of financial liberalization that it had previously championed. This

---

1   Brazil's delegation was tied with Canada's for fourth largest in size.

process culminated in the Fund's widely reported announcement in late 2012 of a new official institutional view that backed the use of "capital flow management measures" (IMF 2012). Critics quickly highlighted, however, the limited nature of the change in the new IMF position. The Fund's statement not only stressed the need for capital account restrictions to be temporary, but also continued to emphasize that "careful liberalization of capital flows can provide significant benefits, which countries could usefully work toward realizing over the long run" (ibid., 13).

The Bretton Woods architects turned their backs on the financial liberalism of the pre-1930s era in a more decisive way. They wrote into the IMF's Articles of Agreement a provision that gave governments the right to control all capital movements on a permanent basis. Their goal was to enable governments to prevent speculative and "disequilibrating" financial movements from undermining stable exchange rates and the policy autonomy of governments. The IMF was also empowered to request that governments introduce capital controls to prevent its resources from being used to finance deficits arising from a "large or sustained outflow of capital" (Helleiner 1994, chapter 2). This strong support for capital controls within the IMF charter is often overlooked by analysts, who describe the Bretton Woods agreements as foundational documents for the liberal international economic order of the postwar period.

The radical nature of this provision at the time also deserves to be underlined. After World War I, governments had endorsed a resolution at an important 1920 League of Nations financial conference that condemned all barriers to the international movement of capital (League of Nations 1920, 9). In 1944, governments embraced the opposite position. As Keynes put it, "Not merely as a feature of the transition, but as a permanent arrangement, the plan accords to every member government the explicit right to control all capital movements. What used to be a heresy is now endorsed as orthodox" (quoted in Helleiner 1994, 25).

Signalling their seriousness about restricting undesirable financial movements, both Keynes and White discussed in their early drafts some innovative ideas about enhancing the effectiveness of capital controls through international cooperation. Both noted that controls would work better if they were implemented, in Keynes' words, "at both ends" (quoted in Helleiner 1994, 38); that is, in both the country exporting the capital and the country importing the capital. As White put it, "without the cooperation of other countries such control is difficult, expensive and subject to considerable evasion" (ibid.).

White even proposed that such cooperation be mandatory. In early drafts of the Fund's charter, all members were required to help enforce the capital controls of foreign governments by measures such as information sharing, blocking capital inflows that were not permitted by the sending country, or making available to foreign governments assets of their nationals that were held abroad illegally. As White noted in mid-1943, his proposal provided "for control of capital movements from both ends. Perhaps this double control will do the job" (Helleiner 2014, 111). Because of opposition from the New York financial community, however, he was forced to remove this provision for mandatory action and the final IMF charter merely permitted cooperation.

Canadian officials fully supported Keynes and White's idea that capital controls had an important place in the postwar international financial order. In their July 1943 plan, the Canadian government proposed that countries be given the right to use capital controls. The Canadian plan also echoed White's proposal that countries should cooperate in enforcing each other's capital control regimes (Helleiner 2006, 81-82). The latter proposal was particularly attractive to Canadian policy makers since it suggested a way to maintain the effectiveness of capital controls without needing to resort to the kind of comprehensive exchange controls that Canada had imposed for the first time with the outbreak of war.

After introducing those controls, Canadian officials discovered quickly that the administration of exchange controls was a massive and complex task. As Governor of the BoC Graham Towers put it in 1940, "from some points of view exchange control in this country is more difficult, more upsetting in a way, than in almost any other country in the world…because of our extremely intimate relations with the United States. It is almost like cutting a body in two to run the line of exchange control across our frontier" (quoted in Helleiner 2006, 71). If the United States could help enforce Canadian capital controls, those cumbersome and unpopular exchange controls might not be necessary. As Rasminsky put it in an internal memo a few months before the Bretton Woods conference, "Could we dispense with this [comprehensive foreign exchange controls covering current account after the war] if U.S. authorities co-operated by giving us information regarding security transactions and bank balances of Canadians?" (ibid., 82).

After the 2008 financial crisis, analysts who favour greater restrictions on capital flows have asked the same kind of question about the prospects for international cooperation. Some have even explicitly resurrected Keynes and White's ideas about the need for controls "at both ends." Interestingly, these analysts include some IMF officials who argued in a September 2012 Fund staff discussion note that countries receiving large speculative capital inflows "would welcome attacking the problem of volatile capital flows at both ends of the transaction" (Ostry, Ghosh and Korinek 2012, 20; see also Blanchard and Ostry 2012). This idea did not find a place in the IMF's official view in December 2012. The principle that international cooperation can help curtail undesirable financial flows, however, has been incorporated de facto into recent international initiatives — endorsed by the G20 — to constrain illicit financial movements associated with tax evasion, corruption, bribery, stolen assets and money laundering.

Echoing their support for cooperative controls at Bretton Woods, Canadian officials have been supportive of these latter initiatives. In the early 2000s, they also backed some creative ideas about the role of internationally endorsed payments standstills to facilitate the resolution of international financial crises (Haldane and Kruger 2001). A few years earlier, in the late 1990s, Canadian officials had also displayed more skepticism than many of their G7 counterparts for the promotion of financial liberalization by the IMF, foreshadowing the more nuanced post-2008 views in IMF circles (Abdelal 2007, chapter 6). In these ways, Canadian policy makers continue to uphold some of the skepticism of free finance that was characteristic of the Bretton Woods negotiators, although in a less comprehensive manner and without any accompanying notion that Canada itself would reintroduce capital controls.

PRIORITIZING SOCIAL PROTECTION GOALS IN GLOBAL FINANCIAL REFORM

The innovative nature of the Bretton Woods vision is also relevant for another issue on the contemporary post-crisis international policy agenda. Responding to the severity of the 2008 crisis, the United Nations and other international institutions have developed a new "Social Protection Floor

Initiative" aimed at supporting governments worldwide to provide universal social protection to those within their territories. Social protection floors are meant to tackle issues such as basic income security, as well as access to services such as health, education, water and sanitation. This initiative is meant to foster a more "fair and inclusive globalization" in which everyone experiences minimum levels of social protection (Social Protection Floor Advisory Group 2011).

The initiative is portrayed as an innovative response to the 2008 crisis; however, it simply resurrects ideas that were at the core of the Bretton Woods vision. Reacting to the experience of the Great Depression, the Bretton Woods architects pioneered the notion that a worldwide social protection floor was needed as a foundation for the postwar international financial order. Most historians have overlooked this aspect of the Bretton Woods plans, but archival evidence reveals its importance.

To begin with, Keynes' papers highlight very clearly that the concept of "social security" was central to his initial thinking about the postwar international financial order. That thinking was triggered in late 1940, when he was asked to develop a radio broadcast to counter Nazi propaganda about the postwar order they proposed for Europe. In his first draft of the broadcast, he noted: "Mr. [Ernest] Bevin said recently that social security must be the first object of our domestic policy after the war. And social security for the peoples of all the European countries will be our policy abroad not less than at home. Indeed the one is hardly possible without the other; for we are all members of one family" (quoted in Helleiner 2014, 209).

The importance of social security was then enshrined in the Atlantic Charter announced by US President Roosevelt and UK Prime Minister Winston Churchill in August 1941. The Charter is widely recognized as the first official statement of the Anglo-American goals for the postwar world, with Roosevelt even comparing its objectives to those of the United States Constitution and British Magna Carta (Borgwardt 2005, 5). The Charter included a call for "the fullest collaboration between all nations in the economic field, with the object of securing for all improved labor standards, economic advancement, and social security" (Helleiner 2014, 210-11). Ernest Bevin (whom Keynes had referred to in his broadcast), the prominent British trade union leader and labour minister in Churchill's government, drafted this phrase. He had been arguing since the autumn of 1940 that postwar peace could only be maintained if human beings across the world were promised "security against poverty, care in sickness and trouble, protection against injury, provision for old age" (quoted in ibid.).

Roosevelt liked Bevin's proposed wording for the Atlantic Charter because he felt it was similar to a prominent commitment he made in January 1941 to promote "freedom from want" worldwide. In Roosevelt's words, that latter commitment "translated into world terms, means economic understandings which will secure to every nation a healthy peacetime life for its inhabitants — everywhere in the world" (Roosevelt quoted in Helleiner 2014, 120). Historian Elizabeth Borgwardt notes that Roosevelt saw provision of "freedom from want" across the world as an internationalization of the New Deal in ways that would provide a key foundation for international peace and political stability. He insisted on its inclusion within the Atlantic Charter in a phrase that promised "all the men in all the lands may live out their lives in freedom from fear and want" (Borgwardt quoted in ibid.).

The commitments to social security and freedom from want in the Atlantic Charter are usually ignored in analyses of Bretton Woods. We have already seen, however, that Keynes' initial thoughts about postwar plans had placed social security at the core of his objectives. Archival evidence also makes clear that White's initial plans were deeply influenced by these ideals in the Atlantic Charter. White's first proposal of the Fund in early January 1942 made explicit reference to the fact it was designed to facilitate "the attainment of the economic objectives of the Atlantic charter," and that membership would be open only to countries that subscribed to the objectives of the Charter (Helleiner 2014, 121). When he developed his first draft of the International Bank for Reconstruction and Development (IBRD) later that month, White also included a provision that all members would be required to "subscribe publicly to the 'Magna Carta of the United Nations'" — a document that he then described in a March draft as "a bill of rights of the peoples of the United Nations" that set forth "the ideal of freedom for which most of the peoples are fighting the aggressor nations and hope they will be able to attain and believe they are defending" (ibid.).

When presenting White's plans to Roosevelt, Morgenthau also went out of his way to link their content to Roosevelt's desire to internationalize the principles of the New Deal. In a memo accompanying White's proposal, he described the plans as "the preparation of specific instrumentalities for what really would be a New Deal in international economics" (Government of the United States 1963, 172). In his opening speech at the Bretton Woods conference two years later, Morgenthau continued to stress Roosevelt's commitment to freedom from want worldwide, telling the delegates that a key objective of the meeting was to establish "a satisfactory standard of living for all the people of all the countries on this earth" (Helleiner 2014, 122). Morgenthau justified this objective in the following way: "Prosperity, like peace, is indivisible. We cannot afford to have it scattered here or there among the fortunate or to enjoy it at the expense of others. Poverty, wherever it exists, is menacing to us all and undermines the well-being of each of us" (quoted in ibid.).

In his opening comments as chair of the committee that finalized the IBRD's charter at Bretton Woods, Keynes also highlighted its goal of "raising the standard of life and conditions of labour everywhere" (Helleiner 2014, 220). Other British officials at the conference also insisted on maintaining a reference in the purposes of the IBRD to its role in "assisting in raising productivity, the standard of living, and conditions of labor in member countries," on the grounds that Bevin would have been "very unhappy" if this language was removed (ibid., 221). These goals of Keynes and Bevin were widely shared in British policy-making circles. For example, even before the Atlantic Charter was announced, mid-1941 discussions of postwar international economic planning within the influential Royal Institute of International Affairs (RIIA) had stressed the need for "the release of all peoples from poverty and its evil consequences, primarily through provision of economic security for everyone who desires it and secondarily through the advancement of standards of living" (ibid., 213). In further discussions in early 1943, the RIIA's analysts had continued to stress the need for a plan "in which the provision of the essential needs of food, clothing, shelter, education and health, should have the first claim on the world's productive resources, whether the recipients can afford to pay for what they receive or not" (ibid.).

These goals also met with strong support from Canadian officials. In a December 1941 memo about the postwar international economic order, the Department of Finance's Robert Bryce noted the following: "During the tempestuous twenty years between the wars we all fell far short of achieving that freedom from want which we now recognized as one of the new rights of man. We must do better after this war — if our civilization is to survive.

We must achieve freedom from want, as Roosevelt said, 'everywhere in the world'" (quoted in Helleiner 2014, 217). Bryce reiterated the point in 1943: "If our wartime protestations of allied solidarity and of a desire to improve the standard of living of all those who live in want are to be carried out... then we must have substantial loans from the richer states to the poorer states of the United Nations....Billions upon billions of dollars must be invested in Asia, Polynesia, South America, and Africa, if the great masses in these lands are to be made productive and eventually brought up to minimum standards of health and decency, let alone comfort" (ibid., 216-17).

In addition to raising living standards abroad, Canadian policy makers were committed to the idea that social security needed to be strengthened at home. In discussing postwar economic planning, Rasminsky noted in May 1942 that "this is in fact a revolutionary war and the object of economic policy after the war will not be to make the institutions of a capitalist or semi-capitalist society work with a minimum of friction but to make sure that...the fruits of production are widely distributed....This point of view [must be] kept constantly in the foreground" (quoted in Helleiner 2006, 76-77). In 1942, in analyzing the benefits of the Keynes and White plans, Graham Towers applauded how greater policy autonomy would mean that countries "would have no legitimate excuse for failure to tackle energetically their domestic problems" (ibid.). He continued: "I hope...that those domestic problems will, in fact, be tackled in a really bold fashion. One thing seems certain, namely, that with the experience of war fresh in their minds, and the recollection of the pre-war depression close in the background, people in this and other countries will be extremely impatient with any state of affairs which involves unemployment on a material scale for any appreciable length of time" (ibid.).

These kinds of ideas were reinforced by the growing popularity of the socialist political party, the Cooperative Commonwealth Federation (CCF), at home. Indeed, two weeks before the Bretton Woods conference, the CCF won a landslide electoral victory in Saskatchewan under Tommy Douglas' leadership, thereby bringing into power the first socialist government in Canada (and North America). As the conference began, Towers privately told a British official that the CCF would either gain a majority of the seats in the next federal election or at least do well enough to dictate Canadian government policies. In this changing political context, the federal government committed to full employment goals in its 1945 "White Paper on Employment and

Income" and proposed initiatives to strengthen a Canadian welfare state (Helleiner 2006, 77-78).

Thus, the post-2008 push to create minimum levels of social protection for everyone in the world is not new. It first emerged in the early 1940s and was central to the initial drafts of the Bretton Woods plans for the postwar international financial order. Indeed, it was accorded much greater priority in those plans than in any official discussions of global financial reform after 2008, discussions that appear rather divorced from the discussion of social protection floors.

In the Canadian political context, this contrast between then and now is certainly apparent. Since the 2008 financial crisis, it has been difficult to detect among leading Canadian policy makers the kind of commitment to bold new initiatives aimed at strengthening social protection — either abroad or at home — that was expressed by officials such as Bryce, Rasminsky and Towers during the Bretton Woods negotiations. Here, once again, is an area where the innovations of Bretton Woods might help inspire those who would like to see more action.

CONCLUSION

Global financial crises usually generate reforms to global financial governance. The crisis of 2008 has conformed to this pattern. Given the severity of the crisis, however, the reforms have been rather tame to date. The Bretton Woods discussions may provide some inspiration for those seeking more significant change. Reacting to the global financial crisis of the early 1930s, the architects of the Bretton Woods agreements developed some highly creative ideas about global financial governance.

This chapter has focused on three such ideas that are often overlooked, but which relate directly to some post-2008 international policy discussions: the importance of inclusive multilateralism in global financial governance; support for capital controls and international cooperation to bolster their effectiveness; and the need to prioritize social protection goals in global financial reform. In each case, the Bretton Woods architects — including Canadian officials — outlined ambitious objectives. Some contemporary reforms are moving in the direction of resurrecting these objectives in modest ways. Whether the ambition and creativity of that earlier age is rekindled will depend on leadership of policy makers, including that of Canadians who are once again playing important roles in post-crisis reform debates.

Acknowledgements

I am very grateful for the helpful comments I received from Jim Haley, Dane Rowlands and the other contributors to this book.

WORKS CITED

Abdelal, Rawi. 2007. *Capital Rules.* Cambridge: Harvard University Press.

Blanchard, Olivier and Jonathan Ostry. 2012. "The Multilateral Approach to Capital Controls." *VoxEU,* December 11. www.voxeu.org/article/multilateral-approach-capital-controls.

Borgwardt, Elizabeth. 2005. *A New Deal for the World: America's Vision for Human Rights.* Cambridge: Belknap Press for Harvard University Press.

Government of the United States. 1963. *Foreign Relations of the United States: Diplomatic Papers, 1942: Volume I.* Washington, DC: US Government Printing Office.

Haldane, Andy and Mark Kruger. 2001. "The Resolution of International Financial Crises." Bank of Canada Working Paper 2001-20.

Helleiner, Eric. 1994. *States and the Reemergence of Global Finance.* Ithaca: Cornell University Press.

———. 2006. *Towards North American Monetary Union? The Politics and History of Canada's Exchange Rate Regime.* Montreal: McGill-Queen's University Press.

———. 2014. *Forgotten Foundations of Bretton Woods: International Development and the Making of the Postwar World.* Ithaca: Cornell University Press.

IMF. 2012. *The Liberalization and Management of Capital Flows: An Institutional View.* November 14. Washington, DC: IMF.

Kirkup, James and Bruno Waterfield. 2008. "Gordon Brown's Bretton Woods Summit Calls Risks Spat with Nicholas Sarkozy." *The Telegraph,* October 15.

League of Nations. 1920. *International Financial Conference, 1920, Vol.1.* Brussels: The Dewarichet.

Morgenthau, Henry. 1945. "Bretton Woods and International Cooperation." *Foreign Affairs* 23 (2): 182–94.

Ostry, Jonathan, Atish Ghosh and Anton Korinek. 2012. "Multilateral Aspects of Regulating the Capital Account." IMF Staff Discussion Note SDN/12/10. September 7.

Social Protection Floor Advisory Group. 2011. *Social Protection Floor: For a Fair and Inclusive Globalization, Report of the Advisory Group Chaired by Michelle Bachelet.* Geneva: International Labour Organization.

Toye, John and Richard Toye. 2004. *The UN and Global Political Economy.* Bloomington: Indiana University Press.

Wardhaugh, Robert. 2010. *Behind the Scenes: The Life and Work of William Clifford Clark.* Toronto: University of Toronto Press.

2

Canada and the IMF: Global Finance and the Challenge of Completing Bretton Woods

James A. Haley

●　●　●　●　●　●　●　●　●　●　●　●　●　●　●　●　●　●

In the wake of the deepest, most synchronized downturn since the Great Depression, the International Monetary Fund (IMF) is once again at the forefront of international policy discussions. Before the crisis, the IMF was suffering existential angst as members eschewed its policy prescriptions and repaid Fund resources. The IMF was at risk of sliding into irrelevancy; worse still for an institution known for enforcing fiscal austerity on members in the throes of financial crises, it was threatened with severe budgetary challenges of its own. These problems reflected the financial integration that had transformed global finance over the previous three decades, transforming the balance-of-payments *problems* of the Bretton Woods era into capital account *crises* of much larger size, and which unfold in a much shorter period of time. The IMF was ill-equipped to deal with these crises, with the result that it was less effective in assisting its members in financial difficulty.

Over a decade ago, Canada led efforts to fill the lacunae in the IMF's tool kit. While important progress was made in terms of crisis prevention, critical issues remained to be addressed; moreover, as the global financial crisis revealed, major risks remained. Part of the problem is attributable to the fact that financial markets outgrew national regulation, as regulatory arbitrage created an unregulated "shadow" banking system that posed systemic threats to the global economy. There was also a failure to address governance weaknesses that undermined the IMF's ability to provide the public good of international financial stability, while the absence of clear "rules of the game" meant that the IMF was unable to secure timely, orderly adjustment of external imbalances. These imbalances contributed to the global financial crisis by dampening the adjustment of exchange rates and global interest rates, creating conditions conducive to asset price bubbles and deteriorating credit assessments. The result was the near collapse of the global financial system, with the potential for a catastrophic decline in output.

That outcome was averted thanks to timely and determined policy actions by governments around the globe. Yet, for many countries at the "core" of the global economy, these extraordinary responses, combined with long-term demographic changes, have bequeathed a legacy of adjustment challenges reflected in high public debt and extraordinary monetary policies. Former US Treasury Secretary Lawrence Summers (2013) has even suggested that the North Atlantic economy, by which he refers to these aging "advanced" industrialized countries, is at risk of protracted stagnation. Protracted stagnation would not be propitious for countries struggling with high debt burdens and aging populations. But as the global financial crisis demonstrated, in a global economy linked through trade flows and financial markets, no country is immune to the problems of others. Sustained economic malaise in the North would have adverse effects on the economies of the South, for which the crisis was less severe.

These rapidly growing, dynamic economies enjoyed a remarkably brief downturn and, for the first time, many countries found they had the policy space to adopt counter-cyclical policies. The global recovery was powered by their growth in the aftermath of the crisis, underscoring the shift in the economic centre of gravity from the North to the South that has occurred over the past two decades. For economies in the ascension, anxious to exercise greater influence in the international institutions of global governance, there was indeed a silver lining to the black cloud of the crisis.

The pre-crisis success of the rapidly growing economies of the "periphery" in raising income levels largely reflected favourable terms of trade effects and export-led growth strategies that were dependent on advanced economies' consumption and asset price bubbles. Such strategies cannot be sustained given ongoing demographic changes in mature economies, which entail a shift in savings-investment patterns. This underscores the need to rebalance the sources of growth in the global economy. At the same time, the international financial architecture, the foundations of which were laid in Bretton Woods, New Hampshire at the end of the World War II, must be strengthened to ensure that it is capable of assisting countries — both North and South — in dealing with the difficult adjustment challenges that lie ahead. These renovations are needed to preserve the global economy as an engine of growth and development.

The IMF is at the centre of this architecture.

This chapter explores Canada's efforts to ensure that the IMF is capable of providing the public good of international financial stability both before and after the global financial crisis. The Fund was designed to fulfill this function through its role in promoting timely, orderly *adjustment* in the balance of payments by providing *liquidity* in the face of balance-of-payments problems so that members avoid policies that create unemployment and deflation or shift the burden of adjustment to others. The Fund also fostered *confidence* to the system and encouraged the efficient allocation of savings and investment in support of global growth and development. That confidence and the trust on which financial intermediation is based has been shaken by the global financial crisis, while large adjustment challenges remain and concerns of global liquidity and capital flows loom large in the face of a tapering down of the extraordinary monetary measures taken by some central banks in the midst of the crisis.

THE GOALS OF BRETTON WOODS: LIQUIDITY, ADJUSTMENT AND CONFIDENCE

The two key architects of the Bretton Woods system — John Maynard Keynes, representing the United Kingdom, and Harry Dexter White of the US Treasury — agreed on the need to sustain full employment and restore global trade. They sought to avoid the perverse effects of the dysfunctional gold standard of the interwar years, in which countries in balance-of-payments deficit already in stagnation were forced to introduce fiscal austerity to generate the deflation and real exchange rate depreciation required for international adjustment.[1] These policies of "internal devaluation," by which similar policies in the euro zone are justified today, were not sustainable in the 1930s: high unemployment led to widening social and political fissures, and countries eventually abandoned the gold standard, adopting measures to protect domestic employment at the expense of others.[2]

Keynes and White recognized that reducing the threat of such beggar-thy-neighbour policies hinged on a judicious balancing of financing and adjustment. Their shared objective was to ensure adequate liquidity to support postwar trade and growth, while promoting timely, orderly adjustment in members' balance of payments. Their approaches to this objective, however, differed. To prevent the hoarding of international liquidity that had led to deflation and global stagnation in the 1930s, Keynes proposed a generously endowed clearing union to facilitate the settlement of international payments and overdraft facilities, under which surplus countries would provide credits to deficit countries to address payments imbalances. In contrast, the White plan called for a much smaller stabilization fund that would make loans to deficit countries to support policies to promote adjustment. The White plan for postwar monetary arrangements reflected the prevailing view that the United States would be in perennial surplus and the one providing these overdrafts. US officials were understandably concerned that Keynes' proposals would impart an inflationary bias to global finance, detrimental to US interests.

Under the compromise plan that Canadian officials helped to broker, the IMF facilitated the pooling of international reserves, thereby avoiding the maldistribution of global liquidity that had marked the interwar period (see Rasminksy 1943). Canada argued that if countries had ready access to internationally accepted liquidity in times of stress, the temptation to shift the burden of adjustment to others through restrictions on trade and payments

---

1   The real exchange rate is a measure of international competitiveness incorporating both the foreign exchange value of the currency, or nominal exchange rate, and relative rates of inflation. For example, a 10 percent depreciation of the currency, making domestic goods more competitive in international markets, could be completely offset by an inflation differential of 10 percent that raises the price of domestic goods relative to foreign goods.

2   These policies, which in Keynes' evocative words were "destructive of national and international prosperity," can take several forms, including competitive devaluations to avoid employment loss; trade protectionism, which elicits retaliation and tit-for-tat trade measures that eat up the gains from trade and shrinks the global pie; unsound domestic policies, including the use of inflationary policies to punish foreign creditors, as was the case in Weimer, Germany; and default and debt repudiation, as domestic residents balk at the adjustment costs associated with servicing foreign debt.

would be reduced. Moreover, by pooling international reserves, the IMF would allow its members to economize on their holdings of gold, which Keynes referred to as a "sterile" asset, freeing resources for investments in health, education and infrastructure offering higher social returns.

The outcome of the Bretton Woods negotiations was an institution significantly larger than the stabilization fund proposed by White, but which, on insistence from the United States, provided short-term balance-of-payments support on "adequate safeguards," rather than Keynes' overdraft facility. The US dollar was the anchor currency against which the par values of other currencies were set, with the dollar fixed in terms of the price of gold. By tying their currencies to the dollar, Bretton Woods members acknowledged an exceptional role for the United States, reflecting the fact that it alone had the financial resources to backstop international financial stability. That being said, stability of the system required that US policies be consistent with price stability; in this regard, while US monetary policy was freed from the strict bonds of the gold standard, that freedom was contingent on other countries having confidence in the dollar.[3]

Keynes and White also agreed on the need to restrict the movement of capital. Their embrace of capital controls reflected the need to finesse the international policy "trilemma," under which countries could choose to fix exchange rates, allow capital flows or pursue independent monetary policies — but not all three. The choice of any two determined the third. And, given the experiences of the interwar period, there was a bias that, rather than act as a stabilizing force in financing balance-of-payments imbalances, capital flows and flexible exchange rates had been sources of instability, which in the 1930s led to insupportable adjustment burdens on countries already in financial difficulty.

The use of capital controls in the Bretton Woods era meant that balance-of-payments difficulties were limited to differences in national saving and investment rates, typically on the order of a few percentage points of GDP. In

---

3 Confidence would not be sustained if monetary policy was subordinated to the need to finance excessively expansionary fiscal policy. In other words, the quid pro quo of US "exceptionalism" was a commitment to sound fiscal policies. This was the case in the early years of the Bretton Woods system. By the late 1960s, however, the United States was fighting the Cold War against the Soviet Union, a "hot" war in Vietnam and a war on poverty at home. The fiscal costs of these commitments undermined confidence in the system and, by the early 1970s, other industrial countries unwilling to absorb the inflationary consequences of maintaining fixed parities with the dollar, allowed their currencies to appreciate.

these circumstances, an IMF-supported program that spread the adjustment process over time smoothed the impact of fiscal or other policy measures designed to compress domestic demand. This facilitated the judicious balancing of financing and adjustment that Keynes and White had sought, and encouraged members to eschew policies that would have negative spillovers to the global economy.

Over time, however, capital controls became increasingly porous as financial markets found ways to evade them and governments sought the benefits that capital account liberalization offered. By the early 1990s, controls were largely removed, heralding a degree of financial integration unimaginable to the architects of Bretton Woods.[4] Capital flows increased in size and, with the inevitable bouts of optimism followed by pessimism, sudden stops and reversals of capital flows ensued. Such problems quickly evolve into crises analogous to bank runs, as foreign and domestic investors attempt to convert domestic assets to foreign currency denominated assets. These capital account crises are typically much larger (reflecting the conversion of asset *stocks*, rather than *flows*) and unfold over a much shorter time compared to the current account problems of the Bretton Woods era.

POLICY CHALLENGES IN THE POST-BRETTON WOODS ERA

The global financial system was tested by a series of such crises, beginning with the Mexican peso crisis in 1994-1995, followed by the Asian financial crisis in 1997-1998 and culminating in the Argentine debt default in 2002.

Following the Asian crisis, international attention turned to the challenge of financial crisis prevention and resolution. The initial response focused on weaknesses in regulatory and policy frameworks in the emerging market economies that had been subjected to sudden capital outflows (Fried and Haley 2010). Canada was the first country to subject itself to a comprehensive review of its financial sector policies, or financial sector assessment,

---

4   This is not to imply that Keynes and White did not anticipate an eventual role for private capital flows. Indeed, the inclusion of Article VI in the IMF Articles of Agreement, which precludes the use of Fund resources to "bail out" private creditors, suggests they foresaw a time when private capital flows would swamp official resources.

conducted by the IMF and World Bank.[5] It soon became clear, however, that because private capital flows dwarfed the resources of the IMF, the adjustment burden borne by crisis-afflicted countries was correspondingly higher. In this respect, some recognized a need to augment the IMF's tool kit so that it could better assist its members in dealing with the vagaries of global capital and allow them to benefit from globalization. Canada assumed a leadership role in these efforts, focusing on the prerequisites for successful capital account liberalization, reforming IMF lending, formalizing a payments standstill and, eventually, supporting efforts to promote the timely, orderly restructuring of sovereign debt.[6]

Road Map for Capital Account Liberalization

The first element of this program reflected the belief that the IMF may have been too hasty in promoting rapid capital account liberalization without a proper assessment of the potential for financial crises or identification of the necessary policy frameworks and legal and institutional support for the efficient use of capital inflows. The result was short-term capital inflows that were subsequently reversed. In effect, in their haste to gain access to global capital markets, too many countries liberalized their capital accounts without first establishing the strong supervisory regimes necessary to safeguard financial stability. For this reason, Canada pushed the IMF to develop a "road map" for capital account liberalization. While these efforts met with substantial opposition and progress was slow, in time the balance of opinion shifted and in 2012, official IMF policy endorsed the key principles that Canada had articulated more than a decade earlier (see IMF 2012).

Lending, Access Limits and Dynamic Inconsistency

The second element of Canada's reform agenda entailed efforts to limit IMF lending into crises in order to avoid distorting the incentives of private creditors to reschedule their claims. The problem with large-scale IMF lending is that it can finance private capital flight, while official sector claims are serviced through improvements in the balance of payments brought

---

5　For an exhaustive discussion of the Financial Sector Assessment Program, see IMF (2005).
6　Canadian priorities were articulated by then Finance Minister Paul Martin at the Commonwealth Finance Ministers' meeting, Ottawa, 1998.

about by a compression of domestic demand. This asset transfer from private investors to the public sector has implications for capital market efficiency, since higher *ex ante* returns on lending were compensation for increased risks that should be borne by private creditors. As noted at the time, the unintended result of IMF rescue packages could be a socialization of risk and the privatization of return.

Financial crises entail a risk of contagion, however, either through direct trade and financial linkages, or indirectly through higher risk premia, making it difficult for the IMF to deny financing if the authorities are prepared to commit to policy measures sufficiently robust to constitute adequate safeguards of repayment. This can be the case even if there are very large implementation challenges and vexing questions regarding the sustainability of the program. And yet, because of its preferred creditor status, IMF financing designed to prevent a suspension of payments can be a double-edged sword: when an IMF-supported program fails to restore confidence and quell capital flight, and the member subsequently defaults, losses to remaining private creditors are magnified by the convention that credits to the IMF are repaid in full before the claims of private creditors are serviced.

In view of these problems, attention was focused on the establishment of strict access limits on the size of IMF support packages, with clearly defined conditions for exceptional access (see Haldane and Krueger 2001).[7] The intent of these efforts was to discipline behaviour on the part of sovereign borrowers and their creditors by influencing expectations of the amount of IMF assistance that would be forthcoming in the event of balance-of-payments difficulties. Some progress was made in clarifying the conditions under which exceptional access would be provided; although such criteria were eventually adopted by the IMF, they have not been the bulwark against large programs that many hoped they would be. Indeed, the size of the financial challenges faced by members, and the perceived risks associated with a disruptive suspension of payments, led to a situation in which exceptional access was the norm, not the exception. In other words, regardless of how desirable strict access limits

---

7 Haldane and Krueger's influential paper, circulated by the Bank of Canada and the Bank of England, set the terms of the debate. It notes that the goal of access limits is to prevent official sector resources from shielding private creditors from the risks they willingly assumed when contracting with sovereign borrowers. In other words, contrary to the impression created by some, the intent is to enhance market efficiency, particularly the efficient allocation of capital and risk bearing, and not enforce some undefined notion of "fair" burden sharing.

are *ex ante*, the potential disruption associated with their enforcement may render them incredible *ex post*.[8] Absent a framework that contains the fallout from limiting financing, attempts to impose strengthened access limits and constrain discretion are not credible and will not affect behaviour.

Standstills, Collective Action Clauses and the Sovereign Debt Restructuring Mechanism

The third element of Canadian efforts to equip the IMF to deal with the capital account crises of the twenty-first century focused on measures to facilitate the timely and orderly restructuring of sovereign debt. Reflecting the Asian crisis experience, these efforts concentrated initially on a debt standstill arrangement that would prevent the panicked exit by investors from a country by requiring the extension of asset maturities. Since a protracted suspension of debt payments would create harmful uncertainty among investors, there was also an overarching need for Fund programs to focus on promoting growth. In this respect, it was argued that a well-designed standstill agreement would give the sovereign time to introduce sound policies that "grow the pie" to the benefit of creditors, as well as domestic citizens. Under such conditions, creditors would hopefully voluntarily roll over claims, confident that strengthened policies would preserve or enhance the values of their assets.

It soon became clear, however, that there could be problems of insolvency as well as illiquidity. These concerns became paramount following the Argentine default in 2002. Efforts focused on measures to promote the possible reduction in the value of private claims. The first step was to address potential creditor coordination problems in the restructuring of sovereign debt issued under New York law. Such bonds required unanimity to amend key payment

---

8   The prospect of IMF financing encourages creditors to delay needed negotiations and for borrowers in distress to "gamble for redemption," even though such choices increase the dead weight losses suffered by both parties. Strict limits on IMF financing would, it is argued, force timely, orderly and "voluntary" restructurings. Yet, the potential consequences of a crisis, should creditors and borrowers fail to agree on a restructuring of claims, render threats to withhold official sector resources incredible. These considerations were prominent in the period preceding the Greek restructuring of 2012. Efforts to increase the IMF's lending capacity were rebuffed by Canadian Finance Minister James Flaherty, who argued that the prospect of additional financing would distort incentives for needed policy adjustments: "We need to remain focused on the Europeans solving this crisis, and avoid focusing on non-central issues like increasing the resources of the IMF" (Thomson Reuters 2011).

terms. The need for unanimity created incentives for opportunistic behaviour, as creditors wanting to extract higher payoffs could withhold their consent in the expectation of avoiding a reduction in the discounted present value of their claims. The potential for opportunistic behaviour accounts for the fact that in earlier episodes of debt problems, such as the debt crisis of the 1980s, bonded debt was treated as *de minimus* and excluded from restructuring. By the 1990s, bonded debt had largely replaced the syndicated bank lending that had previously dominated credit flows to sovereign borrowers.

Canada demonstrated leadership in promoting the use of collective action clauses (CACs), which allow key payment terms to be changed by a supermajority of bondholders. Such clauses have long been a feature of bonds issued under English law in London. By including such provisions in its foreign currency debt issued under New York law, Canada and the other major industrial countries that adopted them helped to dispel potential stigma effects for emerging market borrowers fearful of possible first-mover disadvantages.

The terms of the debate shifted and a cleavage opened between those prepared to support such "voluntary" approaches, in which bondholders would accept contractual modifications that facilitated restructuring, and those who supported the more formal, statutory approach represented by the Sovereign Debt Restructuring Mechanism (SDRM), as developed by the IMF under then First Deputy Managing Director Anne Krueger. The SDRM was proposed to replicate features of domestic bankruptcy with respect to sovereign debt at the international level, including possible writedowns for highly indebted countries suffering from an unsustainable debt burden. The need for the mechanism, however, was hotly debated.

In particular, concerns were raised by private creditors regarding the role of the IMF in determining the size of potential "haircuts" under the SDRM. Private creditors pointed out that as a major potential creditor with preferred creditor status, the IMF could face a potential conflict of interest in recommending proposed debt writedowns. Their argument was that, because IMF lending decisions are subject to political influence and outstanding purchases are de facto senior debt, the interests of private sector creditors could be sacrificed for political expediency. The IMF subsequently modified its proposal so that it would have no direct role in determining potential debt reductions; under the revised proposal, the IMF would facilitate the restructuring process by allowing members to utilize its Articles of Agreement to enforce a stay on litigation. Nevertheless, owing to sustained opposition to the SDRM, further work on the proposal was suspended in 2003 and efforts to promote timely, orderly restructurings focused on the adoption of CACs, which have now become boilerplate covenants in sovereign bond contracts, and the voluntary codes of conduct in sovereign debt restructuring negotiations promulgated by the Institute of International Finance (2004).

Surveillance, Legitimacy and Adjustment

Important progress was made a decade ago in terms of crisis prevention and improving the framework for the restructuring of sovereign debt. Nevertheless, countries traumatized by the effects of financial crises, particularly the massive exchange rate depreciations and draconian adjustment programs they endured, sought to self-insure against the potential risks of future crisis through the accumulation of foreign exchange reserves. In the eyes of many, the Fund had failed to assist its members to strike a judicious balance between financing and adjustment; countries in the throes of financial crisis, they argued, had been asked to do too much adjustment in return for too little financing.[9] And because the IMF was viewed as less effective in assisting its members in dealing with severe balance-of-payments difficulties, it lost credibility with the countries that were most likely to need its support. At the same time, some countries sought to prevent an overly rapid appreciation of their currencies from crisis-induced troughs to sustain export-led growth. Unfortunately, reserve accumulation continued despite the growing risks it posed.

The problem was that reserve accumulation financed large current account imbalances and dampened the adjustment of exchange rates and global interest rates, creating the conditions for asset price bubbles, deteriorating credit assessments and imprudent lending decisions (see Haley 2009). Collectively, countries recognized the mounting risks, but each was reluctant

---

9 The 1980s debt crisis led to similar disenchantment. To raise underlying growth prospects, promote debt sustainability and restore access to capital markets, the IMF encouraged heavily indebted developing countries to implement broad-ranging structural reforms. Such reforms entailed difficult political decisions that many viewed as unwarranted interference in the sovereign affairs of its members. Echoes of these complaints were also heard in the wake of the Asian financial crisis.

to accept the "hot potato" of adjustment and the slower growth or deterioration in trade balances that adjustment would have entailed. Some countries may have viewed their current account surpluses as the by-product of their virtue (i.e., high savings rates), and US deficits as the result of public and private profligacy. Efforts to encourage exchange rate appreciation in Asia were thus viewed as an attempt to shift the burden of adjustment to others. Moreover, consistent with the rules of the game agreed to on US insistence at Bretton Woods, past practice clearly put the burden of adjustment on deficit countries — not surplus countries. Claims that China was "manipulating" its exchange rate through sterilization of capital inflows in contravention of the rules were therefore rebuffed with the argument that sterilization was simply intended to prevent domestic inflation. As the surplus country, there was little pressure on China to adjust. Of course, given the role of the US dollar as the international vehicle currency and reserve asset, the United States had considerable scope (or *exorbitant privilege*) to evade adjustment — as long as it wanted to maintain its exchange rate peg to the dollar, China had little option but to accumulate US dollar assets.

The outcome was a "prisoner's dilemma" (or, as one prominent observer framed it, a "balance of financial terror"; see Summers 2004) in which both sides would benefit from cooperation to reduce the risk of disorderly adjustment, yet in which each was distrustful that the other would do their fair share. The end result was long-term US interest rates that were too low for too long. By 2007, the global financial system was akin to an inverted pyramid balanced precariously on its apex. When problems arose in the subprime mortgage market in the summer of 2007, the pyramid began to teeter. It toppled over in the autumn of 2008 with the fire sale of assets triggered by the failure of Lehman Brothers; the result was the near collapse of the global financial system, with the potential for a catastrophic decline in output.

A policy-led adjustment process would have taken out insurance against this risk. Ideally, the IMF could have — indeed, should have — played an important role in supporting a cooperative solution to this challenge. In fact, prior to the global financial crisis, efforts were made to reduce these risks through special multilateral consultations on imbalances (see IMF 2007). However, the absence of clear rules of the game meant that the IMF was ineffective in promoting the timely, orderly adjustment of external imbalances, with the result that the Fund was unable to provide the public good of international financial stability.

First and foremost, this was a failure of IMF surveillance over members' policies. This being said, the effectiveness of Fund surveillance depends on how members view the institution. The perception that the IMF was both less effective and less credible in the wake of the Asian financial crisis meant that its members were reluctant to listen to its warning and, arguably, even less willing to heed its advice. Part of the problem was a long-standing asymmetry: countries in need of Fund assistance were obliged to follow IMF policy conditionality, while the advanced economies with assured access to private capital markets, and which controlled the institution, were at liberty to ignore the policy prescriptions of the Fund.

In recent years, Canada has been an active participant in efforts to enhance the effectiveness of IMF surveillance. These efforts have led to a series of new policies to strengthen the traction of Fund policy advice and its capacity to speak truth to power, including the *Consolidated Multilateral Spillover Report*, the *External Sector Report* and the *Integrated Surveillance Decision*. The *Integrated Surveillance Decision* clarifies that surveillance should focus on economic and financial stability both at the country and global levels, and establishes Article IV consultations as the basis for both bilateral and multilateral surveillance. If successful, the asymmetry in surveillance observed before the crisis, specifically the lack of focus on surplus countries, should be reduced. The result would be a more comprehensive, integrated and consistent analysis of policy spillovers that enhances the quality, even-handedness and effectiveness of IMF surveillance.

At the same time, because the nature of Fund programs has changed — from filling modest balance-of-payments gaps in the current account to playing a catalytic role in the mobilization of private capital flows in the midst of capital account crises — the Fund has necessarily evolved from a rules-based institution to one in which discretion (i.e., the size of Fund programs and nature of policy conditionality) has increased in importance. Discretion must be based on legitimacy. Regrettably, however, because access to Fund resources in the Asian crisis was notionally constrained by a member's quota (share in the institution) that had not been adjusted to reflect shifts in economic weight, many concluded that the IMF lacked legitimacy. Asian members did not receive adequate financial support, some argue, because their quotas were too small relative to their financing needs, and, where notional access limits based on quotas were exceeded, the Fund extracted unwarranted and overly intrusive conditionality on structural reforms. In short, the argument is that the nature of IMF assistance was fundamentally different for Asian members; that the rules of the game were changed in mid-play.

Regardless of the merits of the argument, it underscores the fact that the IMF is a locus of obligations and responsibilities to which members mutually consent and pool a small share of their sovereignty, subject to transparent rules, for the mutual benefit of all. Prior to the global crisis, the absence of a consensus on those obligations and responsibilities and an erosion of legitimacy led to an institution that was less effective in its role as guardian of international financial stability.

By late 2008 and early 2009, the consequences of this situation were clear. In this environment, the Group of Twenty (G20) emerged as a coordinating committee by which independent sovereign states agree on joint action to the mutual benefit of all. G20 coordination was initially facilitated by a common threat: faced with the prospect of a global financial collapse that would harm all, a common, coordinated response was possible. As countries came out of the crisis at different speeds, however, the nature of the problem changed from "the same policy response at the same time" to "appropriate policy responses at the appropriate times." Needless to say, the latter is a far more demanding task. The necessary differentiated policy requirements are both more difficult to agree on, as opinions differ on the appropriate country-specific targets, and more difficult to monitor.

These are the twin goals of the G20 Mutual Assessment Process (MAP), which Canada has co-chaired since it was established in 2009. The MAP is intended to promote *strong, sustainable and balanced growth* through multilateral reviews of and consultations on members' policies. The objective is to avoid an asymmetric adjustment process, in which countries at, or near, full employment permit their currencies to depreciate in the face of negative shocks, but resist real appreciation. Such efforts could impart a deflationary bias to the global economy. The potential danger in the current situation is that countries facing secular stagnation may view such an asymmetric policy response as a conscious attempt to thwart adjustment, leading to the adoption of protectionist policies and the possible fragmentation of the global economy. The IMF has played an important supporting role in providing the analytical foundations for the MAP. Absent a consensus on the rules of adjustment, however, its ability to enforce, cajole or otherwise convince countries to adhere to a set of policies to maximize joint welfare is limited.

The Obligations of Adjustment and Governance Reform

A more felicitous outcome in which everyone is better off is possible. But there must be agreement on the obligations and responsibilities of members in the global economy of the twenty-first century. And some monitoring mechanism independent of any one member of the G20, but accountable to the collective, is needed to support a cooperative equilibrium. Canada has consistently argued, for example, that the rules of the game for the international monetary system must reflect the new realities of the post-Bretton Woods world of highly integrated capital markets. As former Finance Minister Jim Flaherty (2006a) presciently warned before the crisis: "The global financial and economic landscape has changed considerably over the last two decades and our challenge is to forge a common view on the proper role of the IMF in a globalized international financial and monetary system....Globalization has not only expanded consumption and investment opportunities, but has also allowed imbalances to grow and the scale of crises to increase."

Getting to an agreement on a new set of obligations and responsibilities appropriate for the integrated global economy of today will not be easy. Moreover, while it is a necessary condition for strong, sustained and balanced growth, it is not a sufficient condition.

The IMF must be viewed as legitimate if it is to assist its members attain that objective. Since quotas are the most basic metric determining a member's voice in the institution, as well as determinant of access to Fund resources, efforts at quota reform are of considerable importance. In this respect, governance arrangements that reflect the relative economic weight of members in the mid-twentieth century are not indicative of the global economy in the early twenty-first century. The reality is that a governance structure that does not reflect current realities lacks legitimacy. Recognizing the need to address this issue if the IMF is to be effective in safeguarding international financial stability, Canada played a leadership role in advancing meaningful quota reform. As noted at the time: "Proper alignment of quotas with countries' economic and financial weight in the global economy is essential to the Fund's legitimacy as an international institution. Legitimacy in turn is [the] key to ensuring that the Fund can serve as an appropriate forum for members and that the Fund's policy advice is heeded" (Flaherty 2006b).

At the IMF annual meeting in Singapore in 2006, members agreed to a number of steps to advance quota reform, including an initial ad hoc increase in quotas for the most underrepresented members (China, South Korea, Mexico and Turkey), a new quota formula to guide the assessment of the adequacy of members' quotas, a second round of ad hoc quota increases based on the new formula, as well as measures to address the special needs of smaller, lower-income members. Since then, however, quota reform has stalled. In part, this reflects the intractability of the problem: quota reform is an example of a zero-sum game — one member's quota share increases at the expense of another; no member wants to see their share decline. That said, if quota reform were embedded in a broader package of reforms designed to safeguard the interests of all members of the international community, it might be possible to transform the zero-sum game of quota reform to a positive-sum game of architecture reform.

CONCLUSION: COMPLETING BRETTON WOODS

Reflecting on the origins of the Great Depression, Charles Kindleberger (1971, 292) famously observed: "In 1929 the British couldn't and the United States wouldn't [provide the public good of international financial stability]. When every country turned to protect its national private interest, the world public interest went down the drain, and with it the private interests of all."

The absence of an effective guardian of international financial stability in 1929 prompted Keynes and White to create the IMF in 1944. The system they created was designed to address the adjustment challenges in the global economy 70 years ago — high debt burdens, the threat of secular stagnation and a moribund world trade and payments system that was ensnared in a web of tariff barriers and inconvertible currencies. Likewise, restoring full employment, sustaining growth and promoting adjustment are key policy objectives today. Unlike the bias that prevailed at Bretton Woods, however, there is reason to believe that flexible exchange rates and capital flows will have to play a key part of the adjustment process. Rapidly growing, dynamic economies have large infrastructure shortfalls. Filling these gaps would provide a source of domestic development and help rebalance global growth;

pension funds in the aging, mature industrialized economies, meanwhile, need the higher returns that these investments could provide. Such investments and mutually beneficial gains from inter-temporal trade require clear rules of the game and stability of policy frameworks.

Monitoring clear rules and promoting stable policies should be the role of the IMF and the other institutions in the international financial architecture. It is clear, though, that financial integration has strained the IMF's ability to assist its members in crisis. In this respect, the need today is not so much to reproduce the Bretton Woods consensus as it is to "complete" Bretton Woods to allow countries to better reap the benefits of financial integration by reducing the virulence and contagion of financial crises. This will require international agreement — through work at the Financial Stability Board and other international fora — on the governance of global capital. It will also take a better framework for the timely, orderly restructuring of sovereign debt.

Important progress on debt restructuring was made a decade ago; the Greek restructuring in 2012 and the ongoing legal challenges faced by Argentina have reanimated work on this issue, with many of the same issues framing the debate (see Haley, forthcoming). The likely outcome of these efforts is unclear, but there is clearly room to expand the use of CACs, identify model clauses for the aggregation of outstanding claims, introduce contractual standstill agreements and define how the equal treatment of creditors (the *pari passu* clause) is to work in practice. It would also be beneficial to create a neutral forum in which distressed country governments, their creditors and the IMF can engage in the difficult discussions necessary to restructure sovereign debt (Gitlin and House 2014).

Equally important are governance reforms that align IMF quotas with the shifts that have occurred in economic weight. A better framework for the timely, orderly restructuring of sovereign debt would help the IMF assist its members to achieve that judicious balance between financing and adjustment it was created to promote. But such a framework must be coupled with measures to secure the buy-in that the IMF needs from its entire membership, including the rapidly growing dynamic economies in the ascendancy. Success in both these areas would address the perceived loss of credibility, effectiveness and legitimacy of the IMF, and allow the international community to once more come together around a set of responsibilities and obligations to each other and the system. Failing this outcome, the risk is that the global economy could fragment and resource allocation will be conducted on the basis of opaque state-to-state agreements rather than through open and transparent markets.

Efforts to complete Bretton Woods are enormously important to Canadians. It is true that Canada fared much better in the global financial crisis than most other industrial countries. No bank failed. Unemployment increased, but it never approached the levels of most other industrial countries. And while output contracted sharply, growth was quickly restored, owing to the timely application of fiscal stimulus and the introduction of a range of measures to ensure the flow of credit to the economy. Nevertheless, the crisis demonstrated the extent to which Canadian economic prospects are affected by the global economy. Moreover, looking ahead, the security and the returns of Canadian savings invested abroad are affected by the economic fortunes of others. In short, in a globally integrated economy, Canada's prosperity is tied to the welfare of our trade and investment partners. A reformed IMF in a strengthened international financial architecture would protect national private interest and promote global public interest.

Author's Note

The views expressed in this chapter are strictly those of the author and should not be attributed to the Inter-American Development Bank or the Government of Canada.

Acknowledgements

Helpful comments from the editors, Antoine Brunelle-Cote, Tom Hockin, Doug Nevison and Tony Porter are gratefully acknowledged.

WORKS CITED

Flaherty, Jim. 2006a. Statement to the International Monetary and Financial Committee, April 22.

———. 2006b. Statement to the IMF's Summary Proceedings Annual Meeting, September 17.

Fried, Jonathan T. and James A. Haley. 2010. "Crisis Prevention and Resolution: Lessons from Emerging Markets for Advanced Economies." In *International Monetary and Financial Law: The Global Crisis*, edited by Mario Giovanoli and Diego Devos, 65–95. Oxford: Oxford University Press.

Gitlin, Richard and Brett House. 2014. *A Blueprint for the Sovereign Debt Forum*. CIGI Papers No. 27.

Haldane, Andy and Mark Krueger. 2001. *The Resolution of International Financial Crises: Private Finance and Public Funds*. Bank of Canada/Bank of England Working Paper.

Haley, James A. 2009. "Nominal Anchors, Global Adjustment and the IMF." In *G20 Workshop on the Global Economy: Causes of the Crisis*, edited by Rakesh Mohan and Charles Bean. Reserve Bank of India and Bank of England. http://17g20.pa.go.kr/Documents/g20_workshop_causes_of_the_crisis.pdf.

———. Forthcoming. *Sovereign Debt Restructuring: Old Debates, New Challenges*. CIGI Paper.

IMF. 2005. "Financial Sector Assessment: A Handbook." www.imf.org/external/pubs/ft/fsa/eng/index.htm.

———. 2007. "The Multilateral Consultation on Imbalances." International Monetary Fund Issues Brief 07-03. www.imf.org/external/np/exr/ib/2007/041807.pdf.

———. 2012. "IMF Adopts Institutional View on Capital Flows." IMF Survey Magazine, December 3.

Institute of International Finance. 2004. *Principles for Stable Capital Flows and Fair Debt Restructuring in Emerging Markets*. November.

Kindleberger, Charles. 1971. *The World In Depression, 1929-1939*. Berkeley: University of California Press.

Rasminsky, Louis. 1943. "Tentative Draft Proposals of Canadian Experts for an International Exchange Union." Tabled in the Canadian House of Commons by the Minister of Finance, July 12.

Summers, Lawrence H. 2004. "The United States and the Global Adjustment Process." Speech given at the Peterson Institute, Washington, DC, March 23.

———. 2013. "Economic Stagnation is Not Our Fate — Unless We Let It Be." *Washington Post,* December 18.

Thomson Reuters. 2011. "Don't Focus on IMF, Make Europeans Solve Crisis: Flaherty." Thomson Reuters, October 14.

3

The G8 and G20: Canada's Role

Barry Carin

● ● ● ● ● ● ● ● ● ● ● ● ● ● ● ● ●

A SHORT HISTORY OF THE GROUP OF EIGHT

In 1975, French President Valéry Giscard d'Estaing invited the heads of government from the United States, the United Kingdom, West Germany, Japan and Italy to a summit at Rambouillet, France to discuss the economic difficulties of that time. In 1976, Canada was added to the original group, creating the Group of Seven (G7). In 1993, a personal representative of Russian President Boris Yeltsin met with the G7 Sherpas, and Russia began meeting separately with G7 leaders during their summits, formally joining the group in 1997.[1] Early G8 summits were enjoyed by leaders for their informality and direct personal interaction. Over the years, the turnover of leaders decreased the degree of intimacy, simply because leaders had not been at previous meetings. A lack of language facility began to compromise the informality, and the range of topics on the agenda expanded beyond

---

1   For a historical summary of (Group of Eight) G8 development, see Hajnal (2007). For a useful bibliography, see G20 Research Group (2014). For Canadian work on these subjects, see Centre for Global Studies (2014), the Centre for International Governance Innovation (CIGI) (2013), the Canadian Defence and Foreign Affairs Institute (CDFAI) (2014), and Smith and Heap (2010).

international finance to include security matters, development and climate change.

By 1997, G7 finance ministers and central bank governors had been meeting regularly for a decade. Following the 1997 Asian financial crisis, an Asia-Pacific Economic Cooperation (APEC) decision established the Willard Group or Group of Twenty-Two (G22). The G22 comprised ministers and governors of the G8 plus 14 other countries. Then, in late 1999, Canadian Finance Minister Paul Martin and US Treasury Secretary Lawrence Summers organized the Group of Twenty (G20): finance ministers and central bank governors from G8 countries and key regional powers plus the European Union.[2] The G20 was generally applauded as a necessary innovation in the international architecture. Given the growth of the emerging economies, especially China, the G8 could no longer act as a global steering committee. China was perceived as disinterested in simply transforming the G8 into a "G9."

The chair of the 2005 G8 summit, UK Prime Minister Tony Blair, responded to the changing global power structure by inviting Brazil, China, India, Mexico and South Africa to the meeting at Gleneagles, Scotland. The 2007 Heiligendamm summit was intended to regularize the relationship among the "G8+5," establishing a schedule for regular ministerial meetings among the 13 countries to cover four areas.[3] This process did not succeed — the five leaders were insulted by the apparent second-class status of being the "+5." In 2008, US President George W. Bush called the first G20 meeting at the leaders' level to deal with the worldwide financial crisis.

Paul Martin (2005) noted the advantage of the G20's expanded representation at the leaders' level:

> First, some decisions — no matter how technical — can only be made at the political level. Second, despite the many differences that exist within the group, there are also surprisingly large areas of commonality; all the countries are wrestling with

---

2 Paul Martin jokes that it is not true that the fact there are actually 19 member countries is a rounding error made by finance ministers — Nigeria was originally on the list, but not invited due to political turmoil at the time.

3 The four areas are: "promoting and protecting innovation; strengthening the freedom of investment by means of an open investment climate, including strengthening the principles of corporate social responsibility; determining joint responsibilities for development, focusing specifically on Africa; and joint access to know-how to improve energy efficiency and technology co-operation, with the aim of contributing to reducing CO_2 emissions" (The Press and Information Office of the Federal Government of Germany 2009).

similar issues and have drawn similar lessons from past failures. Third, when national decision-makers discuss issues openly and frankly, it is remarkable how much can be accomplished (never underestimate the value of peer pressure in getting to yes). The G20 has also allowed world leaders to move from a focus on crisis management to a focus on steady improvement in international economic stability and predictability.

THE PROGNOSIS FOR THE G8 AND G20

Recent assessments of the G20 as the "self-described premier forum for international economic cooperation" (G20 Leaders 2009, paragraph 19) and its stewardship of macroeconomic collaboration and financial stability range from the favourable to the very critical. In a recent survey, CIGI experts were asked to respond to the question: "How much progress has been made on macro-economic and international monetary cooperation in the last year?" (Carin and Lombardi 2013). The responses on macroeconomic cooperation were mostly pessimistic:

- "Co-operation on the MAP [Mutual Assessment Process] within the G20 has not advanced and may have gone backwards. The 2010 IMF [International Monetary Fund] reforms have not yet been implemented and further progress on quota reform and governance are stalled."
- "Very little progress on improving crisis resolution framework. Debt restructuring discussion has been stillborn."
- "Surveillance has, if anything, retreated."
- "...the agenda for reforming IMF governance is well specified and has been agreed by G20 leaders....Implementation, however, depends crucially on legislative action by the U.S. Congress, which has no realistic chance of approval in the coming months."
- "There have been very substantial discussions, but the implementation of Basel III is still very uncertain, and financial reform is occurring in quite inconsistent ways in different countries."

- "International momentum behind the international financial regulatory agenda has been fading and, as a result, no meaningful progress has been achieved."
- "Out of the limelight of financial crises, it seems as though the international regulatory regime has hit a standstill." (ibid.)

Responses to the survey that were more favourable to the progress made by the G20 include:

- "Important inroads have been made to develop a holistic/systemic approach to surveillance in the last year."
- "We have to be realistic. When leaders and ministers meet in the G20 context, they spell out mutually acceptable goals and define a strategy to meet them. When they return home, they have to focus instead on national interests and objectives. Short-term challenges dominate in the domestic arena, while global progress requires a longer-term focus." (ibid.)

On balance, if the G20 did not exist, we would have to invent it. It is not realistic to expect the United Nations to be an effective body. The question is how to maximize effectiveness at the same time as representativeness and legitimacy.

CANADA NEEDS A SUCCESSFUL G20

It is important for Canada to be a member of the premier forum for international economic cooperation, because the G20 is where the rules of the global game are made or amended. The G20 will be replaced if a consensus develops among major powers that the forum is ineffective. In all likelihood, if the G20 is replaced, the new format will be smaller — a group of perhaps eight or 10 countries — and it is unlikely to include Canada. Excluded from the rule-making table, Canada will become a rule taker, with potentially unpleasant consequences.

Decisions in complex multilateral negotiations are not made in open plenary sessions — not in the World Trade Organization (WTO), the IMF or the UN Security Council. Trade-offs are always discussed and agreed in a smaller group of the most influential countries, whether it is in the WTO's "Green Room"; "the Invisible Committee," an informal grouping of countries at the WTO in the mid 1990s; a subset of the IMF's executive board; or the permanent five members at the UN Security Council. A package of reforms or action is often crafted by a group of countries who are "friends of the chair," or a small group of countries, such as the Blair House Accord on agricultural trade between the United States and the European Union that took place at the Uruguay Round of multinational trade negotiations, and was then presented to the plenary of the organization as a "take it or leave it" deal. Influence depends on being in the room; intellectual capacity to do the homework and delineate "win-win-win" solutions is not sufficient.

If the G20 lapses in effectiveness, the likelihood is that it will be supplanted. What would the ensuing forum look like? Successors appear to include:

- a "G2," made up of China and the United States, despite China's aversion to claiming leadership and the responsibility that goes along with it. A G2 is unlikely if China remains focused on its significant domestic challenges;
- a "G4" comprising China, the United States, the European Union and Asia;
- a G8, suggested a few years ago by *Forbes* magazine, which would drop Canada and Italy, and add China and India; and
- a "G13," made up of the G8+5 proposed in 2007. Germany, host of the G8 in 2007, introduced the so-called "Heiligendamm Process," which would include Brazil, China, India, Mexico and South Africa (the +5) in a dialogue with the G8 members at the leaders' summit. This original process was doomed, as noted earlier, but there was talk of simply expanding the group to 13.

Much depends on the future of the European Union. If it remains as dysfunctional as it is today, it is improbable that the current overrepresentation of Europe in both the G8 and G20 will persist. In the current G8, Europe has six of the 10 seats — the EU presidency and the European Commission join France, Germany, Italy and the United Kingdom. If the European Union consolidates its power over its member states, the best bet is that the successor arrangement would be a "G6" — limited to Brazil, China, the European Union, India, Japan and the United States — or a G7, which would include South Africa, if it is deemed essential to have an African country in the new group. If the European Union does not consolidate its power over member states, look for a new G8 grouping of Brazil, China, Germany, India, Japan, the United Kingdom and the United States, and possibly South Africa.

France and Italy may not make the cut because they may be perceived to be debtors in apparently dire straits. The United States will be the exception to the convention that the creditors make the rules, because it is too big to fail. The rest of the world has run out of patience with the unreasonable European demand for half the seats at any global table. In any case, if the number of members is decreased, Canada will not be included.[4]

The consequences of the failure of the G20 and its replacement by a smaller grouping will be severe for Canada. The demise of the G20 would result in rules being made without regard for Canadian national interests. The potential impact of decisions being made when Canada is not in the room include an array of trade and international financial issues. For example, permissible national subsidies — when an agreement could be reached where the only "subsidy modes" to be allowed are state equity participation (the EU and Chinese approach) and military procurement (the US approach). Banking rules (over-the-counter [OTC] derivatives and shadow banking) and taxation (tax havens and money laundering) are critical areas where Canada needs to have a voice to promote its own interests.

Canada needs to be at the table when rules for settlement of trade disputes are determined. There is no doubt that Canada will be disadvantaged if it is not included in the "G" group that supersedes the G20.

THE G20 AS GLOBAL ECONOMIC MANAGER

What is the ideal scenario for the G20 to be blessed as manager of long-term oversight of the global economy? Several decisions would be made regarding the functioning of the presidency and the troika, a virtual secretariat, outreach and process:

- The G20 would reverse its agenda creep and focus strictly on international finance issues.
- The troika would be transformed into a "bureau" or executive committee by adding the United States and China. This core group would crunch the issues and do all the work. The bureau's meeting

---

4 This contention is validated by the various attempts to organize Australia, Canada, South Korea, Mexico and Turkey into groups of "middle powers" or "constructive powers."

would be open to the other G20 Sherpas, but the preparatory work would be expected to be done by the five formal members.

- A non-secretariat would reside in the G20 host country, rotating with the presidency. (In diplomatic practice, a non-paper is an informally provided discussion document, without an identified source, title or attribution, provided as an aid to facilitate negotiations.) The non-secretariat would be staffed by seconded officials on three-year terms from the troika governments, the United States and China, who would remain on their own governments' payrolls.
- Spain and other guests would be disinvited. More than 50 people have been seated at recent G20 summit tables — depreciating the summit into a circus where bilateral meetings on the margin have become the reason for leaders to attend.
- International organizations would be removed from the G20 Sherpa process — other than inviting their ideas.
- Outreach would be cut back dramatically, perhaps hosting one annual Davos-type conference early in the presidency. The G20 would stop trying to appease the excessive demands for transparency and accountability; it would announce that it is an informal negotiating forum, not a treaty-based implementation agency.
- In 2012, the US-China Study Group on G20 Reform recommended that any country proposing a new topic should have to provide, in writing, an explanation of a critical gap for which the G20 can usefully provide political guidance, how the G20 can advance the issue and the "sunset provision" for G20 involvement.

One way the body could make the transition from crisis management to effective global steering committee would be for China and the United States to make a joint decision that it was in their mutual self-interest to ensure G20 success and legitimacy. The reality is that if the two powers could agree, their recommendations would, most likely, be congruent with the interests of most other G20 countries. To make this happen, Australia in 2014, or Turkey in 2015, could prepare the ground, with decisions being ratified during a Chinese 2016 G20 presidency. Another option would be for a group of constructive powers — Australia, Canada, Mexico, South Korea and Turkey, for example — to refine a proposal and promote it in the G20 preparatory process.

SUGGESTED SUBSTANTIVE CANADIAN INITIATIVES FOR THE G20

There are differing views on Canadian effectiveness at recent G20 summits. In 2010, Canada chaired the G8 and the Canadian government touted the Muskoka Initiative agreement on maternal and child health. It was criticized in the run-up to the summit for excluding reproductive rights and afterwards for disappearing without effect (Boldosser 2011). The Toronto G20 Summit is remembered primarily for the police mishandling protest demonstrations and not for the summit meeting proceedings. Non-G8 member countries grumbled about Canada's insistence on holding the Muskoka G8 meeting immediately before the Toronto G20, rejecting South Korea's request to reverse the order. The perception was that the G8 caucused beforehand, once again giving the impression that the non-G8 countries were second-class members. South Korea, president for the G20 meeting in fall 2010, was given no substantive role in preparing the Toronto summit. They returned the "favour" at the Seoul summit, with Canada having no privileged influence in its preparation.

At the 2013 St. Petersburg G20 Summit in Russia, Canada played it safe, announcing priorities that were not controversial: macroeconomic strategy combining short-term growth with medium-term fiscal consolidation; implementation of the Basel III standards on bank capital, agreed in 2010; endorsing regional trade agreements and extending the G20's anti-protectionist pledge; combatting corruption; catalyzing market-based solutions to help the poor; and advancing the G20's accountability for delivering on commitments. The skeptic would observe that these Canadian minimalist G20 priorities kept heads below the trench line. The realist would respond that, given the implications of the behaviour of the US Congress, Canada was pursuing the art of the possible.

Expending effort on G20 accountability seems especially misplaced — pandering to civil society activists desperate for a role. It would appear that efforts should be concentrated on finding solutions to problems instead of examining the entrails of past decisions taken in different circumstances, which is especially the case since the G20 is not an implementing body.

Substantive Initiatives

Canadian initiatives for the 2014 Brisbane G20 Summit should be devised, bearing in mind the various constraints faced by the Australian presidency. Australia must steer the preparations in difficult economic conditions with a group of countries in different economic and fiscal situations, and dissimilar norms and strategies. Since commitments are not subject to any binding compliance measures or formal dispute resolution system, initiatives need to be framed to ensure win-win outcomes for each member country. Because the G20 operates by consensus, positive-sum outcomes are not sufficient — each country must be a winner. Formulating such initiatives is a worthy problem.

There are three categories of assistance Canada could consider in preparing substantive proposals. First, to improve international governance, strategies to promote innovations in international institutions and informal arrangements could be suggested. Second, specific initiatives could be elaborated to break deadlocks in negotiations on climate change and in the process on post-2015 UN Millennium Development Goals (MDGs). Third, terms of reference for studies to be commissioned by the Australians for subsequent G20 consideration could be crafted for several specific policy issues on the agenda.

A major raison d'être of the G20 is to be the steward of the international institutional architecture. The Canadian government could champion specific innovations in global governance, formulating ideas to fill recognized governance gaps, where problems with global public goods dimensions are not being adequately addressed by existing formal international institutions or informal arrangements. Examples include new organizations or arrangements to deal with international cooperation on cyber security, sovereign debt resolution, energy, fisheries, water or migration. It could stimulate debate by offering to work with the G20 presidency to help devise proposals and then promote the ideas.

Canada could prepare *aides-mémoires* or "non-papers" — informal discussion documents without attribution or an identified source — suggesting ideas that could be the basis of discussion of a proposed agreement. Providing Australia with non-papers informally does not commit anyone to their contents. For example, Canada could propose a blueprint to transform the Financial Stability Board (FSB) into a treaty-based organization, with concrete suggestions for the resources and approaches to deal with the financial regulatory issues on the table. Investing effort in the FSB promises a higher return than pushing for implementation of the 2010 agreements to strengthen the IMF — "only an inveterate optimist would venture a favourable guess for action [from US Congress] this year or next" (Boughton 2013).

Australia's new government was elected in September 2013. At the 2014 World Economic Forum annual meeting at Davos, Switzerland, Australian Prime Minister Tony Abbott (2014) indicated three specific priority areas for the G20: trade liberalization, combatting tax avoidance and evasion, and encouraging infrastructure investment. Mike Callaghan (2013) of the Lowy Institute's G20 Studies Centre in Australia had suggested that the five priorities should be:

- developing a clearer, more consistent and more coordinated global growth strategy;
- breathing life into the multilateral trading system;
- tackling climate change financing;
- delivering tangible progress on the international effort to combat tax evasion and avoidance; and
- "mainstreaming" development into the G20 agenda and not treating it as an "add-on."

One way to proceed on the global growth strategy is for each G20 country to prepare a report on its own efforts to stimulate growth. Canada should provide an early report of sufficient quality to be used by Australia as a template to elicit national reports from the G20 countries.

We will need an "outside-the-box" approach to breathe life into the multilateral trading system. Perhaps the best way to re-energize the WTO is to encourage it to envision a multilateral investment treaty. The 1995–1998 effort by the Organisation for Economic Co-operation and Development (OECD) to pursue a multilateral investment agreement was doomed because it appeared to be an effort by developed countries to make the rules on regulating foreign investors and then impose the rules on developing countries. This criticism would not apply to a well-crafted G20 effort, with sophisticated outreach and the clear goal to enact the treaty under the WTO umbrella.

To tackle the climate change deadlock, an *aide-mémoire* or non-paper could be crafted to outline first steps. Rather than the G20 vacuously "welcoming progress" at the latest UN Framework Convention on Climate Change failed negotiation, a pragmatic proposal could be presented outlining a package of feasible elements. Another example could be to establish a mechanism to measure emissions. The G20 could establish a publicly funded global institution to catalyze research and publish open-source results. Another element could be triggering an international effort to consolidate and then accelerate all the work being undertaken to develop standards in heavy-emission sectors such as power, transportation, cement, mining, and oil and gas. Imagine if the G20 agreed to phase in rigorous standards over the next 10 years and then established a WTO approach of sanctioned border-tax adjustments to support them.

To combat "base erosion and profit shifting," the focus could be on global companies' exploitation of loopholes, which allows them to shift profits to low taxation jurisdictions. Australia should invite work to be done to enhance international cooperative tax arrangements. It could request China and the United States to jointly propose strengthening the Convention on Mutual Administrative Assistance in Tax Matters. This convention has been signed by Brazil, China, India and Russia, despite being developed by the OECD and the Council of Europe.

There is another opportunity for a non-paper for the development section of the G20 agenda. The St. Petersburg G20 Leaders' Declaration confirmed that members of the G20 "support the ongoing efforts in the UN for the elaboration of the post-2015 development agenda. We commit to participate actively in this process and engage in the discussion on the direction of the new framework and its key principles and ideas and effectively contribute to the timely conclusion of the process" (G20 Leaders 2013).

Unfortunately, the intergovernmental process that will determine the final outcome is unlikely to reach agreement on post-2015 MDGs. There is overwhelming pressure from all sides to highlight specific areas that should be included on the list, which must be limited in number. Lobby groups fight to give prominence to their subject: poverty; employment; inequality; social protection; food security; health; secondary and tertiary education; physical security; gender equality; disaster resilience; connectivity; "energy for all"; human rights; environmental sustainability; climate change; anticorruption; and governance. If everything is included, an important opportunity to establish the next development paradigm will have been lost. The G20 can act to ensure that the current UN process does not result in a post-2015 development agenda that is vacuous. Canada, acting as amicus curiae, could provide a "non-road map" to the Australian presidency, proposing a vision of development, a list of agreed principles and a menu of options of a limited number of goals and measurable targets for the G20 to consider. The UN intergovernmental process would benefit from substantive consideration by the G20.

An important G20 activity is the preparation of complex issues for future consideration by remits to international organizations (for example, the International Energy Agency, the OECD, the Organization of the Petroleum Exporting Countries and the World Bank were requested to jointly prepare a report on inefficient fossil fuel subsidies) or from a key actor (for example, UK Prime Minister David Cameron and Bill Gates at the Cannes summit).[5] Canada could suggest to Australia that it may wish to commission studies and request a series of reports to be discussed at Brisbane or at the 2015 summit in Turkey. The reports could be requested by officials or possibly leader to leader. Canada could provide draft terms of reference for remits on issues, such as arrangements to dampen commodity price volatility, initiatives to lever new official development assistance commitments and private sector investment to promote financial inclusion, or new modalities to encourage public-private partnerships in international infrastructure projects.

SUGGESTED CANADIAN PROCESS INITIATIVES FOR THE G20

The preparatory process for a leaders' level G20 presents a very significant challenge, especially given the high expectations and media scrutiny faced by any G20 meeting. The G20 does not have a permanent secretariat with an experienced staff to provide continuity and institutional memory. Leaders do not generally have the appropriate technical expertise to debate, negotiate and agree on policy approaches to the complex problems on the agenda; this is especially true of leaders who are not former finance ministers. The challenge is compounded by the participants' dissimilar cultural approaches to decision

---

5   David Cameron was asked to present a report on global governance and Bill Gates had been invited to prepare a report on how to finance the development of poor countries.

making. To complicate matters, any G20 summit host will be hard pressed to sift through the cacophony of demands from both civil society and excluded countries, each of which demand to be substantively involved, in addition to officials from international organizations jockeying for visibility. Meeting time is short. Exacerbating this problem is that leaders will not be passively choreographed. Despite the predetermined agenda, leaders will discuss the current crisis and pressing issues that are of concern to them when the summit takes place. The key decisions in the "precooked" final declaration will, therefore, have to be well prepared in advance by G20 officials.

Each G20 leader appoints a personal representative, denoted as a Sherpa — ideally someone with direct access to their leader. The Sherpas are in constant contact with each other and meet several times before the summit to broker agenda items and draft the communiqué language. G20 finance ministers, who meet a few times a year, including on the margins of the semi-annual World Bank-IMF meetings, each appoint a senior official known as the G20 finance deputy. An unfortunate change initiated by Mexico in 2012 was to introduce a two-track system, where finance deputies meet separately from the Sherpa track. This provides unnecessary coordination difficulties and an additional level of complexity to an already overburdened process. Distance from the finance track handicaps work on employment, food security, development and corruption — the issue areas assigned to the Sherpas. All these issues require policy decisions that are prerogatives of finance ministries. Canada should advise Australia to scrap this bifurcated system.

To increase the probability of success of the G20, Canada could pursue several avenues. Canadian officials could confer with counterparts in Mexico, Korea and Turkey with a view to organizing some joint suggestions to help the G20 presidency find win-win solutions for issues on the G20 agenda. Mexico, South Korea and Turkey all have interests similar to Canada's regarding the success of the G20. This middle powers or constructive powers caucus could propose ideas to the Australians. One suggestion is to second officials to the Sherpa team from troika countries, as well as Mexico, South Korea and Turkey. This is not a new idea. There is a history of such secondments over the past 10 years. Australia seconded an official to the Mexican Sherpa team in 2012. Another idea would be to promote a "quintet" rather than a troika approach. While all G20 countries are equal, two are more equal than others. To be pragmatic, Australia should approach the United States and China early to identify common ground and jointly prepare future proposals. A well-argued idea from Australia, endorsed by troika members Russia and Turkey, and supported by the United States and China, will invariably carry the day and gain consensus in the G20.

It is late in the day to substantively influence the Australians. They will have hit the ground running on December 1, 2013. Perhaps the focus should be on Turkey, the 2015 G20 presidency, and the rumoured 2016 Chinese presidency. China's year will be particularly important. The Chinese will want to ensure a widely acknowledged success. Informal discussions in 2014 can lay the groundwork for intensive cooperation in the subsequent years.

The G7/G8 has long outlived its relevance and usefulness. (For example, what impact can a G8 decision have regarding the Syrian issue without Turkey and Saudi Arabia signing on?) The continued existence of the G8 undermines the G20, and it would not be a step in the right direction for the major emerging economies to formalize their group and have the G20 degenerate into a face-off between two caucuses. The BRICS countries (Brazil, Russia, India, China and South Africa) have already met five times. It is time to euthanize the G8. Canada could promote a painless demise and dignified funeral for the European-dominated institution.

The formulation of Canadian positions within the G20 is a black box. Historically, while one might think that several departments and agencies would be involved, the Finance Department and the Bank of Canada held a decided monopoly of advice. It was not a question of the Finance Department being more equal than others — outside opinion or advice was not warmly received. Input from the Foreign Affairs, Trade and Development Department or the Canadian International Development Agency was not welcome, even in cases where their officers were former Finance Department officials.

The Canadian government could push the boundaries of public diplomacy by publishing an annual "Canadian G20 Commentary." It could compile initiatives for the subsequent year's G20 presidency suggested by Canadian think tanks, academics, civil society, business and youth groups. It would be released in the late fall, just prior to the new presidency taking the chair. The call for submissions would solicit ideas, proposing positive-sum approaches to finesse sticking points on items on next year's G20 agenda. This idea would likely be adopted by other countries, including non-G20 countries. It could have the very helpful effect of contributing to decreasing the current heavy burden on G20 officials of outreach activities.

CONCLUSIONS

There is no scientific or arithmetic basis to judge the success of the G20 in managing the financial crisis to date or to assess the prospects to prevent and contain future similar challenges. There is evidence to support both optimists and pessimists.

Idealistic optimists would note the G20's achievements — the London summit coordinated a US$5 trillion stimulus, the creation of the FSB to modernize banking standards and the resurrection of the IMF, which had been withering into irrelevance. The G20 "standstill" agreement on protectionist measures prevented wholesale imposition of Depression-era "beggar-thy-neighbour" tariffs. Supporters would argue the G20's performance should be graded on a realistic scale. Once out of the crisis management mode, it is naive to expect complex multilateral negotiations to result in quick successes. In a context of geopolitical rivalries, unbalanced macroeconomic recovery, sovereign debt difficulties and politically challenging levels of unemployment, patience is required.

Pessimistic appraisers would note the inability of the G20 to implement commitments. The summary conclusion of a 2013 survey of experts was that there is considerable cause for concern in progress on arrangements for international economic governance (Kelly 2013). The assessment was that there has been minimal progress on international cooperation on both macroeconomic policy and on financial regulation. Even the vaunted standstill on protectionist measures is being questioned. The WTO reported as early as 2011 that "policy slippage continues to occur and appears to be increasing" (WTO 2011). Simon J. Evenett (2013) argues "that the current G20 approach to promoting open trade and investment is not working. In recent years G20 members resorted to protectionism more frequently than at the beginning of the economic crisis and, indeed, the stock of crisis-era protectionist measures imposed by the G20 members keeps on growing." Thomas A. Bernes (2013) was trenchant in his assessment that "what is so disquieting about this most recent summit is the sense it leaves with observers that the G20 is falling into a bureaucratic morass — longer communiqués (and annexes), more words and no sense of real progress."

In the medium to longer term, the G20's most significant contribution can be to build the institutions needed to prevent a recurrence of the great financial crisis. Institutions do not create or reform themselves. The strategic vision and brokering function must be provided from the outside. Other than the G20, there is no viable option. It is imperative to identify the most likely prospects for success. The outlook for new or strengthened institutions will be more promising if the proposal can be credibly depicted as win-win. The judgment of what constitutes a win-win in international cooperation is compromised by international politics. An interesting example is the Egmont Group — a relatively informal organization of national "financial intelligence units" to combat money laundering and the financing of terrorism (see Egmont Group 2014). While it would seem a "no-brainer" that China would join the group (Hong Kong is a member), it declines to join because of Taiwan's membership.

Perhaps more important is the criterion for the future agenda that US congressional approval not be required for any proposed G20 initiative. This requires that, in the international financial area, the focus should be on building up the FSB. Efforts to reform and strengthen the IMF should await Republican ownership of the idea. It will be easier in the medium term to make progress on highly technical issues, such as shadow banking and OTC derivatives. The issues of regulating international and too-big-to-fail institutions require international cooperation, and clearly do not have the zero-sum game characteristics of reassigning IMF voting shares or executive board seats.

Canada should take the lead in laying to rest the G8, and work hard to secure the success of the G20. Globalization has resulted in a world where there are many spillovers of policy decisions beyond national borders. Canada is impacted by events in both the real and financial global economy. The global commons has many dimensions, where collective action is required to secure appropriate management of global public goods. Decisions are not taken on the basis of global universal suffrage; the rules are made by a small group of the most powerful countries. If the G20 does not appear to provide effective leadership, it will be replaced by a smaller group that will not include Canada.

Canada should secure its position by being an intellectual leader, formulating ideas and crafting initiatives to enhance the prospects of G20 success. These ideas should cover both G20 process improvements and substantive policy proposals: strategies to improve the international governance architecture; initiatives to break deadlocks in negotiations on climate change and the process on post-2015 development goals; and terms of reference for studies to be commissioned for key G20 policy issues. Canada should enlist the other middle powers — South Korea, Mexico and Turkey — to collectively develop consensus approaches to G20 priorities to assist Australia's presidency.

WORKS CITED

Abbott, Tony. 2014. "This Year's G20: Getting the Fundamentals Right." Speech given at the World Economic Forum Annual Meeting, Davos, January 23. www.pm.gov.au/media/2014-01-23/address-world-economic-forum-davos-switzerland-0.

Bernes, Thomas A. 2013. "Ho Hum…On to Brisbane." CIGI Commentary, September 9. www.cigionline.org/publications/2013/9/ho-hum%E2%80%A6on-brisbane.

Boldosser, Amy. 2011. "What Happened to the G8's Commitment to Maternal, Newborn & Child Health?" Family Care International Blog. June 2. http://familycareintl.org/blog/2011/06/02/what-happened-to-the-g8s-commitment-to-maternal-newborn-child-health/.

Boughton, James. 2013. "Why We Need (But Will Not Soon Get) IMF Reform." CIGI Commentary, October 4. www.cigionline.org/publications/2013/10/why-we-need-will-not-soon-get-imf-reform.

Callaghan, Mike. 2013. "Playbook for the Brisbane G20 Summit." Lowy Institute for International Policy. October.

Carin, Barry and Domenico Lombardi. 2013. "CIGI Survey: Progress of International Economic Governance." CIGI. http://interactive.cigionline.org/survey-of-progress.

CDFAI. 2014. www.cdfai.org.

Centre for Global Studies. 2014. University of Victoria. www.uvic.ca/research/centres/globalstudies/.

CIGI. 2013. CIGI G20 Papers. www.cigionline.org/series/cigi-g20-papers.

Egmont Group. 2014. www.egmontgroup.org/.

Evenett, Simon J. 2013. "Five More Years of the G20 Standstill on Protectionism?" *VoxEU*, September 3. www.voxeu.org/article/five-more-years-g20-standstill-protectionism.

G20 Leaders. 2009. "G20 Leaders Statement: The Pittsburgh Summit: September 24-25, 2009, Pittsburgh." www.g20.utoronto.ca/2009/2009communique0925.html.

———. 2013. "Russia G20: G20 Leaders' Declaration: September, 2013." www.g20.org/sites/default/files/g20_resources/library/Saint_Petersburg_Declaration_ENG.pdf.

G20 Research Group. 2014. "G20 Bibliography: Compiled by the G20 Research Group." G20 Information Centre, Munk School of Global Affairs, University of Toronto. www.g8.utoronto.ca/g20/biblio/index.html.

Hajnal, Peter I. 2007. *The G8 System and the G20: Evolution, Role and Documentation.* Aldershot, UK: Ashgate.

Kelly, Declan. 2013. "Inaugural CIGI Survey on International Economic Governance Reveals 'Considerable Cause for Concern.'" CIGI News Release, September 4. www.cigionline.org/articles/2013/09/inaugural-cigi-survey-international-economic-governance-reveals-%E2%80%98considerable-cause.

Martin, Paul. 2005. "A Global Answer to Global Problems." *Foreign Affairs* May/June.

Smith, Gordon S. and Peter C. Heap. 2010. "Canada, the G8, and the G20: A Canadian Approach to Shaping Global Governance in a Shifting International Environment." The School of Public Policy SPP Research Papers 3 (8). November. www.policyschool.ucalgary.ca/sites/default/files/research/smithfinalfinal.pdf.

The Press and Information Office of the Federal Government of Germany. 2009. "Heiligendamm Process." www.g-8.de/Content/EN/Artikel/__g8-summit/2007-06-08-heiligendamm-prozess__en.html.

WTO. 2011. *Report on G20 Trade Measures (Mid-October 2010 to April 2011).* Geneva: WTO.

4

Canada, the FSB and the International Institutional Response to the Current Crisis

Tony Porter

● ● ● ● ● ● ● ● ● ● ● ● ● ● ● ● ● ●

Early in the global financial crisis, policy makers and regulators worldwide devoted a lot of attention to reforming the international institutions and rules involved in the governance of global financial markets. This reflected the global character of the crisis, the dependence of national rules on global rules and the importance of global institutions and rules for the restoration of confidence in global finance. Canadian policy makers and regulators were heavily involved in this reform effort. Although the Canadian financial system performed better than others during the crisis, it too suffered problems of its own, as well as being harmed by problems that had originated elsewhere. The global integration of Canadian financial market actors and regulatory institutions means that Canada has a lot at stake when changes are made to international institutions and the rules governing global finance — both in times of crisis and in times of stability. Canada's strong track record and expertise in domestic and international financial regulatory matters also mean that policy makers and regulators elsewhere welcome a strong Canadian role in international reform efforts.

Developments in international financial governance, before and after the crisis, exemplify very significant changes in global governance more generally that have been occurring since the 1970s. An older model of global governance, which reached its zenith in the two decades following World War II, was based on the states that governed national political and economic systems working to shape their global interactions through a mix of state-to-state threats and negotiations, and the creation of formal international treaties and bureaucratic organizations such as the International Monetary Fund (IMF). This older model has been complemented, and often displaced, by complex mixtures of institutions and rules that are formal and informal, public and private, and national and international. In the case of global finance, this is evident in a consistent, incremental growth of relatively informal international groupings of national regulatory officials who set standards or best practices that are implemented nationally, but can have a direct effect on private actors in global financial markets. Rules created by public officials often interact with private sector rules created by globally active private financial market actors, individually or in associations.

Canada, like other countries, operates within this changing environment, while also contributing to its ongoing construction. Canada's experience displays some familiar characteristics of Canadian foreign policy in the older state-centric model of global governance, including the need to balance its geographic proximity and ties to its powerful neighbour to the south, its interactions with other more distant and less powerful states, and its integration with the international economy. At the same time, the emergence of more complex global governance mechanisms has introduced new elements into the Canadian role in international financial governance. Yet, these also echo earlier periods where Canadian expertise helped it play a larger role in multilateral institutions than the more conventional measures of power would predict.

This chapter will discuss the evolution of the more complex governance arrangements in global finance and Canada's role in them, as well as the international institutional response to the global financial crisis that began in 2007, highlighting the distinctive role that Canada played.

THE INTERNATIONAL REGULATORY ARRANGEMENTS PRIOR TO THE CRISIS

Since the 1970s, a set of informal international arrangements has played an increasingly prominent role in the governance of global financial markets.[1] In 1971, the Euro-currency Standing Committee was established at the Bank for International Settlements (BIS) in Basel, Switzerland, to monitor the rapid growth of global financial markets that had begun to worry authorities. This committee was renamed the Committee on the Global Financial System in 1999. A number of similar committees have been created that are also hosted by the BIS. The best known is the Basel Committee on Banking Supervision (BCBS), created in 1975, which has established relationships with informal regional groupings of bank regulators around the world. The International Organization of Securities Commissions (IOSCO) was established in 1984, but built on the Inter-American Association of Securities Commissions and Similar Organizations, which was created in 1974. IOSCO is a more conventional formal organization, but until its 2012 reorganization, its most important work was done in its more informal Technical Committee.

A similar process was occurring among private sector actors. The Institute of International Finance, created during the debt crisis of the early 1980s by commercial banks to share information about exposure to sovereign borrowers, has increasingly become involved in consultations with officials at the BCBS and other international institutions. The international standards developed by the private sector International Accounting Standards Board (IASB), created in 2001, have been given force by their recognition by public authorities in almost 120 countries. By the early 2000s, more than 200 international financial associations were playing a variety of governance roles (McKeen-Edwards and Porter 2013).

The informality of the above groups, which primarily involve officials with technical expertise representing national regulatory authorities, has been accompanied by the growing prominence of informal political arrangements at more senior levels. In the 1970s, the Group of Ten (G10) Central Bank Governors, which, for the most part, included the same actors as the board of the BIS, played a key role in coordinating collaboration among regulators.

---

1   This history has been covered elsewhere, including Davies and Green (2008) and Porter (2014).

However, in the mid-1970s, the Group of Seven (G7) was created at the level of both heads of government and finance ministers, and over time, it displaced the G10 and the more formal IMF as a location for political coordination of global financial governance. In 1999, following the Asian financial crisis of 1997, the G7 created the Financial Stability Forum (FSF). This was an informal body hosted by the BIS, which brought together three representatives from each G7 member, along with the key international institutions involved in the governance of global financial markets. The Group of Twenty (G20), also created in 1999, was modelled on the informality of the G7, bringing together finance ministers and central bankers from the G7 countries plus 12 other systemically important countries, together with representatives from the IMF, World Bank and European Union. The creation of the FSF and the G20 further integrated the informal regulatory groupings. By virtue of the weight of the countries participating in the G7, and the effectiveness of the informal institutions involved, the G7 was able to exercise a leadership role in the governance of global financial markets.

Canadian political and regulatory institutions, as well as individual Canadians, have been actively involved in the evolution of these international arrangements. Such individuals include Malcolm Knight, who served as general manager of the BIS from 2003 to 2008, and William White, who was manager of the Monetary and Economic Department of the BIS in 1994 and head of the department from 1994 to 2008. White was one of the few people who warned about the global financial crisis some years before it occurred (*The Economist* 2012).

Canada was a member of the Basel Committee from the beginning, and in the early 1980s was supportive of the work that would develop into the first Basel Accord on capital. However, Canada did not stand out for its strong positions, despite having the longest-serving BCBS representative, Serge Vachon, of all member states from 1975 to 1997 (Goodhart 2011, 65, 149, 547). This is not surprising, since Canada's Office of the Superintendent of Financial Institutions (OSFI), which now has primary responsibility for bank regulation in Canada, was only formed in 1987 through a merger of the Department of Insurance and the Office of the Inspector General of Banks (OIGB). The OIGB was small: at the time of the Basel Committee's creation, it had only four staff (OSFI 2012). There has also been a tradition in Canada of the Bank of Canada (BoC) minimizing its involvement in financial regulation. This lack of regulatory capacity contributed to Canada's lack of prominence in the lead up to the first Basel Accord.

OSFI's creation was accompanied by a commitment to increase staff and a growing prominence in international regulatory discussions. By 2000, OSFI staff had increased to 390 (OSFI 2000, 11). Canada was enthusiastic in its support for Basel II, issued in 2004, when Nicholas Le Pan, then superintendent of OSFI, was chair of the Basel Accord Implementation Group and vice chair of the BCBS.

In the international governance of securities, provincial regulators played an especially visible leadership role. Quebec's securities commission, the Autorité des marchés financiers (AMF), and the Ontario Securities Commission (OSC) were founding members of IOSCO, which had its headquarters in Montreal until it moved to Madrid in 2000. Paul Guy was appointed secretary general of IOSCO in 1986, having previously served as chair of the AMF and director of operations at the Montreal Stock Exchange (see Guy 1992). Key initiatives in IOSCO's early years grew out of US efforts to promote multilateral initiatives on the exchange of information on securities fraud and multi-jurisdictional disclosure systems for securities prospectuses — initiatives that it had not been able to promote effectively unilaterally (Porter 1993, 116-17).

With respect to international accounting governance, Canadians have been especially active internationally, as early as the 1973 formation of the International Accounting Standards Committee (IASC), which was the predecessor to the IASB (Bernhut 2002). Tricia O'Malley and Paul Cherry, who both served as chairs of Canada's Accounting Standards Board, also played prominent roles at the IASB. O'Malley was a founder and member of the IASB from 2001 to 2007, and then served as IASB director of implementation activities until 2009. Cherry, who served as chief accountant of the OSC from 1986 to 1988 and chaired IOSCO's working group on international accounting and auditing standards, was chair of the IASC's Standing Interpretations Committee from 1997 to 2001, a key period leading up to the IASB's 2001 creation (Zeff and Radcliffe 2010). He was also chair of the IASB's Standards Advisory Council from 2009 to 2013. Edward Waitzer served as chair of IOSCO's powerful Technical Committee from 1994 to 1996 while he was chair of the OSC, a period in which IOSCO was engaged in important discussions with the IASC on expectations for international accounting standards. Waitzer then went on to chair the IASC's Strategy Working Party (Zeff 2012, 819). In the early 2000s, the priority was to harmonize with US standards while continuing to work with the IASB, but as the IASB's standards became more widely adopted around the world, Canada also adopted those standards, while maintaining certain exceptions designed to allow it to continue to engage closely with US markets.

At the political level, in 1976, Canada was added — with US support — to the leaders' meetings that had begun in the previous year, constituting the G7. The Halifax G7 Summit of 1995, hosted by Canada in the wake of the 1994 peso crisis, marked a significant upswing in the engagement of G7 leaders with global financial regulatory issues. Former Minister of Finance Paul Martin played a key role in the creation of the G20 in 1999, and Canada hosted the G20's rotating secretariat for its first two years, with Martin serving as its chair. This reflected Martin's own role, but also the advantages of Canada relative to the United States and European member states, which were seen to have already been playing prominent leadership roles in the lead up to the G20's creation (G20 Research Group 2008).

THE INTERNATIONAL REGULATORY RESPONSE TO THE CRISIS

The most significant international institutional reforms in response to the crisis were the transformation of the FSF into the Financial Stability Board (FSB), the upgrading of the G20 to the leaders' level and the transfer of the G7's leadership role in global financial governance to the G20. The FSB was given a written charter and a more differentiated structure. Its membership was expanded to more closely match the membership of the G20, and it adopted a mandatory peer review process to apply to all members, including the United States and China. Six FSB Regional Consultative Groups were added to help expand the FSB's consultative process beyond its own membership. The upgraded G20 began systematically reviewing and endorsing reports from the FSB, in addition to the important role it played during the crisis in coordinating stimulus packages and in making additional funds available to the IMF.

There were a number of other significant international institutional reforms. The membership of the BCBS was expanded and it was given a new charter in 2013 with stronger and clearer accountability mechanisms, including a more formalized relationship to its oversight body, the Group of Governors and Heads of Supervision, and a mandatory public notice and comment procedure for standards. The G20 agreed to establish supervisory colleges designed to foster cooperation among supervisors for particular internationally active financial firms. The G20 also agreed to work to require over-the-counter (OTC) derivatives to be cleared by central counterparties or for banks exposed to risks associated with them to hold higher levels of capital, to shift standardized OTC derivatives onto exchanges and to require that data on trades be recorded in trade repositories. A new international monitoring board of public authorities (initially including the European Commission, IOSCO, the US Securities and Exchange Commission, and the Financial Services Agency of Japan) was created to increase the public accountability of the IASB.

These institutional changes have been accompanied by growth in the strength, number and complexity of the content of international standards. The most important of these are the Basel III standards, which raise the capital that banks are required to hold relative to their risk-weighted assets, as well as establishing standards for managing risks associated with liquidity and funding stability. Standards have also been strengthened with regard to the too-big-to-fail problem, including identifying globally systemically important financial institutions and requiring them to hold more capital, requiring risk-sensitive executive compensation practices, strengthening the regulation of credit rating agencies and developing mechanisms for macroprudential regulation (considering the collective impact of firm activity and not just individual firms). There are many other similar changes that go beyond the scope of the present chapter.

Overall, the degree to which the international response to the crisis builds on existing reforms is striking. Rather than create a new centralized formal regulatory body like the IMF or reverting significantly to national-level solutions, the reform mainly strengthened existing informal arrangements and the standards associated with them. The incremental and path-dependent character of the standards is especially evident with Basel III, which builds directly on Basel II, which in turn built on Basel I. There have been numerous concerns raised and skepticism expressed with regard to the reform effort. Nevertheless, a review of the websites of the FSB, the BCBS and the other bodies confirms that reform is moving ahead in significant ways, even if it falls well short of ensuring that another major crisis will not occur.

CANADA'S ROLE IN THE REGULATORY RESPONSE

Canada's superior performance during the crisis significantly enhanced the reputation of its regulatory system and respect for its regulators. Canadian banks received assistance from the Canadian government through the purchase of insured residential mortgage pools by the government's Insured Mortgage Purchase Program, support of liquidity by the BoC and support for a private sector-led restructuring of the asset-backed commercial paper market when it froze during the crisis. This assistance, however, was much more modest than that of other countries in terms of its volume and the exposure of the government to losses.

The positive features of the Canadian regulatory system facilitated Canada's ability to contribute to international reform initiatives, not only through its reputational effects, but also because it facilitated the ability of Canadian officials to produce knowledge and policy positions that were useful in international discussions. Although regulatory authority is shared among a number of bodies at the federal and provincial levels, there are effective coordination mechanisms linking these bodies, also facilitated by the relatively concentrated character of the Canadian banking industry and the stabilizing role it plays in securities markets.

In Canada, the coordination of regulatory policies relevant to international reform efforts is primarily accomplished through three committees linking the three major authorities. The Superintendent of Financial Institutions chairs the Financial Institutions Supervisory Committee (FISC), which also includes the governor of the BoC, deputy minister of finance, and heads of the Canada Deposit Insurance Corporation and Financial Consumer Agency of Canada. The primary focus of FISC is microprudential regulation. The governor of the BoC chairs the Heads of Agencies Committee, which also includes the Department of Finance, OSFI, the four largest provincial securities regulators (Alberta, British Columbia, Ontario and Quebec) and the chair of the Canadian Securities Administrators. This committee's primary focus is financial markets' regulatory issues. The deputy minister of finance chairs the Senior Advisory Committee, which has the same membership as

FISC, with other agencies included as needed. One of its functions is keeping the minister of finance informed. The committee is concerned with regulatory reform issues and macroprudential regulation. All of these committees also have subcommittees composed of officials who are more involved in the technical working-level details of the regulatory issues.

Prior to the financial crisis, these coordinating mechanisms were relatively passive conduits for monitoring issues, but they became much more proactive, deliberative forums during the crisis. As the FSB's 2012 "Peer Review of Canada" notes, "In spite of Canada's relatively complex regulatory structure, cooperation between relevant agencies during the crisis appears to have been swift and effective" (FSB 2012, 16). It goes on to note that the above mechanisms "enabled the effective exchange of information and facilitated discussions that led to coordinated responses" (ibid.). This then enhanced the effectiveness of Canadian engagement in international discussions.

The comparable US mechanisms provide a contrast. The Financial Stability Oversight Council (FSOC) was established by the 2010 Dodd-Frank Wall Street Reform and Consumer Protection Act to address regulatory fragmentation, with 10 voting members and five non-voting members. The Canadian mechanisms are smaller, less legalistic, more effective and better able to develop a coherent perspective. The FSB's 2013 "Peer Review of the United States" notes that "the FSOC's decisions and actions reflect the views of a wide range of agencies with different mandates and interests. This might affect in some cases the FSOC's ability to take decisions in an effective and prompt manner" (FSB 2013, 6-7). Sharp conflicts among US regulators have influenced their engagements on reform issues at the BCBS and the FSB (Bair 2012, 257–72).

Areas of Canadian leadership in the international reform effort are especially evident in the prominent roles played by Tiff Macklem, senior deputy governor at the BoC; Mark Carney, former governor of the BoC; and Julie Dickson, head of OSFI. For a country of Canada's size, it is unusual to have this number of regulators with this level of recognition. This leadership is due, in part, to their personal qualities, but also reflects the expertise, effectiveness and culture of the Canadian agencies where they have worked. Both Dickson and Macklem developed their careers within government, with less private sector experience than would be typical for senior figures in the regulatory world in the United States. The personal international reputations of all three are associated with their agencies. As a *Euromoney* article says of Carney, he "is investing the country's reputational capital, playing the role of international financial peacekeeper" (Verma 2012). It is useful to briefly consider each of their roles in turn.

Tiff Macklem played a particularly important role in the early stages of the reform. He chaired (with Rakesh Mohan of India) the G20 Working Group 1 on Enhancing Sound Regulation and Strengthening Transparency. When the FSB was first established, he was associate deputy minister of finance and appointed chair of the FSB's Standing Committee on Standards Implementation (SCSI). He also held this position after being appointed senior deputy governor of the BoC in 2010. Macklem's international reputation and contacts have been widely noted in the press. For example, an article in *The Globe and Mail* provides quotes from foreign officials attesting to Macklem's expertise and contributions during the response to the crisis, noting that Mario Draghi, European Central Bank president and head of the FSB at the time, "hand-picked" Macklem to lead the FSB's SCSI due to his expertise (see Carmichael 2013).

In his role as governor of the BoC, Mark Carney also attracted high levels of positive attention for his contributions to international regulatory matters, as was evident in his selection to head the FSB. As a 2012 *Euromoney* article notes, "'When Carney speaks, people listen' is the typical refrain from the financial and policy community, particularly during international meetings, from the IMF to G20 to Davos" (Verma 2012). He was noticed for expanding the central bank's role in regulatory matters. His ability to build consensus and attract positive comments from senior bankers while aggressively defending higher capital charges against banking critics is noteworthy. Carney's widely cited October 2011 comment that the Occupy Wall Street protests were "entirely constructive" is an indicator of his attentiveness to the larger social and political aspects of the financial crisis, as are his efforts to explain the significance of the international reform in a manner that can engage policy makers and the broader public, for instance with the "Narrative Progress Report on Financial Reform" that the FSB has recently started providing to G20 leaders.

In media reports, Julie Dickson has, like Carney, been seen as "an international celebrity of sorts — an A-lister in rarified global financial circles" (Tedesco 2013). While critics have suggested that her aggressive implementation of international standards is a sign of her excessive enthusiasm for this reputation, her commitment to strong regulation was evident well before. She chairs the Committee on Supervisory Intensity and Effectiveness at the FSB, which works on systemically important financial institutions, and she sits on the FSB's Standing Committee on Supervisory and Regulatory Cooperation. In its annual reports, OSFI has noted the leadership it is exercising in the Accounting Task Force of the BCBS and the Accounting and Auditing Issues Subcommittee of the International Association of Insurance Supervisors, and on the consistency of calculations of risk-weighted assets in the Standard Implementation Group of the BCBS.

The role of Canada in international regulatory reform can also be analyzed with regard to how it is implementing international standards domestically, as this is a sign of commitment to the reform. Canada has been particularly aggressive with the implementation of the new banking standards, requiring immediate implementation of Basel III capital standards in 2013, rather than the additional six-year phase-in period it provided, and in the imposition of the surcharge on the big six banks designated as domestically systemically important in 2016, rather than in the longer phase-in the international rules permitted. With regard to the implementation of principles for financial market infrastructures formulated by the Committee on Payment and Settlement Systems and IOSCO, Canada is about as far as its peers in implementation. OTC derivatives reforms have lagged that of other countries, in part due to the greater difficulty of developing them with both federal and provincial regulators, and in part due to the reliance of Canada on other jurisdictions for derivatives trading. The main central counterparty for the most important OTC derivatives for Canada, interest rate swaps, is LCH.Clearnet's SwapClear in London, England, and the BoC will be overseeing this multilaterally with other regulators (Schembri 2013). Global standards implementation issues flagged for vigilance by the 2012 FSB "Peer Review of Canada" include macroprudential surveillance and regulations to govern the relationships between credit rating agencies and the types of structured financial products that contributed to the crisis.

There are a number of ways that Canada's close proximity to the United States and the size and character of Canada's own market influences its relationship to global standards. Canadian political and regulatory authorities lobbied aggressively against the extraterritorial effects of the US "Volcker rule," which aims to prohibit proprietary trading by banks.[2] This would create serious problems for Canadian banks given their operations in the United States. With respect to accounting standards, Canada's Accounting Standards Board has required adherence to the IASB's international standards since 2011, and generally now restricts its role to monitoring the character of the IASB's governance and due process, asking one question to Canadian stakeholders: Do you believe that there are aspects of the proposed standard that make some or all of it inappropriate for Canadian entities, even though it is appropriate for entities in the rest of the world? At the same time, a number of exceptions to the IASB's standards are maintained due to the importance of the United States, such as allowing Canadian companies that are publicly traded in the United States to use US standards. Canada lobbied worldwide against bank taxes when it hosted the G20 meeting in 2010, arguing that its banks shouldn't be required to pay such taxes, given their stability (Goodman 2010).

CONCLUSION

Canada has played an increasingly prominent role in the informal international regulatory arrangements that have characterized governance arrangements for global financial markets. Relatively effective Canadian domestic regulatory arrangements have contributed to the increased prominence of Canadian regulators in international matters, especially after the crisis, both through the positive reputational effects of Canadian stability, and because domestic institutions facilitate the development and implementation of policies and regulatory initiatives that are relevant internationally. This is especially the case in banking-related regulations, where strong international standards and robust Canadian regulations complement one another, but less so in other areas, such as OTC derivatives, where Canada is more reliant on international markets and regulators, and where provincial-federal regulatory collaboration is also needed.

Canada has benefited from its mix of independence, global connections, and political and geographical proximity to the United States, evident in its

---

2   The Volcker rule is part of the Dodd-Frank Act. It restricts the ability of commercial banks to engage in proprietary trading and to invest in hedge funds.

roles in the G7 and G20. This is also apparent in Canada's early prominence in the establishment of IOSCO, which displays a mix of independent Canadian initiatives, such as accounting harmonization, and a willingness to support priorities originating in the United States such as working against cross-border securities fraud. More recently, as Canada has become more aligned with international standards and the political and financial preponderance of the United States has diminished, the idiosyncratic and unilateral character of some US rules, such as the Volcker rule or the US accounting standards, have become more obviously problematic, with Canada's proximity to the United States becoming less of an advantage.

Overall, the Canadian role in international financial regulatory institutions reflects a distinctive mix of national institutions and interests and relationships to a changing global environment, together with the talents of particular individuals. A well-recognized feature of Canadian foreign policy after World War II was its ability to draw on Canadian expertise, and on Canada's ability to mediate between its US and other international linkages in a way that contributed simultaneously to Canada's interests and the strengthening of international institutions. Since then, the informal and private aspects of global governance have grown in importance relative to formal public international organizations and law, and the United States has become less dominant. Canadian engagement with international financial institutions has changed accordingly, drawing on new organizational capacities and expertise in financial regulation, not just in public sector agencies such as OSFI, but also in the private sector (which is evident in accounting), while also displaying continuities with earlier periods in Canadian foreign policy. Combined with the particular characteristics of the Canadian financial system, this has contributed to the distinctive roles that Canada and Canadians have played in the relatively informal, and often highly technical, international financial institutions that have been central to the international response to the global financial crisis.

Acknowledgements

This chapter benefited greatly from advice provided by Lawrence Schembri, deputy governor of the BoC, and from comments provided by other contributors to this volume on an earlier draft of this chapter. Research that informed it was funded by the Social Sciences and Humanities Research Council of Canada (grant 410-2011-2376). Research assistance was provided by Zeina Sleiman-Long and Hooria Raza.

WORKS CITED

Bair, Sheila. 2012. *Bull by the Horns: Fighting to Save Main Street from Wall Street and Wall Street from Itself.* New York: Free Press.

Bernhut, Stephen. 2002. "Setting the Standard." *CA Magazine*, May. www.camagazine.com.

Carmichael, Kevin. 2013. "Macklem's Bank Shot: The Race to Take Over from Mark Carney." *The Globe and Mail*, March 30.

Davies, H. and D. Green. 2008. *Global Financial Regulation.* Cambridge: Polity.

FSB. 2012. "Peer Review of Canada." www.financialstabilityboard.org/publications/r_120130.pdf.

———. 2013. "Peer Review of the United States." www.financialstabilityboard.org/publications/r_130827.pdf.

G20 Research Group. 2008. "The Group of Twenty: A History." www.g20.utoronto.ca/.

Goodhart, C. 2011. *The Basel Committee on Banking Supervision: A History of the Early Years 1974–1997.* Cambridge: Cambridge University Press.

Goodman, Lee-Anne. 2010. "Flaherty Holds Firm in Resistance to G20 Bank Tax, Calling it Punitive." *Canadian Business*, April 22. www.canadianbusiness.com/markets/headline_news/article.jsp?content=b221019417.

Guy, Paul. 1992. "Regulatory Harmonization to Achieve Effective International Competition." In *Regulating International Financial Markets: Issues and Policies,* edited by Franklin R. Edwards and Hugh T. Patrick. Springer.

McKeen-Edwards, H. and T. Porter. 2013. *Transnational Financial Associations and the Governance of Global Finance: Assembling Power and Wealth.* London and New York: Routledge.

OSFI. 2000. "Report on Plans and Priorities for the Years 1999-2000 to 2001-2002." Ottawa: OSFI.

———. 2012. "Our History." www.osfi-bsif.gc.ca/osfi/index_ e.aspx?DetailID=372.

Porter, Tony. 1993. *States, Markets, and Regimes in Global Finance.* Basingstoke and New York: Macmillan and St. Martins.

———. 2014. "Introduction: Post-Crisis Transnational Financial Regulation and Complexity in Global Governance." In *Transnational Financial Regulation after the Crisis,* edited by Tony Porter. 1–25. London: Routledge.

Schembri, Lawrence. 2013. "Born of Necessity and Built to Succeed: Why Canada and the World Need the Financial Stability Board." Remarks at the CFA Society, Ottawa, September 24. www.bankofcanada.ca/wp-content/uploads/2013/09/remarks-240913.pdf.

Tedesco, Theresa. 2013. "In Final Year as Canada's Top Bank Watchdog, Julie Dickson Will Make No Apologies."*Financial Post,* May 22.

The Economist. 2012. "The Curious Case of William White." *The Economist,* September 5. www.economist.com/blogs/freeexchange/2012/09/perverse-effects-easy-money.

Verma, Sid. 2012. "Canada's Carney: Finance's New Statesman." *Euromoney* 42 (522). October.

Zeff, Stephen A. 2012. "The Evolution of the IASC into the IASB, and the Challenges It Faces." *The Accounting Review* 87 (3): 807–37.

Zeff, Stephen A. and Vaughan S. Radcliffe. 2010. "The Ontario Securities Commission on Accounting and Auditing from the 1960s to 2008 — Part 2: The First Four Chief Accountants 1986-1996." *Accounting Perspectives* 9 (2): 97–138.

5

The Global Financial Crisis and Financial Regulation: Canada and the World

David Longworth

• • • • • • • • • • • • • • • • • • • •

The global financial crisis of 2007–2009 had a profound impact on output in the advanced economies, and led to a re-examination of financial regulation and supervision in Canada and internationally. Although Canada's financial sector was less affected than most advanced economies and it had the highest bank soundness rating in the World Economic Forum surveys from 2007-2008 through 2012-2013, the Canadian economy was not untouched. The funding profile of Canadian banks deteriorated because of contagion from abroad, while trade linkages led to a decline in Canadian economic output. The deterioration sparked initiatives to improve certain aspects of Canadian financial regulation, during the crisis and afterwards, and, together with the trade-linkage effect, led the Canadian government and its agencies to work with their international counterparts to improve minimum standards for financial regulation and supervision internationally. This chapter deals with both of these actions.

The need for regulatory reform largely resulted from inadequate attention to systemic risk — the risk of financial system collapse or severe instability. This risk can arise either from the pro-cyclical nature of credit creation and the financial cycle (in which the cycle is amplified by the nature of decision making, risk management and regulation), or from the interrelationships among financial institutions, particularly the largest ones. Many of the fundamental policy changes that have been made in Canada and internationally since the financial crisis deal with implementing so-called macroprudential policies aimed at mitigating these systemic risks. At the same time, the international reform agenda has dealt with failures of microprudential regulation and supervision.

CANADIAN DOMESTIC FINANCIAL POLICY RESPONSES

During the crisis itself, especially following the failure of Lehman Brothers in mid-September 2008, the key financial policy response was liquidity provision to banks and borrowers by the Bank of Canada (BoC) (see chapter 6 in this volume for more information) and the federal government (Department of Finance Canada 2009), in response to both the contagion from global bank funding markets and the reduced ability of foreign and non-bank financial institutions to lend in specialized lending markets. In addition, the government progressively tightened Canada Mortgage and Housing Corporation's (CMHC's) requirements for obtaining mortgage insurance and broadened statutory authorities for itself and the Canada Deposit Insurance Corporation. As well, as a result of the freeze in the Canadian non-bank, asset-backed commercial paper market in August 2007, both the federal government and various provincial securities regulators began to examine the need for more transparency of securitized products and greater attention to systemic risk. As the crisis progressed, Canada began to work on what it would like to see as new international standards, subsequently adopting domestic regulations that were more stringent than required by those standards.

CANADA'S ACTIVE ROLE IN INTERNATIONAL REFORMS

Two days before the Group of Twenty (G20) Summit on Financial Markets and the World Economy in Washington, DC on November 15, 2008, former Canadian Finance Minister Jim Flaherty published a piece in the *Financial Times,* in which four of the main themes were: dealing with the tendency to underestimate risk in good times; having adequate capital buffers (and dealing with leverage); strengthening international coordination, review and surveillance; and improving market infrastructure (systems used to record, clear or settle payments or other financial transactions among institutions) — including for over-the-counter (OTC) derivative trades (Flaherty 2008).[1] That summit's *Action Plan to Implement Principles for Reform* had a section on "Enhancing Sound Regulation," which echoed these four themes in making reference to four areas (among others) that, in hindsight, are the areas where Canada made its greatest contribution to international regulatory reform: mitigating pro-cyclicality in the financial system; maintaining adequate bank capital; committing to peer review of national regulatory systems; and improving the infrastructure for the OTC derivatives market (G20 2008).

At the G20 level, to follow up on the Washington summit commitments and prepare for the London summit, several working groups were established. Tiff Macklem, then associate deputy minister of finance for Canada, co-chaired the G20 Working Group 1 on Enhancing Sound Regulation and Strengthening Transparency in early 2009 (G20 Working Group 1 2009). The working group's recommendations dealt with all four of the major areas of Canada's contribution: recommendation 3 dealt with macroprudential tools to deal with systemic vulnerabilities (most of which represented elements of pro-cyclicality); recommendations 12 and 14 dealt with bank capital (including, implicitly, its role in countering pro-cyclicality); recommendation 11 dealt with regulatory review through the Financial Sector Assessment Program (FSAP) and self-assessment by national authorities of their regulatory frameworks; and recommendations 17 and 18 covered the infrastructure for the OTC derivatives markets, including the regulation of relevant central counterparties (ibid.). The London G20 Summit in April 2009 followed up in all these of areas with its *Declaration on Strengthening the Financial System* (G20 2009).

In total, the G20 Working Group 1 made 25 recommendations covering a wide range of areas, in addition to the above, which required reforms: a system-wide approach to financial regulation; the scope of regulation; oversight of credit rating agencies; private pools of capital (including hedge funds); liquidity; compensation; transparency; enforcement; and technical

---

1   Many of these ideas were already circulating internationally, whether from ongoing work (as summarized by the Financial Stability Forum [2008]) or individual viewpoints.

assistance. In most of these areas, there was general agreement internationally that something needed to be done. As well, Canada did not have as great a comparative advantage in these additional areas as in the four areas of its major contributions.

In the financial area, good regulatory reform now requires appropriate decisions at four levels: the G20, to set suitable objectives; the Financial Stability Board (FSB), previously the Financial Stability Forum, to coordinate policy development and implementation monitoring to help ensure that a comprehensive and coherent financial reform agenda is enacted; the standards setters — including the Basel Committee on Banking Supervision (BCBS), the International Organization of Securities Commissions (IOSCO) and the Committee on Payment and Settlement Systems (CPSS) — to set international standards; and various subcommittees, task forces and working groups of the FSB, standards setters and the Committee on the Global Financial System (CGFS), which reports to central bank governors at the Bank for International Settlements (BIS), to study the issues and make specific policy proposals. Thus, at the same time that these G20 processes were going on, various Canadian agencies were preparing themselves to make useful contributions in standard-setting organizations and elsewhere.

The Office of the Superintendent of Financial Institutions (OSFI) was well aware that regulation is typically ineffective without strong supervision. Superintendent Julie Dickson (2010c) stressed this need for supervision and headed up the Supervisory Intensity and Effectiveness Group of the FSB. This group focuses on how regulations and guidelines should be turned into day-to-day supervisory practice, especially for systemically important financial institutions (FSB 2010b). Equally important, OSFI was active from the start in examining improvements to Basel II and what was needed for a new Basel III.

As well, the BoC undertook a much greater involvement in the BCBS — particularly through co-chairing or participating in various subcommittees and taskforces — to ensure there was sufficient emphasis on macroprudential policy. OSFI and the BoC often cooperated in developing the various regulations being debated in Basel.

The BoC initiated a policy research program on pro-cyclicality — laying out some of its early priorities between mid-November 2008 and mid-January 2009 in two speeches each by then Governor Mark Carney (2008a; 2008b) and then Deputy Governor Pierre Duguay (2008; 2009). This program reported on early findings in its *Financial System Review* in June 2009, and followed up with reports related to a macroprudential approach to regulation in its December 2009 review (BoC 2009a; 2009b). In late 2008 and early 2009, the BoC encouraged the CGFS at the BIS to adopt a macroprudential policy research agenda.

There was a growing interest in the provincial securities commissions, especially the Ontario Securities Commission (OSC) and the Autorité des marches financiers (AMF) in Quebec, in systemic risk in general and derivatives markets in particular, including how they were being dealt with internationally. This is illustrated by Jean St-Gelais, president and CEO of the AMF, and Howard Wetston, chairman of the OSC, chairing an IOSCO task force that published a discussion paper on mitigating systemic risk (Technical Committee of IOSCO, 2011).

THE FOUR CORE AREAS OF REFORM

There are four core areas of financial policy reform that Canada focused on in its international efforts to promote a more stable global financial system: mitigating pro-cyclicality; bank capital regulation; peer review; and OTC derivatives markets reform. In all of these areas, Canada was able to successfully push for reforms that resonated with its experiences and interests in enhanced financial sector regulation and supervision.

Mitigating Pro-cyclicality of the Financial System

The global financial crisis brought to light many areas where the pro-cyclicality of the financial system had amplified the boom and provided less of a cushion of bank capital than had been intended. Canadian regulatory agencies wanted to ensure that pro-cyclicality be taken explicitly into account in the design of new regulations in some key areas, and they were largely successful.

In particular, the declining risk weights (especially in bank trading books) in the boom that were used to calculate risk-weighted capital to asset ratios had meant that banks took on more of the same risk or freed up capital for other areas of risk taking. The problem of declining risk weights was somewhat less problematic in jurisdictions such as Canada and the United States (in the case of their commercial, but not investment, banks), which also had capital ratios based on unweighted assets to supplement the Basel requirements for risk-weighted capital to asset ratios; these "simple leverage ratios" were seen as being useful. Another deficiency was that when credit was expanding rapidly, there was no recognition that credit expansion would be associated with higher risks and, therefore, that required capital ratios should rise.

Canadian regulatory agencies were also concerned about the way in which value at risk (VaR) calculations were made for portfolios of traded assets and how those affected the amount of capital that had to be held against them. VaR calculations were typically done based on volatilities (and covariances) over the previous one to two years. This meant that information in the longer historical period — including periods of high stress — was ignored (Youngman 2009). Canada felt that this was inappropriate and successfully sought to change it in Basel III.

A similar concern existed in the market for repurchase transactions (repos), where lenders protected themselves against the risk of declining asset values by lending less than the value of the borrower's offered collateral, with the percentage difference between the value of the collateral and the value of the loan being referred to as a "haircut." The magnitude of these haircuts tended to be set based on volatilities over short historical periods, not longer ones that included times of financial stress. Thus, very high amounts of credit were made available in repo loans in boom times and, when haircuts on risky assets rose during the crisis, that credit partly dried up. BoC representatives emphasized this in two CGFS study groups (CGFS 2009; 2010), and OSFI representatives covered this area in the BCBS as it applied to bank regulation. At a later date, Canadians participated in discussions of these matters in shadow banking working groups at the FSB. In all these committees, the emphasis of Canadian officials has been on "through-the-cycle" calculations. International standards now seem to be moving in that direction.

Enhancing Bank Capital Regulation

Various Canadian representatives on the BCBS and its numerous subcommittees drew on Canada's experience with a leverage ratio, higher quality Tier 1 (equity) capital and higher capital requirements — as well as its research on a counter-cyclical capital buffer and contingent capital — to encourage the adoption of all of these elements in Basel III capital regulations. They were broadly successful, as significant additions or improvements were adopted in all these areas (BCBS 2011). Financial crises typically start with the creation of too much credit against the background of too little bank equity: as credit decisions are revealed to have been poor, there are potential solvency problems for banks. Regulation of bank capital is, therefore, extremely important in preventing crises.

In its earliest minimum standards for international banks (known as Basel I and Basel II), the BCBS had focused entirely on the ratios of capital to risk-weighted assets, with risk weights depending on the riskiness of the assets involved. This focus was maintained despite criticism of the risk-weighting procedures. In comparison, OSFI and US banking regulators (with the exception of the US Securities and Exchange Commission, which regulates investment banks) had regulations for the minimum ratio of capital to unweighted assets, including some off-balance-sheet exposures. In Canada, this minimum ratio was expressed in reciprocal form as the maximum assets to capital multiple, which was between 20 and 23, depending on the bank. At the beginning of the global financial crisis, actual ratios of assets to capital (but not taking into account off-balance-sheet exposures) ranged from 35 to above 50 for all US investment banks, large Swiss banks and many large continental European banks (Bordeleau, Crawford and Graham 2009). It has been shown that these ratios based on unweighted assets were better than ratios based on weighted assets in predicting which banks would go under or require government capital injections during the crisis (Haldane 2012). In Basel III, the BCBS has followed a "Canadian" (and US) approach by adopting a minimum ratio of capital to unweighted assets plus specified off-balance-sheet exposures (simple leverage ratio) of three percent.

The definition of capital was put to the test by the global crisis. The conclusion was that the key capital concept had to be the kind that was fully loss absorbing: common equity (including retained earnings) net of assets that may have questionable realizable value in times of stress. The key capital requirements in Basel III are based on this concept (see Table 1). In Basel I and II, the capital of highest quality had been denoted as Tier 1 capital. In addition to common equity, it could include preferred shares and innovative/

hybrid instruments with up to a 50 percent share. OSFI, on the other hand, only allowed non-common equity up to a 25 percent share prior to the crisis.

Basel I and II capital requirements were a four percent Tier 1 capital ratio and an eight percent total capital ratio, which included subordinated debt. OSFI's requirements were higher at seven percent and 10 percent, respectively. On a broadly similar basis, Basel III requirements are essentially six percent for Tier 1 (not including the capital conservation buffer), seven percent for common equity capital (including the capital conservation buffer) and 10.5 percent for total capital (including the capital conservation buffer).

Table 1: Basel III Risk-weighted Capital Ratios
(Required Ratio of Common Equity Capital to Risk-weighted Assets, in %)

Component	Minimum Common Equity Capital Ratio	Capital Conservation Buffer	Add-on for Systemically Important Banks (SIBs) (G=Global; CDN=Canadian)	Counter-cyclical Capital Buffer
Capital Ratio	4.5	2.5	0 (if not SIB) 1–2.5 (G-SIB) 1.0 (CDN-SIB)	0–2.5
Cumulative Capital Ratio	4.5	7.0	7.0–9.5	7.0–12.0

Sources: BCBS (2011) and author.

In Basel III, there are also additional capital requirements in boom times (consistent with the recommendation of the G20 Working Party 1 and the London summit declaration) and for SIBs. The BoC was a major proponent of a counter-cyclical capital buffer (Arjani 2009; Chen and Christensen 2010) and, with others on the BCBS and at the BIS, led research for an appropriate formulation. In the end, what was agreed upon was a 0–2.5 percent buffer that would be triggered by the behaviour of the ratio of credit to GDP, relative to its trend.

The crisis reminded the world that systemic risk is often closely associated with large, interconnected banks that tend to have similar exposures to risks. The collapse of these too-big-to-fail banks would create a potentially devastating decline in credit availability, which would likely provoke government intervention to prevent their failure. This anticipated government intervention creates an incentive to be less cautious (moral hazard) and allows large banks to borrow at lower interest rates. To avoid these distortions, governments must establish a system to ensure that management, shareholders and debt holders know that when a bank becomes non-viable, they will suffer in the same ways as they would in the bankruptcy of a non-financial corporation, while allowing the institution to continue. In the context of Basel III, there are three key aspects to such a structure. The first is higher capital levels for all banks and even higher levels for SIBs. G-SIBs have to have 1–2.5 percent higher common equity risk-weighted capital ratios, and CDN-SIBs must have one percent higher ratios. The second and third are contingent capital and bail-in debt, which transform debt into common equity when a bank is declared non-viable by its supervisor or needs to be resolved. In a letter to the *Financial Times* and in a speech, Superintendent Julie Dickson (2010a; 2010b) outlined an approach to embedded contingent capital that made clear that OSFI was working together with its partners at the BoC — confirmed by Governor Mark Carney (2010) — and the Department of Finance, as well as international counterparts, on this topic (see D'Souza et al. 2010). The approach also noted that the minister of finance was more inclined to this approach than to others that had been floated internationally to deal with systemically important institutions and too-big-to-fail banks. The BCBS incorporated contingent capital into its capital accord by ruling that preferred shares and subordinated debt — the part of total capital that was not also common equity Tier 1 capital — would have to be contingent capital. Subsequently, in the 2013 budget, the minister of finance announced that there would be a study of how to implement bail-in debt in Canada (Department of Finance Canada 2013).

Establishing Peer Review

The crisis was due in part to poor implementation of international standards and domestic regulations elsewhere, as well as poor supervision. Indeed, large countries such as the United States and China had refused to participate in the FSAP, while Canada had participated in the trial FSAP in 2000 and had a second FSAP completed in 2007-2008. Canada, therefore, successfully pushed for all G20 countries to participate in the FSAP process and, with the United States, for peer review to be a major responsibility of the FSB. Tiff Macklem was named the first chair of the FSB's Standing Committee on Standards Implementation, which oversaw country and thematic peer reviews. This committee also oversaw the preparation of a Framework for

Strengthening Adherence and the "Handbook for FSB Peer Reviews" (FSB 2010a; 2011). The first peer review was published in March 2010.

Mandating and Implementing Central Clearing of OTC Derivatives

Another area where Canadian representatives played a major role was the international standards for the central clearing of OTC derivative products, particularly taking into account the needs of small- and medium-sized countries — such as Canada — and their banks. At the 2009 Pittsburgh G20 Summit, leaders decided that to reduce counterparty credit risk and thereby increase the safety and resilience of the financial system, all standardized OTC derivative contracts should be cleared through central counterparties (CCPs) — something that was rare before the crisis.

The Canadian OTC Derivatives Working Group (2010) — composed of members from the BoC, OSFI, the Department of Finance, the OSC, the AMF and the Alberta Securities Commission — was given the task of "providing advice and coordinating efforts to meet Canada's G-20 commitments related to OTC derivatives" with an eye to the "stability and vibrancy of the Canadian financial system." It also helped to provide a perspective on issues that were particularly important to Canada as implementation details of the broad G20 recommendation were worked out internationally.

Deputy Governor Timothy Lane of the BoC was asked to chair a CGFS study group that dealt with the implications for financial stability and efficiency of various configurations of access by banks to central counterparties in OTC derivatives markets, against a background where direct access was dominated by the largest global dealers, a category that does not include Canadian banks that would likely participate in large international CCPs. The study group report (CGFS 2011) was an important input into the decision by the FSB in January 2012 to adopt four safeguards for a global framework of CCPs: "fair and open access by market participants to CCPs"; "cooperative oversight arrangements between all relevant authorities"; appropriate "resolution and recovery regimes" for CCPs; and "appropriate liquidity arrangements" (Carney 2012).[2] These safeguards were essential to the approval by Canada

---

2   As chair of the FSB, Carney was a member of the FSB OTC Coordination Group.

and other similarly sized countries for their banks to participate on an ongoing basis in large international CCPs.

Canadians also actively participated on the CPSS and IOSCO task forces dealing with detailed OTC derivatives and CCP issues. For example, James Turner, a vice chair of the OSC, was co-chair of IOSCO's Task Force on OTC Derivatives Regulation that published a report on derivatives market intermediary oversight (IOSCO 2012).

REASONS FOR CANADA'S INTERNATIONAL INFLUENCE AND SUCCESS

There are six major reasons why Canada had influence and success in the policy areas discussed above:

- As is often the case, Canada is willing to invest in international processes, listen and seek acceptable compromise. Regarding the latter, it often found itself between the hawks and doves in the BCBS.[3] As well, Canada's historical relationship with the United States and the United Kingdom, including their central banks, has often made cooperation with them on international issues much easier.
- At various levels of the international process, Canada brings ideas to the table, including the ideas of others — such as academics and BIS staff members.
- Canada had come through the crisis well — while the United States, United Kingdom and euro area had not — and therefore was seen as having something to offer from its experience, including where its standards had exceeded the international ones.
- Canada's narrow parochial interests in the financial area are less visible than those of larger countries.
- As a result of the above four points and some very talented individuals, Canada was able to chair some important bodies, committees and subcommittees. In chapter 4 of this volume,

---

3   Sheila Bair, former head of the US Federal Deposit Insurance Corporation, has noted that in the days of BCBS negotiation over Basel III, France and Germany were very much the doves (Bair 2012, chapter 22).

Tony Porter notes the prominent roles played by Mark Carney, Julie Dickson and Tiff Macklem in particular. Howard Wetston became vice chair of the board of IOSCO. Various BoC deputy governors, OSFI deputy superintendents and senior officials of the Department of Finance, the BoC, OSFI, the OSC, the AMF and other agencies had important roles on various international committees, subcommittees, working groups and task forces.

- The various parts of Canada's financial agencies are less like silos than in many such agencies abroad, and the agencies themselves are used to working together domestically on formal committees (see chapter 4). Not only are the heads of the regulatory agencies involved in these processes, but key officials meet regularly in support of these processes. This close working relationship allows broad ideas to be pursued at various levels within the same international committee, as well as in various international committees at the same time. As an example, cooperation within the BoC informs the participation of its members in processes taking place in the BCBS, the CGFS, the CPSS and the FSB. Similarly, cooperation between OSFI and the BoC enhances work in the BCBS.

CONCLUSION

The process of dealing with the fallout of the global financial crisis is not yet finished, either internationally or domestically. For example, there is still more to come from the FSB on shadow banking. Domestically, there are issues related to governance, banking competition and resilience versus credit smoothing (smoothing of the credit cycle) that should receive more attention and action.

In the governance area, Canada still lacks a national capital markets regulator to deal with systemic risk issues (including those related to derivatives), although the federal government is moving in that direction. As well, contrary to best practice, Canada does not have a formal macroprudential regulatory committee with a statutory basis. The informal Senior Advisory Committee is playing that role instead, but lacks an explicit macroprudential framework and a transparency requirement (Jenkins and Thiessen 2012).

Canada has historically tended to choose to emphasize stability more than efficiency in both regulation and banking competition policy. This has led to good results on the stability side, including during the recent global crisis. Questions remain, however, as to whether too much is being sacrificed on the efficiency side in competition policy, with the recent takeovers of ING Direct Canada and Ally Canada by the big six banks being a case in point.

In Canada, as elsewhere, the emphasis on new regulations has been on the resilience of the banking system and the financial system more generally, rather than on credit smoothing. It is, as yet, unclear as to whether this is the best policy for both financial stability and macroeconomic performance overall. Canada and other small countries that largely escaped the crisis, such as Australia and Sweden, have experienced credit and housing price booms in recent years and there is still some question whether these booms will end badly. One specific question for Canada is whether there should be a more explicit counter-cyclical policy with respect to key minimum requirements for mortgage insurance that would be used to smooth the mortgage-credit cycle.

Although the global financial crisis did not lead to any Canadian bank failures, it did provide a wake-up call to both Canada and the world that the pre-existing regulatory and supervisory system was insufficient to deal with large systemic shocks. In particular, the pro-cyclical nature of the financial system had not appropriately been taken into account and the overall capital ratios for large banks were insufficient. Canada saw these as core areas for reform both internationally and domestically, was able to have the main elements of these priorities incorporated into international standards and has implemented the key Basel III capital regulations domestically, well before the internationally required dates.

Canada wanted the particular position of small- and medium-sized countries to be recognized internationally, especially when it came to the openness and regulation of CCPs for OTC derivatives. It achieved its aims in these areas. It also wanted to reduce the chances that severe problems would begin abroad, as in the global financial crisis, and have strong effects on the Canadian economy. In addition to the above core areas, Canada stressed standards for supervision and peer review of the adoption of international standards. Both of these have been accepted internationally in FSB processes and should reduce the probability of future large systemic crises.

WORKS CITED

Arjani, Neville. 2009. "Procyclicality and Bank Capital." *Bank of Canada Financial System Review* June: 33–39.

Bair, Sheila. 2012. *Bull by the Horns: Fighting to Save Main Street from Wall Street and Wall Street from Itself.* New York: Free Press.

BCBS. 2011. "Basel III Phase-in Arrangements." www.bis.org/bcbs/basel3.htm.

BoC. 2009a. *Financial System Review.* June.

———. 2009b. *Financial System Review.* December.

Bordeleau, Étienne, Allan Crawford and Christopher Graham. 2009. "Regulatory Constraints on Bank Leverage: Issues and Lessons from the Canadian Experience." BoC Discussion Paper 2009-15, December.

BCBS. 2011. *Basel III: A Global Regulatory Framework for more Resilient Banks and Banking Systems (Revised).* June.

Canadian OTC Derivatives Working Group. 2010. "Reform of Over-the-Counter (OTC) Derivatives Markets in Canada: Discussion Paper." October 26.

Carney, Mark. 2008a. "Building Continuous Markets." Remarks to the Canada-United Kingdom Chamber of Commerce, London, England, November 19.

———. 2008b. "From Hindsight to Foresight." Remarks to Women in Capital Markets, Toronto, December 17.

———. 2010. "The G-20's Core Agenda to Reduce Systemic Risk." Remarks to IOSCO, Montreal, June 10.

———. 2012. "Statement by Mark Carney, Chairman, Financial Stability Board." Remarks to International Monetary and Financial Committee of the International Monetary Fund, April 21.

CGFS. 2009. "The Role of Valuation and Leverage in Procyclicality." CGFS Reports 34, April.

—————. 2010. "The Role of Margin Requirements and Haircuts in Procyclicality." CGFS Reports 36, March.

—————. 2011. "The Macrofinancial Implications of Alternative Configurations for Access to Central Counterparties in OTC Derivative Markets." CGFS Reports 46, November.

Chen, David Xiao and Ian Christensen. 2010. "The Countercyclical Bank Capital Buffer: Insights for Canada." *Bank of Canada Financial System Review* December: 29–34.

Department of Finance Canada. 2009. *Budget 2009: Canada's Economic Action Plan.*

—————. 2013. *Economic Action Plan 2013: Jobs Growth and Long-term Prosperity.*

Dickson, Julie. 2010a. "Protecting Banks Is Best Done by Market Discipline." *Financial Times*, April 8.

—————. 2010b. "Too-big-to-fail and Embedded Contingent Capital." Remarks to the Financial Services Invitational Forum, Cambridge, Ontario, May 6.

—————. 2010c. "Too Focused on the Rules: The Importance of Supervisory Oversight in Financial Regulation." Remarks to the Heyman Center on Corporate Governance, New York City, March 16.

D'Souza, Chris, Walter Engert, Toni Gravelle and Liane Orsi. 2010. "Contingent Capital and Bail-In Debt: Tools for Bank Resolution." *Bank of Canada Financial System Review* December: 51–56.

Duguay, Pierre. 2008. "Fostering Financial System Stability." Remarks to Pictou County Chamber of Commerce, Pictou, November 27.

—————. 2009. "Financial Stability through Sound Risk Management." Remarks to Risk Management Association, Toronto Chapter, Toronto, January 8.

Flaherty, Jim. 2008. "'Boring' Canada's Financial Tips for the World." *Financial Times*, November 13.

Financial Stability Forum. 2008. *Report of the Financial Stability Forum on Enhancing Market and Institutional Resilience.* April 7.

FSB. 2010a. "FSB Framework for Strengthening Adherence to International Standards." January 9.

———. 2010b. "Intensity and Effectiveness of SIFI Supervision: Recommendations for Enhanced Supervision." November 2.

———. 2011. "Handbook for FSB Peer Reviews." December 19.

G20. 2008. "Action Plan to Implement Principles for Reform." In *Declaration of the Summit on Financial Markets and the World Economy.* Washington, DC: G20.

———. 2009. *Declaration on Strengthening the Financial System.* London: G20.

G20 Working Group 1. 2009. "Enhancing Sound Regulation and Strengthening Transparency." March 25.

Haldane, Andy. 2012. "The Dog and the Frisbee." Paper given at The Changing Policy Landscape, the Federal Reserve Bank of Kansas City's 36th economic policy symposium, Jackson Hole, August 31.

IOSCO. 2012. "Derivatives Market Intermediary Oversight." Task Force on OTC Derivatives Regulation.

Jenkins, Paul and Gordon Thiessen. 2012. "Reducing the Potential for Future Financial Crises: A Framework for Macro-Prudential Policy in Canada." C. D. Howe Commentary 351, May.

Technical Committee of IOSCO. 2011. "Mitigating Systemic Risk: A Role for Securities Regulators." Discussion paper, February.

Youngman, Peter. 2009. "Procyclicality and Value at Risk." *Bank of Canada Financial System Review* June: 51–54.

6

Success under Pressure: The Bank of Canada and the Global Financial Crisis — Actions and Lessons

Eric Santor and Lawrence Schembri

• • • • • • • • • • • • • • • • • • •

INTRODUCTION

For the Bank of Canada (BoC) and other central banks, the global financial crisis of 2008-2009 and the subsequent Great Recession represented an unprecedented challenge to their two core policy functions: monetary policy and financial stability. These events were the most severe since the Great Depression of the 1930s, when several central banks — including the BoC — were established to help prevent future financial crises and limit their economic fallout. Central bankers were well aware of the policy mistakes made during the Great Depression, but unfortunately this did not prevent the most recent crisis from occurring. Nevertheless, central banks, by effectively executing a broad and seemingly radical set of policy actions, and coordinating among themselves and with fiscal authorities via the newly reconstituted Group of Twenty (G20), stopped the crisis from spiralling into another Great Depression.

The purpose of this chapter is to examine the actions taken by the BoC (sometimes jointly with other central banks) in response to the crisis and to draw lessons for the future of central banking. At its heart the crisis was clearly a massive failure in financial regulation and oversight, bringing to the fore central banks' role in the financial system and the relationship between financial stability and monetary policy. Since financial systems are highly integrated across countries, the crisis also stressed the need for coordination in its management (even for countries that were not the source of the financial instability), and for developing and implementing policies to remedy structural vulnerabilities in financial regulation and oversight.

Canada's experience during the financial crisis and its aftermath stands out among the Group of Seven (G7) as one of the best of a very severe set of outcomes. In Canada, output fell by 4.2 percent and the unemployment rate rose by roughly 2.6 percentage points, which compares favourably to the United States (4.3 percent fall in output and unemployment rate increase of 5.5 percentage points), the United Kingdom (7.2 percent fall in output and unemployment rate increase of 3.1 percentage points) and the euro area (5.7 percent fall in output and unemployment rate increase of 4.7 percentage points).

This relatively strong performance can be explained, in part, by the fact that Canada did not experience a banking crisis: no banks failed or needed to be bailed out at taxpayers' expense. Nonetheless, the financial system experienced considerable turmoil. As liquidity in most globally integrated financial markets dried up and markets seized, the BoC, along with all other major centrals banks, was quick to respond with a variety of measures to inject liquidity into the financial system. Likewise, as the real economy and confidence faltered, the BoC and its peers aggressively reduced policy interest rates while their governments introduced substantial fiscal stimulus. However, it did not need to introduce large-scale asset purchases or quantitative easing, as was done by the central banks of the United States, the United Kingdom and Japan.[1] Instead, when confronted by the lower bound on the policy interest rate, the BoC introduced forward guidance — namely, a commitment to hold the target for the overnight rate at its effective lower bound from April

---

1 The European Central Bank (ECB) implemented two rounds of long-term refinancing operations in December 2011 and February 2012 that provided three-year financing to euro-area banks at very low interest rates, in return for high-quality collateral.

2009 to the end of the second quarter of 2010 conditional on the outlook for the inflation rate (BoC 2009b).[2] Overall, these measures were judged to be very successful in stabilizing financial conditions in Canada, so that firms and households had continuous access to credit, which thus fostered the economic recovery.

It is important to note that many of the actions taken by the BoC were done in coordination with the federal government (i.e., liquidity measures) and with other central banks (i.e., the interest rate cuts in October 2008). Likewise, the financial reforms promulgated by the G20 have been developed and implemented under the coordinating leadership of the Financial Stability Board (FSB) to address the underlying structural weaknesses that contributed to the crises. The BoC, along with other major central banks and financial agencies, have worked together to develop and implement remedial financial reforms.

Apart from the need for coordination to respond to and prevent financial crises, central banks learned many crucial lessons since 2009. First, monetary policy can be implemented via a variety of instruments when policy rates are close to zero.[3] Second, central banks had to be more aware of the indirect impact of monetary policy on financial stability. Achieving macroeconomic stability via monetary policy is not a guarantee of financial stability. Third, the crisis caused central banks to revisit their role in the financial system. Traditionally, that role was largely seen as a "lender of last resort" to solvent, but illiquid, financial institutions. Lastly, the crisis demonstrated that financial markets were as (if not more) important than financial institutions in facilitating effective intermediation between savers and lenders. Consequently, the central bank's financial stability role also included promoting resilient and continuous core financial markets — that is, central banks also became the "market makers of last resort."

---

2 The BoC normally carries out monetary policy by setting the target for the overnight rate — the interest rate at which major financial institutions borrow and lend one-day (or "overnight") funds among themselves.

3 In some ways, this was relearning, as many of these instruments had been used in the past and had recently been put in the closet with the advent of inflation targeting and the "Great Moderation" in macroeconomic outcomes over the period from 1992 to 2007. See, for example, Borio and Disyatat (2009).

THE GLOBAL FINANCIAL CRISIS AND CANADA

The 2008-2009 financial crisis was, at its source, caused by inadequate regulation and supervision, primarily in the United States and Europe. Regulators and supervisors failed to keep up with the tremendous pace of financial innovation and globalization that had occurred in the previous two decades. New markets and new institutions had arisen, most notably: market-based credit intermediation or shadow banking;[4] banks that had become too-big-to-fail; and enormous, opaque and largely unregulated over-the-counter (OTC) derivatives markets. Moreover, the belief that traditional economic arguments for financial regulation and oversight[5] were no longer valid, because the global financial system had entered a new era of self-governance and self-regulation, proved to be hopelessly naïve.

The emerging fault lines in the regulatory and supervisory frameworks in advanced economies were pried open by global imbalances. These imbalances, in turn, reflected the global "savings glut" — a situation where global savings appeared to exceed global investment. The resulting large US trade deficits and equally large investments in US dollar assets created an environment of ample global liquidity and low long-term interest rates. The consequences were excessive leverage and credit growth in most advanced countries that supported unsustainable consumption, housing and government expenditures, especially in the United States, but also, for example, in Spain and Ireland. When US housing and other asset prices stopped rising and starting falling, the pyramid of leverage unravelled and massive investor runs occurred on a wide range of institutions and markets.

While Canada did not suffer from weak regulation and supervision or the buildup in excessive leverage, it could not escape the fallout from the financial crisis because of the high degree of integration of its financial system with the rest of the world. In the immediate aftermath of the Lehman Brothers default,

---

4 Shadow banking activities include money market mutual funds, commercial paper, securitized mortgage and other credit instruments, repurchase agreements (repos) and security lending. These examples are market-based, but bank-like, credit intermediation, which involves credit and maturity transformation and leverage, and are therefore subject to bank-like risks (such as bank runs).

5 These traditional economic arguments for financial regulation and supervision were primarily based on market failures due to information asymmetries and misaligned incentives — including from moral hazard and adverse selection — and systemic risk — including common exposures, interconnectedness and contagion, and pro-cyclical behaviour.

liquidity in Canadian financial markets and access to funding by Canadian banks started to dry up and, as a result, asset prices declined sharply. Canada was also severely affected through its trade links to the most distressed economies, most importantly the United States, which is the destination of about three-quarters of Canadian exports. Despite having strong policy frameworks — a sound fiscal position, a credible commitment to inflation targeting and a flexible exchange rate, all of which allowed the Canadian authorities and the economy to respond quickly to the crisis and mitigate its impact — the Canadian economy could not be completely sheltered from the crisis.

The resilience of the Canadian financial system also helped to limit the fallout on economic activity by continuing to provide credit throughout the economic downturn and thereby facilitating the transmission of the stimulative monetary policy, which was enacted in the wake of the crisis. The Canadian financial system is largely bank-based, with the banks holding approximately half of all of the assets in the system. Within the banking sector, the big six banks constitute more than 90 percent of all bank assets.[6] They are large, universal banks, which provide traditional deposit-taking and lending activities, as well as being engaged in capital market and investment-banking activities. They are also critical participants in most Canadian financial markets, including the OTC derivatives market and various shadow banking markets, including repos, securitized mortgages and commercial paper.[7] Canadian banks use these markets for funding and to facilitate the economic activities of their clients. An important impact of the financial crisis was to severely reduce the liquidity of these core markets, in part through confidence effects, and thus limit bank access to funding. It is important to note, however, that while these financial markets transmitted the shocks stemming from the crisis to Canada, they were not, in general, a source of

---

6   The big six banks are the Bank of Montreal, the Canadian Imperial Bank of Commerce, the National Bank, the Royal Bank of Canada, Scotiabank and Toronto-Dominion Bank. All were identified by the Office of the Superintendent of Financial Institutions as systemically important to the Canadian financial system and therefore subject to higher regulatory and supervisory requirements. For details on the Canadian financial system, see FSB (2012).

7   In Canada, the majority of mortgages are securitized via the National Housing Authority Mortgage-Backed Securities and Canadian Mortgage Bond programs, run by the Canada Mortgage and Housing Corporation (CMHC). These mortgages are fully insured by the CMHC, which is guaranteed by the Government of Canada. See Crawford, Meh and Zhou (2013) for more details.

instability. In this regard, Canada's experience differed from that of other advanced countries.

THE CRISIS AND THE POLICY RESPONSE

As noted, core financial markets in Canada and in many other countries began to freeze up as a result of the crisis. Because the real economy faltered in response to these tightening financial conditions, the BoC responded quickly with policies targeted to address different aspects of the crisis.

BoC Liquidity Measures

Stress in short-term funding markets for Canadian banks began to mount in the second half of 2007, forcing them to attract funds by offering increasingly higher short-term rates above the expected future policy rate of the BoC. Consequently, the difference between the three-month Canadian Dealer Offered Rate (CDOR) and the overnight indexed swap (OIS) rate, or three-month CDOR-OIS spread, widened from a historical average of about seven basis points (bps) to over 40 bps.[8] In response, the BoC intervened through its standard overnight facility (see Figure 1). CDOR-OIS spreads declined through the fall, but the situation worsened again toward year-end. To address this renewed pressure, the BoC announced the term Purchase and Resale Agreement (PRA) facility, providing longer-term collateralized funding to market participants. In these transactions, the BoC essentially purchases securities for their market value less a percentage haircut to cover the risk of future price movements and resells them for the same price plus interest.[9]

---

8 The CDOR is the average bid rate on Canadian bankers' acceptances for specific terms to maturity, determined daily from a survey of principal market makers, and provides the basis for a floating reference rate in Canadian dollar wholesale and interest rate swap transactions. Because the CDOR rate is not collateralized, whereas the OIS rate is, the spread between the two is a rough measure of interbank confidence. A basis point is equivalent to one-hundredth of a percentage point — i.e., an interest rate increase of 100 bps is equivalent to a one percent rise in the interest rate.

9 Term PRA operations were conducted exclusively with primary dealers for Government of Canada securities.

Figure 1: Timeline of BoC Policy Actions

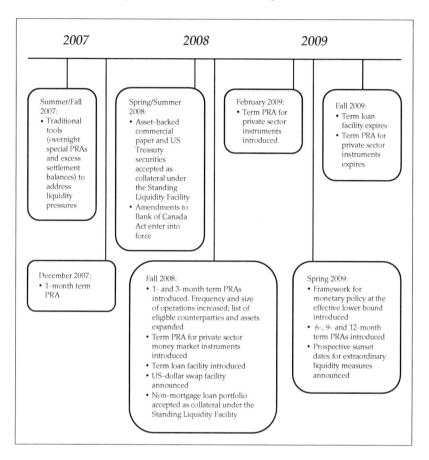

Source: Zorn, Wilkins and Engert (2009).

This dramatic expansion of the BoC's tool kit was guided by five principles (see Zorn, Wilkins and Engert 2009):

- **Target distortions of system-wide importance,** mitigating those market failures that it is best placed to rectify. In practice, interventions should generally be concentrated on liquidity disruptions.

- **Intervention should be graduated,** commensurate to the breadth and magnitude of the disruption. In the extreme case, direct intervention as the market maker of last resort.

- **Intervention tools must be well designed** to match the market failure. For example, the existence of a central bank backstop at a slight penalty rate may be sufficient to restart the endogenous liquidity generation process for minor market failures.
- **Minimize unintended market distortions** by ensuring that transactions, to the extent possible, occur at market-determined prices and conditions (such as through auction mechanism). Facilities should be designed to preserve existing market structures.
- **Mitigate moral hazard.** In addition to those above, there are several measures that could help mitigate moral hazard, including time limitations to ensure that market participants do not permanently change their behaviour, and appropriate pricing so that the program has a natural and market-determined end date.

The initial term PRA operations were relatively modest, consisting of two auctions of CDN$2 billion each, and with maturities of less than one month. These one-month operations were renewed until July 2008. The brief respite ended in September 2008, as funding conditions deteriorated rapidly in the aftermath of the failure of Lehman. The BoC responded by expanding the scope of the term PRAs (see Zorn, Wilkins and Engert 2009 for more details):

- The frequency and size of the term PRAs was increased (biweekly to weekly and the maximum size reached CDN$12 billion).
- The range of eligible counterparties was widened to include all primary dealers and all members of the domestic payment system, and the range of acceptable collateral was expanded to include the private sector assets.

The BoC also introduced a term PRA for private sector money market instruments and signalled a willingness to take non-mortgage loan portfolios as collateral for standing liquidity facilities. These actions demonstrated that the BoC was prepared to "do what it takes," subject to the five principles above, to ensure the stability of the Canadian financial system.[10]

The enhancement of the term PRA facility led to a dramatic expansion of the BoC's balance sheet, as the outstanding amount of term PRAs peaked at CDN$37 billion. BoC funding spreads declined fairly rapidly following the

---

10 Moreover, it would act even when the source of the problem was coming from global markets.

implementation of the term PRA program (see Figure 2). While there were many factors that led to an improvement in bank funding conditions, term PRA announcements had both transitory and persistent effects on reducing the liquidity premium in funding costs (see Enenajor, Sebastian and Witmer 2010). More generally, when complemented by the actions of the Canadian government, these measures helped to underpin confidence in the financial system and to ensure that the monetary transmission mechanism worked, which was crucial for the recovery (see Zorn, Wilkins and Engert 2009, appendix 2).

Figure 2: Term PRA Outstanding

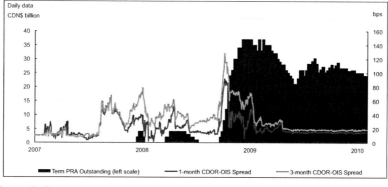

Source: BoC.

Conventional and Unconventional Monetary Policy

In order to stimulate the economy and restore confidence, the BoC used its conventional tools aggressively, initially cutting the target for the overnight rate from 4.5 percent in November 2007 to three percent by the spring of 2008. In response to the collapse of Lehman and the onset of the recession, the BoC lowered the policy rate to the effective lower bound of 0.25 percent by April 2009 and, as noted earlier, published a framework for providing further monetary stimulus (BoC 2009b). This framework included several options, including conditional statements about the future path of policy rates, quantitative easing and credit easing. Of the options presented, the BoC introduced forward guidance in the form of a "conditional commitment." A key element of forward guidance was clear communication — this is why the

BoC introduced regular six- and 12-month term PRA auctions to reinforce the commitment to holding the policy rate at the effective lower bound.[11] Specifically, the BoC stated that "conditional on the outlook for inflation, the target overnight rate can be expected to remain at its current level [the effective lower bound] until the end of the second quarter of 2010 in order to achieve the inflation target" (BoC 2009a).[12] The conditional commitment succeeded: yield-curve expectations declined after the announcement, strengthening the rebound in growth and inflation (see Carney 2012; He 2010).

Central Bank Coordination

An often overlooked aspect of the BoC's response was the role of coordination with other central banks, which took several forms. In September 2008, the BoC expanded its existing swap line with the US Federal Reserve, along with the announcement of swap lines among the Bank of England (BoE), the ECB, the US Federal Reserve, the Sveriges Riksbank and the Swiss National Bank. This allowed the central banks to provide foreign currency liquidity to their respective domestic banking systems. For example, the Federal Reserve swap line with the other major central banks peaked at more than US$550 billion. While the BoC's swap line with the Federal Reserve was never drawn, it provided a useful liquidity backstop (Goldberg, Kennedy and Miu 2011). The BoC, along with several other central banks, cut policy interest rates in October in a coordinated move and as part of a larger effort by the G7 to put in place measures to restore confidence in the financial system and support the real economy.

The BoC engaged closely with other central banks, both formally and informally, throughout the crisis period. This engagement included sharing information on a regular basis on program efficacy, as well as on the spillovers from unconventional measures. Much of this cooperation occurred through regular meetings at the Bank for International Settlements and, in particular, the Markets Committee and the Committee on the Global Financial System. This constant interaction among central banks promoted best practices and

---

11 The term PRA auctions were conducted at the minimum bid rate at the effective lower bound rate of 25 bps and the maximum bid rate at 50 bps.

12 It is important to note that the BoC cooperated with the Government of Canada in such a manner to ensure its independence in the conduct of monetary policy.

provided better understanding of the policy objectives of the respective institutions.

Comparison to Other Major Central Banks

The implementation of liquidity measures was typical of most central banks during the crisis. Programs such as the BoC's term PRA were very similar in nature to the US Federal Reserve's Term Auction Facility and the BoE's Special Liquidity Scheme. Likewise, most central banks also relaxed collateral requirements on existing and new facilities. To a large extent, the use of forward guidance was pioneered by the BoC in 2009, to be subsequently used by the Federal Reserve and the BoE (both of which included thresholds on the unemployment rate).

The BoC differed from its peers in that it did not engage in asset purchases or schemes to facilitate lending to the private sector in order to provide credit easing or further monetary accommodation at the effective lower bound. For example, the US Federal Reserve purchased commercial paper, in addition to its more well-known purchases of mortgage-backed securities and US Treasury bonds as part of quantitative easing. Likewise, both the Bank of Japan and the BoE have established programs to purchase government debt as a means to provide additional monetary accommodation. As noted earlier, the BoC outlined the framework by which it would conduct such programs, if the need arose.

LESSONS LEARNED, THE CANADIAN EXPERIENCE AND THE ROAD AHEAD

Central banks and other public authorities learned several important lessons from the financial crisis. The most important is that an economic contraction spawned by a financial crisis is very costly because the impacts on the real economy can linger for years as financial institutions, firms and households repair their balance sheets (see Reinhart and Rogoff 2009). Thus, every effort should be made to reduce the likelihood of such financial crises and lessen their impact should they occur. This imperative has two implications for central banks — one domestic and one global.

Domestically, central banks realized that because financial crises can have a severe impact on economic activity and greatly affect inflation outcomes, and because central banks have a unique system-wide perspective among oversight authorities, they must step up their efforts to promote financial stability and be intimately involved in the formulation of macroprudential policy designed to mitigate systemic risk. In the past, financial stability was not given the same prominence as monetary policy within central banks. The financial crisis and Great Recession changed that view. Central banks are now devoting more attention and more resources to strengthening their efforts to identify and mitigate systemic risk. In collaboration with other oversight authorities, central banks are collecting more data and developing tools and models to analyze it.

At the international level, central banks and other public authorities have realized that because of global financial integration, they cannot protect themselves entirely through their own actions, but instead need to act in concert to develop and implement minimum standards for the financial system to prevent regulatory arbitrage across jurisdictions and preserve a level playing field. To coordinate these efforts, the FSB was established in 2009. The BoC has played an important role in the FSB because, like other central banks, it has a system-wide perspective on financial stability,[13] and because Canada relies on having open access to global capital markets to support economic activity.

In addition to recognizing the benefits from and helping to lead efforts to promote domestic financial stability and to develop and implement fundamental financial reforms, central banks have better appreciated their pivotal crisis management role. They now have a set of battle-tested policy measures that allow them to respond quickly and effectively to a crisis, often in conjunction with other authorities, in order to maintain the functioning of core financial markets.

With respect to monetary policy, central banks have learned from the crisis that achieving low, stable and predictable inflation is not sufficient to maintain financial stability. In other words, central banks must take into account financial stability considerations in formulating monetary policy, recognizing that other instruments, such as micro- and macroprudential measures, are

---

13 Former BoC Governor Mark Carney has served as chair of the FSB. Senior Deputy Governor Tiff Macklem was chair of the FSB's Standing Committee on Standards Implementation.

also available to mitigate risk and preserve financial stability. To this end, the BoC, in its recent agreement to renew its inflation control target with the Government of Canada, developed a *flexible* inflation-targeting framework, which allows it to incorporate financial stability considerations in its interest rate decisions by adjusting the time horizon over which inflation will return to the two percent target.[14]

Central banks have also learned important lessons about the conduct of monetary policy in a low interest rate environment, especially with respect to the use of unconventional monetary policy tools, including forward guidance and asset purchases. While such measures have proved to be effective, their effectiveness critically depends on the initial circumstances and clarity of communication (Santor and Suchanek 2013).

CONCLUSION

The actions of central banks were a key factor in the recovery from the financial crisis. The timely and aggressive implementation of a wide range of measures prevented the Great Recession from becoming a Great Depression. Five years later, however, the effects of the crisis continue to play out. The recovery has been anemic, with growth held back by ongoing deleveraging across the advanced economies and a lack of rotation in global demand to fast-growing emerging market economies (EMEs), in part due to a lack of timely, real exchange rate adjustment. Consequently, central banks will continue to need to provide considerable monetary stimulus to support the economy as households, banks and governments repair their balance sheets.

Central banks, including the BoC, will also continue to play a key role in financial sector reform. The reform agenda set out by the FSB, which is necessarily ambitious, will take years to complete and implement. There is a risk that the momentum for reform will fade as the crisis falls from view. This would be a mistake. The crisis is a stark reminder that the resilience of the real economy is only as good as that of the financial system.

---

14 Normally, the BoC determines the setting of its policy interest rate to return inflation to its two percent target in six to eight quarters. For more information on the flexible inflation-targeting framework, see BoC (2011).

Financial sector reforms are not enough. Other reforms are needed to ensure that global recovery continues. To this end, the reforms and policies set out by the G20 Framework for Strong, Sustainable and Balanced Growth need to be implemented fully, including: appropriately timed fiscal consolidation in the advanced economies; structural reforms in the euro area, Japan and China; and a move toward greater exchange rate flexibility in surplus EMEs. More broadly, central banks will need to be mindful of the ongoing evolution of the international monetary and financial system and their role within it.

WORKS CITED

BoC. 2009a. "Bank of Canada Lowers Overnight Rate Target by 1/4 Percentage Point to 1/4 Per Cent and, Conditional on the Inflation Outlook, Commits to Hold Current Policy Rate until the End of the Second Quarter of 2010." BoC press release, April 21. www.bankofcanada.ca/2009/04/publications/press-releases/fad-press-release-2009-04-21/.

———. 2009b. "Framework for Conducting Monetary Policy at Low Interest Rates." *Monetary Policy Report.* www.bankofcanada.ca/wp-content/uploads/2010/03/mpr230409.pdf.

———. 2011. *Renewal of the Inflation-Control Target: Background Information.* www.bankofcanada.ca/wp-content/uploads/2011/11/background_nov11.pdf.

Borio, C. and P. Disyatat. 2009. "Unconventional Monetary Policies: An Appraisal." BIS Working Papers No. 292.

Carney, Mark. 2012. "Guidance." Speech given to the CFA Society, Toronto, December 11. www.bankofcanada.ca/2012/12/publications/speeches/guidance/.

Crawford, A., C. Meh and J. Zhou. 2013. "The Residential Mortgage Market in Canada: A Primer." *Financial System Review,* December. www.bankofcanada.ca/wp-content/uploads/2013/12/fsr-december13-crawford.pdf.

Enenajor, E., A. Sebastian and J. Witmer. 2010. "An Assessment of the BOC's Term PRA Facility." Bank of Canada Working Paper 2010-20.

FSB. 2012. "Peer Review of Canada." www.financialstabilityboard.org/publications/r_120130.htm.

Goldberg, L. S., C. Kennedy and J. Miu. 2011. "Central Bank Dollar Swap Lines and Overseas Dollar Funding Costs." *Economic Policy Review* (May): 3–20.

He, Z. 2010. "Evaluating the Effect of the Bank of Canada's Conditional Committment Policy." Discussion Paper 2010-11. www.bankofcanada.ca/wp-content/uploads/2010/08/dp10-11.pdf.

Reinhart, C. and K. Rogoff. 2009. *This Time Is Different: Eight Centuries of Financial Folly.* Princeton: Princeton University Press.

Santor, Eric and Lena Suchanek. 2013. "Unconventional Monetary Policies: Evolving Practices, Their Effects and Potential Costs." *Bank of Canada Review* (Spring).

Zorn, Lorie, Carolyn Wilkins and Walter Engert. 2009. "Bank of Canada Liquidity Actions in Response to the Financial Market Turmoil." *Bank of Canada Review* (Autumn): 2–22.

7

The Bank of Canada and the Global Financial Crisis: Quietly Influential among Central Banks

Domenico Lombardi and Pierre Siklos

• • • • • • • • • • • • • • • • • • • •

INTRODUCTION

By some accounts, central banks are believed to have acquitted themselves well since financial markets practically collapsed in 2009 (see Blinder 2013). Of course, mistakes were made prior to the financial crisis, as well as in some of the responses to the extraordinary shocks hitting the global economy. While the economic repercussions for Canada were far from trivial, the consequences were largely felt elsewhere, especially in the United States.

The global financial crisis upset the goal of many central banks to be seen as dull[1] but competent and, perhaps unwillingly, thrust them to the forefront of efforts among policy makers to enact policies whose aim was to return to the "Great Moderation" (Bernanke 2004) that endured for roughly two decades previously. The global financial crisis also put a stop to some elements of the

---

1   Lord King (2007), the governor of the Bank of England (BoE) until June 2013, famously explained in 2007 that his ambition was for monetary policy to be "boring."

consensus about the role and functions of monetary policy (see Bernanke 2013). This can be summarized as seeking low and stable inflation, while ensuring that economies would remain at or near potential economic activity. Financial stability would naturally follow in such an environment. Price stability remains in favour worldwide, even in Europe where monetary union is in peril. The United States and the United Kingdom are mired in quantitative easing, but inflation shows signs of being too low for comfort in several parts of the world. Central bank independence is under attack as monetary authorities are being called upon to fill a void that fiscal policies are unable or unwilling to fill. Moreover, many observers no longer subscribe to the free movement of capital. Several economies, including Brazil and Malaysia, introduced taxes and other controls to stem the flow of capital to limit their impact on exchange rates and, more generally, the economy. Even Cyprus, a euro-zone economy, limits financial flows. Finally, monetary stability is no longer seen as sufficient for the maintenance of financial stability.

In central banking, the Bank of Canada (BoC) has been at the forefront in providing lessons about how a central bank should behave and the role it ought to play in stabilization policy. This was often accomplished quietly. It was only with the arrival of the global financial crisis that Canada's policy successes came more prominently into view in international policy circles. From exchange rate policy to elaborating the type of monetary policy strategy that can deliver price stability, the BoC is seen as a central bank that has followed best practices. Moreover, until the global financial crisis struck the world economy, the governance structure that defined how governments, regulators, supervisors and the central bank coordinated or cooperated with each other remained largely unnoticed both inside and outside Canada. Canada's financial regime has since emerged as one from which other countries can draw lessons.

While Canada escaped the worst of the global financial crisis, the events of 2008–2013 provide some fodder for the critics of the BoC. The recession of 2008-2009 was short-lived, but among the sharpest of the postwar era (see Cross and Bergevin 2012). Even if the two percent inflation target has proved to be a durable anchor, observed inflation has been below target roughly half of the time since 2005, including all of 2009 and 2013. Prior to 2005, consumer price index (CPI) inflation also remained below two percent between 1998 and early 2001 (BoC 2014).

The excesses of financial markets that came to haunt the US economy did find their way into Canada, although on a much smaller scale.[2] Moreover, the BoC was occasionally reduced to having to rely on bully pulpit speeches and other forms of communication to convey the dangers of rising property prices and debt levels. Much of this effort has not been entirely effective for the simple reason that the BoC's ultra-low interest rate policy does not appear to work seamlessly with macroprudential measures, largely the purview of the political authorities, or able to avert a property or credit bubble. The resulting tensions threaten the BoC's credibility and reputation. Finally, for all of its apparent success, the existing statutory governance structure seems antiquated and out of step with developments elsewhere. The BoC's success in enhancing transparency is being undone by a conflict between a de jure decision-making structure that is at variance with the de facto approach that is closer to worldwide standards, albeit at some cost in the form of a loss of clarity and transparency.

THE STATE OF PLAY ON THE EVE OF THE GLOBAL FINANCIAL CRISIS

It is no accident that the period of the Great Moderation also coincides with the ascendancy of monetary policy, governed by independent and, eventually, transparent central banks (see Bohl, Mayes and Siklos 2011). Meanwhile, fiscal policy became passive and was no longer viewed as being a policy-making tool with the capacity to contribute effectively to stabilization policy. It is against this backdrop that the BoC became one of the first central banks to develop a coherent monetary policy strategy. In 1991, the government acknowledged, not via legislative fiat but as part of a budget announcement,

---

2   This refers to problems with the market for so-called asset-backed commercial paper (ABCP) that emerged in 2007. As the name implies, these are instruments sold in the private sector and ostensibly "backed" by some underlying asset. Many retail investors were inadequately informed of the underlying risks in holding such instruments. The BoC's role was largely limited to applying moral suasion. Although the problem was largely outside its control, the BoC felt the need to intervene. For a brief overview of the problems and the significance of ABCPs for financial stability in Canada, see Dodge (2007).

the desirability of low and stable prices.[3] Canada's approach was cautious, blending a commitment to deliver price stability over time under a largely unchanged institutional structure. For the first few years, the goal was merely to reduce inflation gradually via inflation reduction targets (Crow 2002). When inflation fell faster than expected, monetary policy shifted to outright control targets.

To underscore the importance of accountability, the BoC and the Government of Canada agreed to review the targets on a regular five-year schedule. It is a measure of the success of the regime that the one to three percent inflation target range in consumer prices has been in place since 1993. Few countries can boast of a monetary policy strategy that has, essentially, remained unchanged for more than two decades. Nevertheless, the decision to focus on an inflation objective originally took place at the same time as a severe recession was underway. Not surprisingly, some academics saw the desire to achieve a price stability objective as a major contributor to the economic slump of the early 1990s (see Fortin 1996). The BoC, among others, offered a defence of its policies (see Freedman and Macklem 1998).[4] A lesson that Canada can offer others, and that others have since learned, is that a monetary policy strategy cannot survive without firm and consistent political support. The commitment to low and stable inflation in Canada is a joint one, publicly agreed to by different governments and governors of the BoC for over two decades.

Canada's record of inflation can be characterized as consistent with the objective of maintaining low and stable inflation rates, although periods of persistently below-target rates of change in the CPI have been common. Moreover, for the past 15 years, Canada's average inflation rate has been

---

3   The federal government's 1995 budget was also a landmark, as it both recognized the desirability of low and stable inflation and indicated the government's intention to bring monetary and fiscal policies in harmony with each other. See Laidler and Robson (1993). For the background of the introduction of inflation targeting elsewhere in the industrial world, see Siklos (2002).

4   When it comes to deciphering which interpretation of history is correct, the difficulty lies in identifying the relative importance of contributing factors. In any event, even the BoC later admitted that inflation fell more quickly than anticipated and this, perhaps, explains the short transition from inflation reduction to inflation control targets. As a result, there is at least the possibility that the policy regime made economic recovery more difficult. Whether doing nothing to reduce inflation would have produced better results is, however, an entirely different matter.

lower than that of the United States and the United Kingdom.[5] Former BoC Governor Gordon Thiessen sought to align the BoCs' practice with ones already in place elsewhere (most notably in the United States), while improving the transparency of policy. This led to the creation during the 1990s of the Governing Council, consisting of the BoC's governor and deputy governors. The creation of this body was meant to convey that policy decisions are taken by consensus within a committee structure even if, statutorily, the governor remains solely responsible for delivering monetary policy decisions. Equally important was the decision implemented in 2000 to set, in advance, dates when monetary policy decisions were to be announced on a regular and predictable schedule. Announcements were not enough; it was also necessary to explain a monetary policy decision even if the policy rate was not changed. Accordingly, the press releases accompanying policy rate decisions quickly began to take on an importance that is now acknowledged to be the focal point of the media's reactions to BoC policies.

The worldwide spread of central bank autonomy, combined with measures to enhance the accountability of the monetary authorities, led many small open economies, including Canada, to adopt a form of inflation targeting. By the time the global financial crisis erupted, approximately 30 economies adopted a form of inflation targeting. Even the United States finally announced a price stability objective in 2012.[6] The world's other major central bank, the European Central Bank (ECB), although steadfast in avoiding the inflation-targeting label, does place primacy on price stability and also follows a numerical price stability objective. The pre-crisis adoption of an inflation-targeting regime clearly places the BoC at the forefront of central banks that adopted best practices in the area of monetary policy.

It is worth reminding readers, however, that central bank practices since the 1990s had their origins following an earlier series of "global" crises, namely the supply shocks of the 1970s, and a previous failure in the industrial world of fiscal policy to prevent the stagflation of the 1970s (see Volcker 1984;

---

5 Canada's inflation performance in the 2000s has been so impressive relative to previous decades that it can be likened to a price level target with a two percent drift. See Siklos (2014).

6 Before he became Federal Open Market Committee Chairman, Ben Bernanke (2003) pointed out that inflation targets would likely be viewed by Americans as "foreign, impenetrable, and possibly slightly subversive." Why this is the case is unclear, since US economic history of the twentieth century is full of attempts by Congress to impose price stability rules on the Federal Reserve (see Siklos 2002).

Bordo and Orphanides 2013). Economic thought, together with the view that policy makers' hands ought to be tied lest too much discretion result in poor economic performance, ushered in the twin revolutions of central bank independence and a "do-no-harm" attitude in carrying out monetary policy.

The desire to appear accountable and competent led to both visible and less visible developments. Beginning in 1995, the BoC began to publish an account of its decisions in its quarterly *Monetary Policy Report*, and sought to publicly explain why monetary policy had to be forward-looking. Inflation targeting required the BoC to provide an outlook for the Canadian and global economies, and hint at how it might respond to such developments. Still, the BoC delayed for a few years, only to begin releasing its own forecast of inflation and economic growth in Canada in 2005. The most visible forward-looking element in monetary policy arguably took place in April 2009, when, in the midst of the global financial crisis, the BoC announced a conditional commitment (CC) to keep the policy at the effective zero lower bound (ZLB) for a year.[7] The only condition leading to the removal of the commitment was a serious threat to miss the inflation target. The policy's aim was to highlight the fact that the central bank was doing whatever it would take to create conditions for a successful economic recovery. The CC policy, now termed forward guidance, has been emulated by several other major central banks (for example, the US Federal Reserve, the BoE, the ECB and the Bank of Japan).

Less visible to the public was a long and proud tradition in Canada of developing economic models for analysis and forecasting (see Côté et al. 2006 and references therein). Without the tools to provide informed accounts of the likely future course of the Canadian economy, how global shocks might impact the domestic economy or how monetary policy decisions might play out, decision makers cannot properly perform their tasks. Instinct and judgment, while critical, are not enough.

Of course, there were other forces at play in fostering a new consensus, at least among most policy makers and academics, about what a central bank can and should do. First, there was growing recognition that excessive exchange rate manipulation was not only ineffective, but symbolizes the

---

7 The ZLB refers to the fact that, at least in principle, interest rates cannot fall below zero. While it is possible for lenders to actually accept subsidizing borrowers with negative interest rates, this is a rare occurrence.

failed beggar-thy-neighbour policies attempted several decades earlier. After all, exchange rate flexibility was seen as an essential ingredient in an inflation-targeting strategy. Nevertheless, it is now apparent that freedom of movement in financial flows jeopardizes some of the benefits of a flexible exchange rate regime. Even the BoC now admits that exchange rate flexibility can, under some circumstances, threaten financial system stability (Murray 2010).[8] Second, there existed a view that macroeconomic stability could be paired with financial stability (Schwartz 1995). Third, impediments in the movement of goods, services and capital were considered counterproductive at a time when markets became more global. Finally, the inexorable movement to a single currency in Europe, which combined a price stability objective and an independent central bank, put the seal of approval on a common international understanding of what constitutes good practice in the field of monetary policy (James 2012). Additionally, it became an accepted principle that monetary and financial policies required a certain degree of harmony and that this is conducive to making different economies look more alike. The latter was a precondition for membership in the common currency area.

HOW THE BoC AND OTHER CENTRAL BANKS WEATHERED THE GLOBAL FINANCIAL CRISIS

We now know from a vast literature on the events of 2007–2010 that the so-called global financial crisis originated from a series of structural and governance weaknesses in monetary and financial stability policy strategies. First, the blind eye that the Fed turned toward growing domestic financial imbalances and ineffective financial oversight contributed to create a housing bubble. Next, a liquidity crisis quickly turned into a credit crisis when financial institutions ceased lending to each other. In view of the "exorbitant privilege" standing of the US dollar, combined with a dramatic rise in the connectivity of financial institutions worldwide, the crisis of confidence spread worldwide.[9]

---

8 Nevertheless, there are no signs that the BoC is reconsidering its commitment to a floating regime.

9 The reference to imbalances is in recognition of differences of opinion between those who argue that a global savings glut (primarily in Asia) versus a US monetary policy that was too loose created conditions conducive to a global financial crisis.

Less than three years later, the buildup of sovereign debt among some euro-zone economies created a debt crisis in Europe. The situation was made worse with serious missteps both by the ECB and certain sovereign governments of the euro zone (i.e., Ireland and Spain), which either chose or were forced into underwriting bank losses through state guarantees that turned a funding or banking crisis into a worsening sovereign debt crisis. The patchwork of responses by individual member state governments and the ECB have, so far, calmed markets, even if doubts remain about the survival of the euro zone.

Conventional central bank actions, via changes in a central bank policy rate, became less effective and appeared inoperative once the ZLB was reached. Consequently, much of the advanced world adopted unconventional monetary policies. The shift implies an emphasis on policies that impact the balance sheet of the central bank. More generally, such policies amount to an expansion of central bank influence in the financial system, which happened in the United States, the United Kingdom and the euro zone. While the total assets of most central banks in advanced economies rose in the immediate aftermath of the 2008-2009 crisis, balance sheets have returned to normal in Canada, while remaining inflated elsewhere.

Canada remained in the eye of the storm that was creating havoc in other industrialized economies. A sound banking system and little bubble-like activity in the housing sector meant that two direct channels that propagated the financial crisis in the United States were absent in Canada. Nevertheless, the BoC could not avoid the movement of policy rates toward the ZLB. Regardless, the accommodative monetary policy stance still failed to dent the unease about negative spillovers from the deepening US recession, a phenomenon that was apparent throughout the industrial world.

Even if it was believed that Canada's economy was relatively resilient to the sizable adverse shocks from abroad, why could the Canadian economy not fully avoid a recession and the rapid fall in inflation?[10] The global financial crisis appeared to raise questions about the efficacy of the inflation-targeting regime, which, crucially, relies on a floating exchange rate regime believed to act as a shock absorber. Consequently, the BoC once again was

---

10 Cross and Bergevin (2012) create a business cycle chronology for the Canadian economy that mirrors the well-known National Bureau of Economic Research recession and expansion dates for the United States. They estimate that the recession of 2009 was brief by historical standards, but among the deepest recessions in Canada in decades.

thrust at the forefront of monetary policy actions when it unveiled its forward guidance policy in April 2009. The aim was to convince the public that the midpoint of the inflation target would not be abandoned and, to underscore its determination to return inflation to its two percent goal, that the policy rate would remain at its ZLB for up to a year. The BoC, worried about the possibility that inflationary expectations might become unanchored, raised the policy rate prior to the expiry date of the CC policy. By some accounts, the exit was credible (see Siklos and Spence 2010). Of course, the CC strategy was modest, took place under crisis conditions and had a limited horizon.

While the BoC has been a leader in promoting the virtues of forward guidance to good effect, it occasionally appears incapable of providing clarity about when the economy might return to a state that calls for a more "normal" monetary policy stance. For example, in the April 2010 *Monetary Policy Report*, the BoC first sought to justify why monetary policy might remain loose, even after signs of inflation and a return to capacity might otherwise have led markets to believe that the policy rate would rise. Unfortunately, the explanation was predicated on an inflation rate below target, at a time when observed inflation was above target. As a result, there is the risk that policy can be too loose for too long and that the BoC will not easily be able to tighten policy when, and if, this becomes necessary. Elsewhere, major central banks around the world also struggle with the tension between forward guidance as a tool to reassure the public and financial markets, while simultaneously promoting its policies as ones that will see a return to some form of normalcy in an increasingly distant future. These opposing forces occasionally result in central banks miscommunicating their intentions, such as in May 2013, when the US Fed originally floated the idea of "tapering" its government bond purchases.

The BoC's governance structure is an anachronism reflecting the 1934 Bank of Canada Act, which concentrates too much statutory authority in the hands of the governor. In spite of former BoC Governor Gordon Thiessen's administrative changes to create a committee structure as the vehicle that deliberates and conducts monetary policy, the public and financial markets continue to focus on what the governor alone has to say. The 1992 report on

BoC governance, which essentially concluded that "if it ain't broke, don't fix it," seems less defensible in the post-crisis era (Manley and Dorin 1992).[11]

The BoC has the legal authority and flexibility to act as a lender of last resort through the provision of emergency liquidity assistance or by conducting outright asset purchases. Similarly, the Fed was granted significant flexibility and authority in acting as the lender of last resort by section 13(3) of the Federal Reserve Act. This flexibility allowed the Fed to respond quickly and aggressively in response to the near collapse of the US and global financial systems. Nevertheless, that flexibility has arguably been restricted post-crisis, since the Fed can no longer count on "unusual and exigent circumstances" to take action. Instead, the central bank must adopt policies "consistent with sound management practices."

Other major central banks face legal and political constraints that restricted or delayed similar actions. For example, the actions of the BoE were delayed due to institutional frictions requiring coordination between the BoE, the financial regulator and the US Treasury. On the other hand, although the Treaty of the European Union does not explicitly assign a specific institution the role of lender of last resort, due to political constraints, the ECB left these functions to the national central banks. Political pressures restrained the ECB from acting quickly and aggressively; instead, it implemented liquidity provisions and outright asset purchase programs with caution.

Like other major central banks, the BoC responded to the crisis by significantly extending its lending facilities and aggressively lowering the policy rate. After hitting the ZLB on interest rates, and worried that the expansionary macroeconomic policies were not sufficient to spark a recovery in the real economy, the BoC used a calendar-based conditional commitment to maintain the policy rate at the ZLB. Other major central banks were more hesitant in making such commitments, and acted cautiously when they did.

The Fed had previous experience with guiding market expectations concerning the future path of the policy rate in response to a sluggish recovery in 2003, indicating that the rate would remain low for a "considerable period." In response to the global financial crisis, the Fed was quick to provide guidance; however, the guidance was vague, stating that rates would

---

11 It could be argued that changes in the internal operations of the BoC, instituted during Thiessen's governorship, were a quiet response to the findings of the commission. See Laidler (1991).

remain low for "some time," and later "an extended period." By 2011, the Fed became more explicit in providing calendar-based conditional commitments: this form of guidance was similar to that of the BoC, although, the Fed did not actually state that it was a commitment.[12] Most recently, the Fed has implemented threshold-based conditional commitments in an attempt to communicate more clearly that the monetary policy decision-making process is dependent on developments in the real economy, rather than predetermined (Williams 2013).

The BoE and the ECB were more hesitant to guide market expectations, out of fear that they would either default on their primary objective of maintaining price stability or lose credibility if they reneged. The BoE made a threshold-based conditional commitment immediately after former BoC Governor Mark Carney took his post as governor of the BoE in the summer of 2013. The ECB introduced guidance around the same time as the BoE when Mario Draghi (2013), president of the ECB, stated that "the Governing Council expects the key ECB interest rates to remain at present or lower levels for an extended period of time." The guidance provided by the Fed, the BoE and the BoC were used as an alternative tool for achieving their objectives when the standard and unconventional policies were found to be not enough. The ECB's guidance, on the other hand, does not represent a change in its policy strategy and is not a conditional commitment to a specific policy path, but rather reflects its expected policy stance given its projections concerning the real economy (Praet 2013).

With continued stress in the financial system, unsuccessful attempts to calm markets through expanded liquidity facilities, key policy rates approaching their effective ZLB and the hesitation in making a commitment to the path of the policy rate, the BoE, the Fed and the ECB implemented their own forms of quantitative easing programs. These programs have differed significantly in both size and composition; however, they have all carved a role for the central bank in fiscal policy and have had distributional impacts that have increased discontent concerning the accountability of unelected policy makers.

The major central banks each pioneered their own unconventional policies, designed in accordance with their legislated authority and the ills

---

12 Even though the Fed did not commit to maintaining the policy rate at its ZLB until the specified dates, markets treated these statements as if they were a commitment, rather than projections. See Campbell et al. (2012) and Woodford (2012).

characterizing their financial markets. For example, in partnership with Her Majesty's Treasury, the BoE launched the Funding for Lending Scheme (FLS) in 2012, wherein the BoE can lend UK Treasury Bills to banks and building societies for up to four years against eligible collateral, for a fee. The amount that a financial institution is able to borrow depends on the initial size of its loan portfolio and the expansion of its portfolio over a given period; furthermore, the size of the borrowing fee will depend negatively on the expansion of its loan portfolio. An extension of the program in 2013 increased the incentive to lend to small- and medium-sized enterprises. The purpose of the FLS is to decrease the cost of lending to financial institutions in order to decrease market segmentation, an intractable problem in the euro periphery.

Geographical market segmentation is one of the main reasons for the persistence of the euro crisis (see chapter 10 of this volume). The ECB's ability to address market segmentation is largely prohibited by the Treaty on the Functioning of the European Union. Specifically, the ECB and other EU institutions are prohibited from providing credit facilities or privileged access to public institutions, with the exception of publicly owned credit institutions, and prohibited from assuming liability of public debt. In a bold move to restore confidence in the euro and to reduce market segmentation, Mario Draghi (2012) confirmed that "the euro is irreversible" and introduced the Outright Monetary Transactions (OMT) program. The program consists of purchases of government bonds in the secondary market with no *ex ante* limits, conditional on participation in, and satisfactory adherence to, an adjustment program under the European Stability Mechanism. To date, there have been no operations conducted under the OMT program due to political backlash, especially from Germany, as well as a perceived reluctance of potential euro zone borrowers to sacrifice sovereignty. Nonetheless, OMT succeeded in calming financial markets and, should this become necessary, effectively prepares the ground for the ECB to implement a form of quantitative easing. A legal case arguing that this program represents a breach of the ECB's legislated authorities and violates the German national constitution was upheld by a decision of the German Constitutional Court in February 2014. However, the legality of OMT now also awaits a decision by the European Court of Justice, since the matter has been referred to them by the German Constitutional Court. Interestingly, independence was one of the most important features of the design of the ECB because it would be faced with a surfeit of political influence and without independence, "monetary policy can rapidly become a cause of disintegration and political fragmentation" (James 2013). Yet, despite being one of the most independent central banks in the world, competing domestic interests may be creating such a fate.

De jure and de facto powers of most central banks and their relationships with fiscal authorities have undergone changes since the onset of the global financial crisis. For example, the BoE has been granted more independence in conducting its function as the lender of last resort in an effort to improve its ability to effectively respond to future distress in the financial system.[13] In addition, the UK government introduced a new regulatory framework bringing micro- and macroprudential regulation under the authority of the BoE. In the United States, the 2010 Dodd-Frank Wall Street Reform and Consumer Protection Act expanded the Fed's supervisory and regulatory powers by authorizing it to supervise systemically important financial institutions, including non-bank ones. It also expanded the Fed's power to oversee and regulate specific segments of the financial market. Dodd-Frank has, however, limited the Fed's ability to act quickly and aggressively in proving emergency liquidity as it did in 2008. Specifically, the Fed can no longer provide bailouts for specific institutions and is now required to gain the approval of the Secretary of the Treasury in order to establish emergency lending programs or facilities for non-member banks and non-bank financial institutions. These reforms were implemented to decrease the responsibility and increase the accountability of the unelected officials of the Federal Reserve.

The ECB, on the other hand, has been forced to act as an "institution of a last resort" due to the absence of a well-established fiscal or banking union. However, the ECB has been cautious in intervening in the financial system. Its outright asset purchase programs, including purchases of covered bonds and public and private debt, amount to less than 10 percent of the size of the Fed's quantitative easing program, while most of its non-standard policies consist of the provision of longer-term loans through repurchase agreements. Slow progress in the establishment of fiscal and banking unions, and stagnation

---

13 The aim is to limit losses that may be incurred when a central bank holds long-term government debt on its balance sheet. Otherwise, the public may see bond purchase programs as creating a risk for taxpayers.

of structural reforms within sovereign institutions themselves, is forcing the ECB to take responsibility for the economic recovery and extend its actions beyond what politics permits. The new single supervisory mechanism, to be enacted in 2014, will increase the responsibilities of the ECB through supervision of systemically important financial institutions and the authority to provide bailouts. These measures will improve the ability of the ECB to foster financial stability and decrease market segmentation, aligning its role more closely with that of other major central banks.

The BoC might, at times, have trouble communicating the timing of the return to more "normal" monetary policy, but exit will be implemented through standard measures accomplished by tightening the policy rate. The return to a normal policy stance will probably take longer, create more economic and financial volatility, and will be more complex for other major central banks. There is little sign of a sustained recovery in the euro zone, and it is likely that the ECB will have to further ease monetary conditions and take a commanding role in repairing specific market segments. Meanwhile, the United States has been showing signs of a stronger recovery, and the Fed will soon have the difficult task of unloading US$3 trillion of assets without significantly disturbing the financial system and triggering another recession. The negative reaction of financial markets in May and June 2013 gave a small foretaste of the difficult road ahead, when hints of tapering in government bond purchases were being seriously considered by the Federal Open Market Committee (FOMC). By December 2013, the FOMC decided on a very modest tapering approach, coupled with a firm intention to leave the policy rate at the ZLB for the foreseeable future. The future of monetary policy in other major advanced economies is uncertain, but more stable economic conditions in Canada, in principle, offer its policy makers the opportunity to focus on the future of central banking and financial regulation.

LESSONS LEARNED AND THE WAY FORWARD

While Canada escaped the worst of the global financial crisis, its central bank is not immune to the forces that are reshaping, or will reshape, the conduct of monetary policy. Indeed, we may well have reached a tipping point, when rewriting the "contract" between the fiscal and monetary authorities is in the air (see Carney 2013).

What might a revised central bank contract look like? The general principles required to ensure that Canada remains at the forefront among nations in best monetary and financial policy practices should include the following: first, recognition that monetary policy strategies are not timeless. These should be reconsidered on a regular basis, much like the Bank of Canada Act that defined rules of conduct for commercial banks and are regularly revised.[14] Central banks also need to acknowledge mistakes and engage in periodic self-assessment to clearly establish what lessons have to be learned. Second, the task of maintaining financial system stability requires effective cooperation, if not coordination, among several public institutions. Consequently, the roles and responsibilities of each vis-à-vis the others must be clearly articulated and accountability properly assigned. Furthermore, the global financial crisis heightened the importance of central bank cooperation in securing global financial stability. However, cooperative efforts may have diminished in recent years due to the increase in the costs of ensuring such stability and reluctance to allow the central bank to contribute funds for stabilizing global markets. An example of these circumstances is the difficulty in securing financial stability in the euro zone because sovereigns are reluctant to make individual sacrifices for the common good (James 2013).

The global financial crisis triggered the realization that we are operating in a tightly knit international financial system subject to significant spillover effects. The relative ease with which Canada weathered the crisis prompted other advanced economies to review the Canadian institutional and regulatory environment during their reassessment processes. On the other hand, the hardship that the United States, the euro zone and the United Kingdom have faced, and the significant structural reforms they have undergone suggest that Canada has much to learn from the feats and failures of its peer group. Clearly, part of Canada's success is attributable to its conservative banking system and prudent regulatory bodies supported by a central bank with a credible monetary policy strategy.

---

14 There is some element of self-study each time the BoC and the government renew the inflation target. The analysis is limited, however, to the conduct of monetary policy and focuses on areas of future research and policy improvements that might be contemplated. It is not conducted externally, does not consider improvements to the governance of the BoC — whether the level of transparency is adequate or needs revisiting — nor does it consider whether the relationship between the government and the central bank could be improved.

The BoC has the institutional authority and flexibility to respond appropriately to problems in the financial system through its functions as a lender of last resort. This authority allows for prompt and aggressive actions when necessary, but also improves market confidence in the central bank by knowing that the bank can respond appropriately if necessary. Similar authority was observed in the United States, and the Fed was applauded for its quick and aggressive actions in response to the crisis. On the other hand, restrictions to the authorities of the BoE and the ECB created delayed or cautious reactions to market segmentation. In contrast, the BoC is well positioned to take prompt and aggressive action in the event of a crisis without having to worry about political interference.

Although the BoC effectively did not resort to using unconventional policies, it established a plan and a set of guiding principles for implementing extended liquidity facilities and unconventional monetary policies (see BoC 2008; 2009). Establishing and clearly communicating guiding principles for central bank actions in extraordinary circumstances is important for enhancing the transparency of the central bank's actions, as well as improving the consistency of the decision-making process under rapidly changing circumstances. Furthermore, guiding principles allow for both flexibility and structure in its policy actions. The major central banks all demonstrated flexibility in their policy actions. Nevertheless, it is possible to reduce uncertainty by communicating clearly articulated guiding principles. For example, the consensus in macroeconomics, pre-crisis, argued that monetary policy should not be employed to deliberately stimulate economic activity beyond the short to medium term. More than five years after the global financial crisis erupted, central banks are still perceived as being overly interventionist. Even if the accusation is false, the monetary authorities in some of the advanced economies have not convinced many that the scope, size and duration of their unconventional policies is warranted. If this were not the case, we would observe far fewer criticisms about the current stance of monetary policy.

The major economies have formalized a framework for macroprudential regulation — regulation of the aggregate financial system — but the role of the central banks within these frameworks has yet to be clearly defined. Although Canada already has a system for monitoring and responding to systemic risks, it has not assigned responsibilities and established formal mechanisms for macroprudential supervision and regulation (see chapter 5 of this volume; Jenkins and Thiessen 2012). Similarly, the global financial crisis was a wake-up call to the economies that were hit the hardest: it mobilized them to reassess and redesign their regulatory landscape. In the aftermath of the crisis, these developments have led central banks to expand their influence and authority over stabilization and regulatory policies. Some have argued that the complexity of the financial system demands such a response (see Haldane 2013). Yet, these arguments are unconvincing as larger, more complex institutions are no less prone to policy errors, nor are they necessarily more transparent.

Hopefully, when the next financial crisis arrives, Canada can continue to claim that it was able to remain at the forefront in following central banking best practices. Even if the BoC remains quietly influential, future events may well conspire to remind policy makers around the world of Canada's ability to design effective monetary and financial stability strategies.

Acknowledgements

Comments by David Laidler, Bill Robson, Eric Santor and conference participants on an earlier draft are gratefully acknowledged. Samantha St. Amand provided excellent research assistance.

WORKS CITED

Bernanke, B. 2003. "A Retrospective on Inflation Targeting." Remarks at the Annual Washington Policy Conference of the National Association of Business Economists, Washington, DC, March 25. www.federalreserve.gov/boarddocs/speeches/2003/20030325/default. htm.

———. 2004. "The Great Moderation." Remarks delivered at the Eastern Economics Association, February 20. www.federalreserve.gov/ boarddocs/speeches/2004/20040220/.

———. 2013. *The Federal Reserve and the Financial Crisis.* Princeton, NJ: Pricenton University Press.

Blinder, A. 2013. *After the Music Stopped: The Financial Crisis, the Response, and the Work Ahead.* New York: The Penguin Press.

BoC. 2008. *Financial System Review.* June. Ottawa: BoC.

———. 2009. *Monetary Policy Report.* April. Ottawa: BoC.

———. 2014. "Summary of Key Monetary Policy Variables." www.bankofcanada.ca/rates/indicators/key-variables/.

Bohl, M., D. Mayes and P. Siklos. 2011. "The Quality of Monetary Policy and Inflation Performance: Globalization and Its Aftermath." *Manchester School* 79 (June, S1): 617–45.

Bordo, M. and A. Orphanides, eds. 2013. *The Great Inflation.* Chicago: University of Chicago Press.

Campbell, J. R., C. L. Evans, J. D. M. Fisher and A. Justiniano. 2012. "Macroeconomic Effects of Federal Reserve Forward Guidance." Brookings Papers on Economic Activity, Spring.

Carney, Mark. 2013. "Monetary Policy After the Fall." Speech given at the Eric Hanson Memorial Lecture, University of Alberta, May 1. www.bankofcanada.ca/2013/05/publications/speeches/monetary-policy-after-the-fall/.

Côté, D., John Kuszczak, Jean-Paul Lam, Ying Liu and Pierre St-Amant. 2006. "A Comparison of Twelve Macroeconomic Models of the Canadian Economy." *Journal of Policy Modeling* 28: 523–62.

Cross, P. and P. Bergevin. 2012. "Turning Points: Business Cycles in Canada since 1926." C. D. Howe Commentary No. 366, October.

Crow, J. 2002. *Making Money.* Toronto: John Wiley & Sons.

Dodge, D. 2007. "A Clear Case for Transparency." Remarks delivered to the Canada-UK Chamber of Commerce, September 12. www.bankofcanada.ca/2007/09/publications/speeches/clear-case-for-transparency/.

Draghi, M. 2012. Remarks made by Mario Draghi and Vítor Constâncio of the ECB, Frankfurt am Main, September 6. www.ecb.europa.eu/press/pressconf/2012/html/is120906.en.html.

————. 2013. Remarks made by Mario Draghi and Vítor Constâncio of the ECB, Frankfurt am Main, July 4. www.ecb.europa.eu/press/pressconf/2013/html/is130704.en.html.

Fortin, P. 1996. "The Great Canadian Slump." *Canadian Journal of Economics* 29 (November): 761–87.

Freedman, C. and T. Macklem. 1998. "A Comment of 'The Great Canadian Slump.'"*Canadian Journal of Economics* 31 (August): 646–65.

Haldane, A. 2013. "Why Institutions Matter (More Than Ever)." Speech given at the Centre for Research on Socio-Cultural Change Annual Conference, School of Oriental and African Studies, London, September 4. www.bankofengland.co.uk/publications/Pages/speeches/2013/676.aspx.

James, H. 2012. *Making the European Monetary Union.* Cambridge, MA: Harvard University Press.

————. 2013. *Essays on International Finance: International Cooperation and Central Banks,* vol. 1. CIGI Special Report.

Jenkins, P., and G. Thiessen. 2012. "Reducing the Potential for Future Financial Crises: A Framework for Macro-Prudential Policy in Canada." C. D. Howe Institute Commentary 351.

King, M. 2007. "Monetary Policy Developments." Speech given to the Birmingham Chamber of Commerce. www.bis.org/review/r070125a.pdf.

Laidler, D. E. W. 1991. "How Shall We Govern the Governor?: A Critique of the Governance of the Bank of Canada." The Canada Round, 1. Toronto: C.D. Howe Institute.

Laidler, D. E. W. and W. P. Robson. 1993. *The Great Canadian Disinflation: The Economics and Politics of Canadian Monetary Policy in Canada, 1988-93.* Toronto: C.D. Howe Institute.

Manley, J. and M. Dorin. 1992. *The Mandate and Governance of the Bank of Canada: First Report of the Sub-Committee on the Bank of Canada: Eighth Report of the Standing Committee on Finance.* Ottawa: Government of Canada.

Murray, J. 2010. "Re-Examining Canada's Monetary Policy Frameworks: Recent Research and Outstanding Issues." Remarks at the Canadian Association of Business Economists, August 24.

Praet, P. 2013. "Forward Guidance and the ECB." In *Forward Guidance: Perspectives from Central Bankers, Scholars and Market Participants*. London: Centre for Economic Policy Research.

Schwartz, A. J. 1995. "Why Financial Stability Depends on Price Stability." *Economic Affairs* 15 (September): 21–25.

Siklos, P. L. 2002. *The Changing Face of Central Banking*. Cambridge: Cambridge University Press.

———. 2014. "Communications Challenges for Multi-Tasking Central Banks: Evidence and Implications." *International Finance* 17 (1): 77–98.

Siklos, P. L. and A. Spence. 2010. "Face-Off: Should the Bank of Canada Release Its Projections for the Interest Rate Path?" C. D. Howe Backgrounder 134, October. www.cdhowe.org/pdf/Backgrounder_134.pdf.

Volcker, P. 1984. Remarks at the 78th Commencement of the American University, Washington, DC, January 29.

Woodford, M. 2012. "Methods of Policy Accommodation at the Interest-Rate Lower Bound." Presented at The Changing Policy Landscape, 2012 FRB Kansas City Economic Policy Symposium, Jackson Hole, August 30-September 1.

Williams, J. C. 2013. "Forward Guidance at the Federal Reserve." In *Forward Guidance: Perspectives from Central Bankers, Scholars and Market Participants*. London: Centre for Economic Policy Research.

8

Canadian Autonomy and Systemic Financial Risk after the Crisis of 2008

Louis W. Pauly

• • • • • • • • • • • • • • • • • •

INTRODUCTION

Canadian policy makers were tested during the 2008 global financial crisis. Subsequent journalistic and scholarly accounts commonly assert that they had passed with flying colours. In fact, stories told before, during and after the crisis seemed to readily fit an old pattern: sound Canadian regulatory principles and supervisory practices had helped offset the potentially devastating effects of manic shocks emanating from turbulent US and European financial markets. Those stories were not false, but most missed deeper truths concerning the origins of those principles and practices, and about the tightening constraints around Canada's broader economic policies.

Canada's success in avoiding the worst effects of the crisis of 2008 reflected the legacy of its own financial disasters in the distant and not-so-distant past. Its preference for stability in the face of systemic risk was hard won. In the context of much deeper financial market integration across the 49th parallel, Canada increasingly depended on more intensive collaboration with the United States and other economic partners. Systemic risks cumulated across financial intermediaries that were active internationally. When they threatened to overwhelm integrated payments systems, central bankers became the market-makers of last resort. In the wake of the crisis, governments and central banks in Canada and other leading countries moved to complement microprudential supervision with macroprudential measures designed to enhance the resilience of markets they hoped would remain integrated. Political interaction would determine whether that hope was justified.

Complex interdependence only begins to suggest the existential situation of Canadian financial policy makers today. Canada is not alone in this new world, where intergovernmental coordination on financial crisis management and prevention is hardly voluntary. Its past experiences and geographic location, however, have prepared Canada to be among the first to pragmatically understand the implications of deep integration in financial markets. The scope for the country's economic policies to be crafted autonomously had become quite limited, even if past policy choices favouring open but concentrated capital markets, national control of key intermediaries and a flexible exchange rate still provided tactical room for manoeuvre.

Tony Porter, David Longworth, Lawrence Schembri and Eric Santor concisely summarize the key policy decisions accounting for Canada's enviable performance during the crisis in their chapters in this volume and elsewhere (see also Porter 2010; Lynch 2010, 12–15). This chapter provides historical context and an assessment of the future implications of those decisions.

THE FINANCIAL CRISIS IN CANADA AND ITS LEGACY

Despite its confederal structure, by the 1980s Canada had successfully consolidated its regulation of banks, insurance companies, investment dealers and trust companies. The process was rooted in the path-breaking recommendations of the Royal Commission on Banking and Finance (Porter Commission) in 1964, which originally opened up the postwar financial system and expanded the scope of competition. The big six banks now compete energetically, but they also own the largest investment dealers and trust companies, and are permitted to sell limited types and amounts of insurance, such as travel and personal accident insurance.

In the years before 2007-2008, Canadian authorities, priding themselves on a combination of intensive supervision and principles-based regulation that put the onus for soundness and stability on individual financial institutions, clearly encouraged greater managerial prudence than was evident south of the border. For example, despite a regulatory cap on leverage of CDN$20 in assets for every CDN$1 in capital, the biggest Canadian financial institutions maintained average ratios of 18 to 1 in 2008; their peers in the United States and Europe averaged ratios between 25 and 35 to 1. The so-called Basel Tier 1 bank capital standards, moreover, were generally more rigorous in Canada than elsewhere and, as Longworth notes in his chapter, loss-absorbing capital was of higher quality (see chapter 5 of this volume).

More generally, if concentration and barriers to entry are a force for stability, the Canadian banking system has long been stable. The big six banks have come to dominate a system that spans the country's regions and, most importantly, gathers its retail banking deposits. That retail market is not closed, but, as discussed later in this chapter, it is no accident that foreign banks together have never held more than 10 percent of all banking assets in the country.

Complementing the Canadian banks' retail deposit base are requirements and practices governing the country's home mortgage market. Before the crisis of 2008, about 25 percent of Canadian mortgages were packaged as securities and sold off by the originating banks. The rest were held on the banks' books. In the United States, the comparable number was around 60 percent (Ratnovski and Huang 2009, 11). Also, by way of contrast, only some five percent of Canadian mortgages would have failed to meet a "prime" standard when the Canada Mortgage and Housing Corporation, a federally controlled entity, stopped insuring them in 2008. The banks subsequently grew more cautious. Even before the crisis, however, the overall mortgage business in Canada was quite safe: down payments on house purchases tended to be high, almost half of all mortgages were insured and mortgage interest payments were not deductible for tax purposes. Cautious bank management, intensive supervision, tax policy and government-sponsored insurance all reinforced one another.[1]

Notwithstanding their solid domestic foundations, Canadian banks were among the key beneficiaries of both Canadian and American monetary and fiscal largesse during the darkest days of the crisis. In the immediate aftermath of the collapse of Lehman Brothers in September 2008, Canadian banks, like their counterparts around the world, confronted a drastic shortage of liquidity. In coordinated operations, central banks pumped billions of dollars into money markets. US authorities also took the unprecedented step of lending the insurance giant American International Group (AIG) US$85 billion in exchange for nearly 80 percent of its stock. At the same time, leading governments moved to ban the speculative short selling of financial stocks. Then, during the first days of October 2008, US President George W. Bush signed the US$700 billion Emergency Economic Stabilization Act into law. Fearing a global economic collapse, central banks simultaneously slashed short-term interest rates. On October 14, the US Treasury announced its intention to take US$250 billion from the new US$700 billion fund to purchase troubled assets from US banks and the US operations of Canadian and other foreign banks.

On December 17, the Fed lowered its base interest rates to near zero percent, and initiated a massive government bond purchasing program. Two days later, President Bush announced plans to lend General Motors and Chrysler US$17.4 billion to prevent their collapse; their Canadian subsidiaries were quiet beneficiaries. The Canadian federal and Ontario governments supplemented this bailout with funds of their own, totalling CDN$3.3 billion in loans and equity purchases. The Canadian component was agreed to be about 20 percent of the value of the American package, commensurate with the relative size of the auto industry in Canada.

On February 10, 2009, the US Treasury announced a Financial Stability Plan involving purchases of convertible preferred stock in eligible banks, the creation of a Public-Private Investment Fund to acquire troubled assets from financial institutions, complemented by massive expansions in the Fed's

---

1 Note the less-than-cautious behaviour of Canadian financial consumers. By mid-2013, International Monetary Fund (IMF) data suggested that Canadian household debt as a percentage of GDP at 95 percent remained on an increasing trajectory, while the equivalent ratio in the United States was just above 80 percent and falling.

discount window liquidity operations as well as in its special and temporary Term Asset-Backed Securities Loan Facility and Commercial Paper Financing Facility. One week later, a new US$787 billion fiscal stimulus plan, the American Recovery and Reinvestment Act of 2009, was signed into law. On March 1, the US Treasury provided US$30 billion in capital to AIG and took over two divisions of the company after it announced a US$61.7 billion loss, the largest in US corporate history. Subsequent decisions were made to use some of the proceeds, US taxpayer dollars, to pay AIG's obligations in full to major counterparties — dollar for dollar, without a haircut. Major foreign intermediaries benefited directly (Broz 2012). Canadian banks featured prominently among the leading, and lucky, beneficiaries.

The following table gives a sense of the scale and scope of the liquidity assistance provided to Canadian banks by the Federal Reserve.

Table 1: Federal Reserve Bank Loans
(August 1, 2007–April 30, 2010, in US$ billions)

Beneficiary	Peak Amount of Loans	Average Daily Balance	Number of Days in Debt	Peak Loans/ Market Value (in %)
Bank of Nova Scotia	9.5 (1/2/09)	1.9	798	40
Royal Bank of Canada	6.9 (12/18/08)	1.8	588	21
Toronto Dominion Bank	6.6 (4/19/09)	2.3	679	28.5
Canadian Imperial Bank of Commerce	2.2 (4/19/09)	0.4	364	16.5
Bank of Montreal	1.8 (10/9/08)	0.4	462	11.5

Source: Data from US Federal Reserve data, summarized at www.bloomberg.com ("The Fed's Secret Liquidity Loans"). For comparative purposes, note peak amounts of loans for Citibank (US$99.5 billion); Morgan Stanley (US$107.3 billion); Bank of America (US$91.4 billion); and Goldman Sachs (US$69 billion).

In turn, US authorities asked the Canadian banks simultaneously to provide more high-quality capital to their US operations. This led former Canadian Minister of Finance Jim Flaherty to propose a new ministerial authority to veto the future expansion plans of the banks and insurance companies (see

The Globe and Mail 2011, 1).[2] More threat than follow-through, Flaherty's reaction underlined the increasing political sensitivities involved in cross-border policy interaction in the financial sector.

The banks also benefited indirectly from domestic emergency facilities, both official and officially backed.[3] One program involved asset-backed commercial paper (ABCP). The market for ABCP in Canada stood at CDN$115 billion in 2007, CDN$32 billion of which was based outside the mainstream banking system. In August 2007, the non-bank ABCP market froze. With the finance minister's encouragement, creditors formed the Pan-Canadian Investors Committee of Third Party ABCP Investors in an attempt to restructure and resuscitate the ABCP market. Their plan, dubbed the "Montreal Proposal," is widely understood to be unique in that it was initiated and run by the private sector. Unlike rescue efforts in the United States, an explicit transfer of public funds was not used to prop up the Canadian version of the shadow banking system. However, the quiet encouragement of the federal government, along with the governments of Ontario, Quebec and Alberta, should not be discounted. In fact, they provided critical support for the plan. They collectively agreed to act as the ultimate backstop for the newly created multi-billion dollar margin funding facilities, which, if needed, would make funds available to cover potential shortfalls on margin calls on the credit default swaps at the centre of the frozen ABCP market. Failure to make good on margin calls could have resulted in the collapse of the non-bank ABCP market and spilled over into the bank-centred payments system. The implicit official backstopping of these facilities shed light on another key difference across the 49th parallel. Unlike their American peers, Canada's regulators did not lack the authority to govern domestic institutions that can deliver bank-like services.[4]

In addition, the federal government created the Insured Mortgage Purchase Program, which allowed the official buying of up to CDN$125 billion in securitized mortgages from the banks. By the time the program ended in

2   The proposal specified that ministerial approval would be necessary for any bank or insurance company to increase its consolidated assets by more than 10 percent through a foreign acquisition. In between mandated reviews of the major act governing financial institutions, such a proposal may be interpreted as firm guidance in the absence of final parliamentary action.

3   For more information on the principles guiding liquidity support from the Bank of Canada (BoC), see Longworth (2010).

4   For details on how an equivalent form of deposit insurance was created in the American shadow banking system, see Pozsar et al. (2010).

March 2010, CDN$69 billion had been injected into the banking system. The program was justified by the overriding interest in increasing liquidity within constrained credit markets, as well as by providing a level global playing field with newly "subsidized" foreign competitors. So too were monetary measures designed to lower funding costs for banks at the core of the national payments system. Even though such programs were wisely structured to ensure a long-run profit to the national treasury and thus to mitigate somewhat the moral hazards implied, one could hardly defend the argument that Canadian markets functioned efficiently during this period without assistance from the visible hand of government. Indeed, one analysis estimates the net flows of official funds from US and Canadian sources to the Canadian banks at CDN$114 billion between 2008 and 2010, with the scale of this support at the most extreme moments exceeding the market value of three of them (Macdonald 2012).

Notwithstanding this emergency support, the journalistic and policy literature since 2010 suggests that there is much for others to emulate in recent Canadian experience. Beyond the issue of whether larger political and social conditions permit such emulation, more fundamental questions remain: how did the effective microprudential supervision in place in 2008 actually arise, and what does the emergency support nonetheless provided to Canada's financial intermediaries tell us about residual gaps in the global supervisory system? A look back at the distant past is useful to help answer these questions.

CRISIS AND STABILIZATION IN THE EARLY CANADIAN BANKING SYSTEM

Before Confederation, banking in Canada was characterized by repeated growth phases followed by catastrophes. New banks were not difficult to start and they could operate under either royal charters or licences from colonial legislatures. Fifty-four charters were granted by the Crown or by colonial legislatures between 1820 and 1867 (Neufeld 1972, 553-54). Ease of entry and lax oversight increased competition and expanded credit, but eroded bank profits and encouraged excessive risk taking. Unlucky banks failed, and if they had not put aside a sufficient cushion of capital, their depositors were left with worthless claims. Indeed, spectacular and frequent bank failures were on the minds of Canada's founding fathers in 1867, as well as in 1871 when they promulgated the first Bank Act (Turley-Ewart 2004).

After 1871, granting new bank charters became the sole responsibility of the federal government. Nationwide branching put Canadian banks under a uniform regulatory setting, something the fragmented American system of the day did not offer. It also provided a natural hedge against regional economic downturns, not uncommon occurrences in the boom-bust cycles of Canada's early economic development (Bordo, Redish and Rockoff 2010; Carr, Mathewson and Quigley 1995). Regional instability, however, often did leave local bank depositors with outright losses. Bank failures were in fact quite common and geographically quite widespread during the final decades of the nineteenth century (Breckenridge 1910, 117). In the run-up to the Bank Act of 1890, fearing political threats to their operational autonomy, leading banks proposed a Bank Circulation Redemption Fund, an early form of deposit insurance. The new fund required all banks to deposit five percent of their annual note circulation at the Finance Department, which would be used to compensate depositors in the event of a failure. The quid pro quo was that the federal government would remain on the sidelines with respect to the day-to-day banking activities. The idea soon bore fruit, and the Canadian Bankers' Association (CBA) was established with the stated objective of securing the assets of the fund (Turley-Ewart 2000). In practice, however, a CBA fragmented by geography and bank scale was incapable of serving as the government's night watchman. The Redemption Fund, moreover, proved inadequate on many occasions and depositors continued to face losses when mismanaged banks failed. Most were accompanied by news of fraud and incompetence, and other banks proved reluctant to compensate either perpetrators or victims.

Up until 1910, bank failures averaged one every two years and new bank charters did not keep pace with the number of banks going out of business. In principle, this Darwinian process promised to leave the group of surviving banks larger and more stable. Enhanced capital requirements and mandatory auditing were included in the 1913 revision to the Bank Act, revisions that also favoured large and diversified banks.

On the eve of World War I, steady consolidation had reduced the number of banks to less than half of the 50 in existence in 1875, despite the economy becoming almost five times as large in real terms (Neufeld 1972, 77–80).

Also gone by this time was the serious prospect that Canada might be annexed outright by the United States. The two facts reinforced one another. The big six banks were beginning to emerge as dominant weavers of a resilient national fabric, and they would prove most useful to a federal government preparing for war. Their new obligations to help finance the war effort — directly by way of loans and taxes, and indirectly by selling government bonds — were enshrined in the Finance Act of 1914; in exchange, the federal government agreed to act as their lender of last resort.

One of the first banks to seek out an emergency loan under the new regime was the Home Bank, which was incorporated in Toronto in 1903. The government acquiesced. Despite the failure of the Bank of Vancouver in 1911, the years following 1914 proved to be a relatively stable time in Canadian banking. No bank failed outright again until 1922, although 11 weaker banks merged with stronger ones. In 1922, 17 chartered banks remained. The lender-of-last-resort policy and the often-quiet compensation or regulatory deference offered to merger partners facilitated the process of consolidation. The policy was kept in place inside the Finance Department until 1935, when it was delegated to the new BoC.

With moral hazard issues much in mind, Parliament incorporated more rigorous regulation into the Bank Act in 1923. The Home Bank, however, propped up by an emergency loan and dubious accounting, found it impossible to comply and maintain the confidence of its depositors. Shortly after the death of its general manager and the son of its founder, its parlous condition was uncovered in an audit. Actual losses soon dwarfed all those that had come before in Canadian history, and both the government and its correspondent banks were overwhelmed by the scale and suddenness of the shock (Macmillan 1933).

The bank failed catastrophically. Among other immediate consequences, 60,000 prairie farmers soon saw their life savings vanish (Johnson 1986, 11). The national press also made much of the ensuing struggle of a group of disabled miners from Fernie, British Columbia to cover their medical expenses after the only bank in town had simply closed its doors (Turley-Ewart 2004, 39). Committees of aggrieved depositors were set up across the country in a vain attempt to receive compensation. Both a paralyzed government and competing banks stood back and refused to bear the extravagant losses. The unthinkable had now happened and political passions ignited right across the country.

If observers of Canadian politics today wonder why the image of Toronto and its banks remains capable of generating antipathy across the provinces, they need only recall that painful episode. For Canada, it was akin to the failure of Lehman Brothers in the United States in 2008. It turned out to be the last outright bank failure in the country until the 1980s, not coincidentally because it led to tough-minded federal supervision by the new Office of the Inspector General of Banks (OIGB). Modelled on a similar institution created in the United Kingdom in similar circumstances, the OIGB oversaw the continuing consolidation of the banking system. It also continued to rely on principles-based discipline by the banks themselves; its staff consisted of no more than four permanent employees as late as 1974.

Despite its humble beginnings, the OIGB signified the end of five decades of policy patchwork at the federal level. The mindset of national policy makers had decisively shifted. From the time of Confederation, new regulations were aimed at creating an essentially private incentive structure to reduce moral hazard and the risk of contagion. Revisions of the Bank Act incrementally filled gaps exposed by repeated failures, and the government moved decisively toward more intensive supervision. In contrast to the situation a few decades earlier, the impulse to encourage competition took a back seat to an overarching national interest in financial stability. Bank customers might grumble about credit availability and pricing, but the underlying political trade-off proved enduring.

The Great Depression was as severe in Canada as it was in the United States. GDP fell by 40 percent, and national unemployment reached 27 percent in 1933. Yet, for all of the macroeconomic similarities between the two countries, the ensuing record of the banking industry on either side of the border could hardly have been more different. To the astonishment of many observers abroad, the only Canadian bank to close was Weyburn Security, a small bank concentrated in southern Saskatchewan, which was quietly merged into the Imperial Bank of Canada in 1931, with no loss to its depositors.[5]

Unlike many of their forebears, the remaining 10 banks became renowned for their cautious management. Owing to this caution, loans that were not made surely reduced the losses those banks could have faced when the Great Depression began. Moreover, that risk aversion was deliberately constructed by national policy makers. Affirmed in the Weyburn case, an implicit government guarantee existed, and was matched by intensive supervision when possible and regulatory forbearance when not (Brean, Kryzanowski and Roberts 2011, 252).

The BoC was established in 1935, and by 1944 it had finally achieved a monopoly over currency issuance. After the war, as in the United States, currency and price controls eased only gradually. Again, interest rate ceilings on personal loans were not completely abolished until 1967, when Porter Commission reforms were adopted. That same year, banks were permitted to issue home mortgages for the first time, and a new Canadian Deposit Insurance Corporation (CDIC) formalized the system that had long since evolved in practice. The few bank mergers during the 1950s and 1960s occurred quietly. Also advancing from the late 1950s through the early 1980s was increasing mobility of capital, especially across the 49th parallel as American and Canadian banks and their customers sought direct access into one another's home markets, a theme that is discussed in the final section below (see also Pauly 1988).

CRISIS AND STABILIZATION IN THE CONTEMPORARY CANADIAN SYSTEM

The spectre of past Canadian banking disasters made a surprising reappearance in the mid-1980s. Two Alberta-based banks, the Canadian Commercial Bank (CCB) and the Northland Bank, had built up risky loan

---

5 Although clearly in trouble, the Weyburn Security Bank was deemed solvent at the time of the merger by the Inspector General of Banks (Carr, Mathewson and Quigley 1995, 1150). Weyburn's underlying troubles, associated with crop failures and declining local markets, were hardly unique. Indeed, reliable estimates would later indicate that nine out of the 10 banks operating during the Depression would have been insolvent if they were in fact forced to value their assets at market prices (Kryzanowski and Roberts 1993).

portfolios by lending to the local oil industry and funding their positions on wholesale markets. Without a retail deposit base to fall back on, this left them vulnerable to new-style runs at the first sign of trouble. Questionable accounting tactics allowed the two banks to survive for a time, but a rapid fall in oil prices following the worldwide recession of the early 1980s and collapsing real estate prices in Western Canada soon brought the banks' problems into the open. CDIC guarantees were limited to CDN$60,000 per depositor and, in any case, they failed to impress large, sophisticated dealers in short-term and increasingly global money markets. Why should they risk even the hassle of legal proceedings if a counterparty failed? Better to run first and ask questions later.

The response from policy makers was swift, as the emergency immediately spread beyond the troubled Alberta banks (Estey 1986). The BoC publicly reminded the government that its legal mandate prevented it from lending to insolvent institutions. When markets began to believe that the banks faced more than liquidity problems, and that there was some confusion over whether the finance ministry or the central bank was responsible, confidence quickly collapsed. Naturally, dealers in wholesale instruments began to wonder if other Canadian financial institutions would be implicated. As usual, ever since 1923, moral hazard considerations disappeared from regulatory calculations as fast as cash flew out of the two failing banks. Bailout packages were quickly put together by the CDIC, a consortium of the big six banks, the federal government, and the governments of Alberta and British Columbia. And, despite its solvent counterparty rule, the BoC opened its spigot.

The details of this support are as fascinating for the aficionado of clearing and settlement systems as they are tedious for the casual observer. What is important to note is that, at the crucial moment, when Canadian clearing banks were left with unrecoverable claims on the defunct banks, such as cheques payable to wholesale depositors of those banks on the day of effective closure, the BoC assumed the obligations and maintained them on its balance sheet as "other assets" (Dingle 2003, chapter 5). It was a convenient conceit that this was construed as "liquidity support" and not as a straightforward cash transfer from public coffers to private parties, resident or non-resident in Canada.

In the end, other banks were caught up in the turmoil. With wholesale depositors now highly risk-averse and threatening to run, the Bank of British

Columbia was quickly judged by Canadian authorities to be solvent and merged with the Hongkong Bank of Canada (Chant et al. 2003). Continental Bank was sold to Lloyd's Bank, and later passed on to the Hongkong Bank of Canada when Lloyd's closed its Canadian operations. Mercantile Bank, which had once been a subsidiary of the First National City Bank of New York and was still 25 percent owned by Citibank, had to be backstopped with emergency facilities from the big six Canadian banks and its US parent before being sold to Canada's sixth-ranked bank, the National Bank of Canada. Two small banks, the Bank of Alberta and the Western Pacific Bank merged to become the Canadian Western Bank, and Morguard Bank was sold to the Security Pacific Bank of Canada. Meanwhile, residual claims on CCB and Northland Bank that were already in the payments system were being unwound and shared by the big Canadian clearing banks and other counterparties. As a definitive BoC study later concluded, "The reversals required by the default-sharing procedure had the effect of widely redistributing the financial burdens associated with the event — often in unforeseen ways....The result was most painful for the corporate and government treasurers involved" (Dingle 2003, 29-30).

Despite the fact that the assets of CCB and Northland Bank comprised no more than 0.75 percent of total banking assets in Canada, the cost of their failure amounted to about 0.3 percent of Canada's 1985 GDP. In his study of the affair, Charles Goodhart (1995, 377) estimated the ultimate losses to Canadian taxpayers at about CDN$900 million; he also underlined the fact that the big six Canadian banks were left with significant and uncompensated losses.[6] Although it could have been worse, the impact on the national payments system was profound: "In addition to developments caused by 'contagion' among similar institutions, the extensive court proceedings surrounding the closures of the CCB and the Northland continued for a full 15 years" (Dingle 2003, 30).

One longer-term effect of the crisis came in the supervisory system. Despite the much-vaunted caution of Canadian bankers, the OIGB was judged to have had too little power to prevent individual banks from building

---

6 In contrast to the recent AIG case, where taxpayers essentially bought the firm at rock-bottom prices, sold the shares in a restructured profit-making entity back to the private sector and reaped large capital gains, it is important to underline the fact that CCB and Northland Bank were simply liquidated.

up excessively risky portfolios. It had been tasked with devising regulatory principles for safe banking operations, and with closing insolvent banks in an orderly fashion. The risk of contagion, including contagion across diverse but integrating financial sectors, demanded greater powers of pre-emption and liquidity provision for banks judged to be potentially solvent during and after a crisis. The government, therefore, decided to merge the OIGB with the federal Department of Insurance to create a new and more fully staffed body, the Office of the Superintendent of Financial Institutions (OSFI). The powers of this new agency were then greatly expanded to include an "early resolution" mandate allowing it to pre-empt problems it saw brewing in any financial institution. For example, OSFI now had the power to close a bank down, at its discretion, if it approached a position of negative equity.[7]

The bank failures of 1985 had another effect, more subtle but more profound. Stanley Hartt, deputy finance minister at the time, later explained it this way:

> The conventional wisdom about what happened next is that Canada tried to emulate the 1986 development in Margaret Thatcher's United Kingdom that has come to be known as the "Big Bang." While there is an element of truth to this, Canada was actually driven more by its own domestic policy needs. The CEOs of the Big Six banks asked the minister of finance, Michael Wilson, for an emergency meeting....The bankers made a plea to be allowed to enter the securities business, which had been denied them for decades so as to minimize the risk to bank capital resulting from securities market volatility....The banks' best customers could [now] finance themselves directly in the London Interbank Market, in essence in competition with the banks themselves, by issuing Eurodollar securities, leaving to the banks the worst credits....Dick Thomson of the Toronto-Dominion Bank, speaking for the group, pointed out that while we were still dealing with the frightening implications of the recent run on virtually all of the country's smaller banks, the government needed to consider the possibility of failures among the Big Six. (Hartt 2005, 74)

---

7   That discretion, again, likely manifested itself in some regulatory forbearance during 2008.

Not unlike the US government later contemplating the final end of Glass-Steagall Act restrictions — indeed, helping to hasten that end — the Canadian government soon agreed with the bankers. Competitive impulses reasserted themselves (as they often do) after, not during, crises. In 1992, most functional restrictions on Canadian financial institutions fell away. The banks were transformed into comprehensive institutions analogous to Europe's universal intermediaries, able to bring under one corporate roof activities as diverse as retail deposit taking, and investment underwriting and trading. Although this set the stage for the cascading events of 2008, bank failures such as those witnessed in 1923 and 1985 did not recur. To be sure, the legacy of those earlier crises placed the full faith and credit of the Government of Canada behind dominant national intermediaries, which span all geographic and virtually all functional limits. Together with a decision taken in 1998 to prevent those intermediaries from engaging in voluntary mergers to increase their scale and capacity to take on new risks, it is tempting to conclude that the microprudential policies in place in 2008 adequately protected all stakeholders in Canadian banks. Nevertheless, individuals and institutions providing vital funding to Canada's dominant intermediaries still plausibly threatened to run that same year.

POLICY AUTONOMY IN OPEN MARKETS

Why would any investor run from a triple-A national credit risk in uncertain times? Much hyperbole concerning debts, deficits and commodity busts notwithstanding, the time to finally flee from contemporary Canada — and the American markets within which it is now deeply integrated — is when the serious prospect looms that all paper claims denominated in Canadian dollars are about to become worthless. The panic in 2008 at least suggested that many investors and depositors believed that such claims could soon be significantly devalued. In this context, the effective microprudential policies born of Canada's experiences in 1923 and 1985, and of American and European experiences in the 1930s proved to be inadequate. What was needed were the macroprudential foundations necessary for the next phase of transnational competition in finance.

To the extent that a more centralized and vigorous OSFI was a harbinger of things to come in more integrated North American markets, it is worth noting that its mandate was tested during several turbulent periods from the late 1980s through 2008. Its success throughout this period was likely reinforced by one other long-standing element of continuity in Canadian financial policy — namely, the assurance that dominant intermediaries would remain accountable to the federal government and the BoC. Although ownership structures were loosened over time, the institutions at the core of the payments system remained under national control through a "widely held" rule. This prevents any domestic or foreign entity from owning more than one-fifth of the voting shares (or 30 percent of any non-voting shares) of large financial institutions. The rules were adjusted in 1992 and again in 2012 at the request of banks and demutualized insurance companies concerned about their own ability to compete in external markets, especially in the United States where provisions of bilateral freer trade arrangements had come into play. For the big institutions, expansion in US markets became ever more important. A few years after the crisis of 2008, moreover, the intermediaries at the top of a more concentrated American system hardly seemed to be in retreat from global markets. The coordinated interventions of Canada and the United States in 2008, therefore, likely set the pattern for the future. Prudential policies now had to be more collaborative — regionally and, apparently, globally — and they had to have a macro dimension. Intermediaries competing for the same business would certainly complain if they faced highly differential capital requirements, required leverage ratios and other general operating strictures.

Canada's leading financial institutions and many of their customers are today deeply integrated into American markets, which are now clearly backed by the US Federal Reserve and the US Treasury. At the same time, they have also managed to maintain a dominant position in their home markets with the backing of the BoC and other agencies of the Canadian state. Canadian policy makers can present the price of their remaining autonomy as reflective of a deep-seated and prudent national preference for financial stability. Hard-earned by their constituents and ancestors, that preference is on full display during crises. Just as noteworthy today, however, is the new role of foreign governments and central banks in helping to underwrite that stability.

It cannot be denied that moral hazard is now reinforced in unbounded, but state-backed markets. As central bankers and finance ministers certainly recognized in 2008, key financial intermediaries in Canada, and now across most advanced and emerging market countries, are too big and too interconnected to fail. The post-crisis response from leading countries, including Canada, is that clearer multilateral understandings on burden sharing between the home and host states of the most systemically important financial institutions must be underpinned by tighter and more collaborative macroprudential oversight. This constituted the post-crisis agenda for financial supervisors, and it was apparently fairly easy to agree upon in principle. In practice, and in the absence of emergency conditions, robust, common and enforceable macroprudential policies are proving elusive. Policy makers are pressed once again to preserve national advantages. Also obvious once more are long-standing differences between countries that prefer statutory rules and competition among domestic regulatory agencies and countries that complement basic rules and standards with intensive supervision and consolidated authority. Canada is in the latter camp, while its markets are tightly integrated with the United States, the key exemplar of the former approach. This core dilemma is compounded by deep macroeconomic imbalances and the massive global liquidity that accommodates them.

Effective governance of the systemic risks embedded in markets dominated by intermediaries that are too big and too interconnected to fail depends on finding a workable compromise for the time being. An extreme alternative is to break apart those intermediaries and prevent the expansion of alternative and equally risky investment and financing vehicles in the shadows of vital payments systems. Although the years immediately following the crisis of 2008 were marked by renewed debates on the value of short-term capital movements and by heightened home bias in certain financial markets, there was little evidence of political appetite for seriously downsizing or limiting the operational range of national champions or of returning to the Bretton Woods ideal of "inclusive multilateralism" outlined by Eric Helleiner in chapter 1. Instead, the revealed preference of the leading states inclined in the direction of returning to the status quo observed before the crisis of 2008: open capital markets and low-profile, and often frustrating, technical work on convergent or at least tolerably different national and regional regulatory standards. Behind that inclination lies the market stabilizing faith that "ad hoc" coordination by leading central banks and finance ministries will again prove adequate to the task of managing systemic risks during the next great financial crisis. Although much discussed, "resilient" markets are hardly assured.

In such a context, the scope for autonomous policy making in Canada is ever more highly constrained as commodities remain vital to the national economy and flows of goods, services, financial claims and people across North American and international borders intensify. It also remains true, however, that history has made Canada's financial policy makers masters at exploiting their tactical room for manoeuvre — by relying on a flexible exchange rate, restraining public-sector indebtedness and intensively supervising Canadian intermediaries, and by promoting their preferences for official discretion and effective macroprudential oversight in every global forum available.

Author's Note

A version of this paper was first presented on October 6, 2012 at the University of Oxford conference Governing the Fed, organized by Larry Jacobs and Desmond King. I thank Don Brean and Johan Krijgsman for sharing their research and insights, Lawrence Broz for sharing data, Riley Quinn for providing research assistance, Michael Gavin for drafting an early version of the sections on late nineteenth and early twentieth century history, and the editors and especially Paul Jenkins for detailed and most helpful comments. Of course, responsibility for remaining errors remains mine alone.

WORKS CITED

Bordo, M., A. Redish and H. Rockoff. 2010. "Why Didn't Canada Have a Banking Crisis in 2008 (or in 1930, or 1907, or 1893)?" NBER Historical Working Paper No. 67.

Brean, D., L. Kryzanowski and G. Roberts. 2011. "Canada and the United States: Different Roots, Different Routes to Financial Sector Regulation." *Business History* 53 (2): 249–69.

Breckenridge, R. M. 1910. *History of Banking in Canada.* Washington, DC: National Monetary Commission.

Broz, L. 2012. "The Federal Reserve as Global Lender of Last Resort, 2007–2010." Paper presented at the annual meeting of the International Political Economy Society, University of Virginia.

Carr, J. F. Mathewson and N. Quigley. 1995. "Stability in the Absence of Deposit Insurance: The Canadian Banking System, 1890–1966." *Journal of Money, Credit and Banking* 27 (4): 1137–58.

Chant, J., A. Lai, M. Illing and F. Daniel. 2003. *Essays on Financial Stability.* Technical Report No. 95. Ottawa, BoC.

Dingle, J. 2003. *Planning an Evolution: The Story of the Canadian Payments Association, 1980–2002.* Ottawa: BoC and the Canadian Payments Association.

Estey, W. Z. 1986. *Report of the Inquiry into the Collapse of the CCB and Northland Bank.* Ottawa: Supply and Services Canada.

Goodhart, C. 1995. *The Central Bank and the Financial System.* Cambridge, MA: MIT Press.

Hartt, S. 2005. "From a Bang to a Whimper — Twenty Years of Lost Momentum in Financial Institutions." *Policy Options.* September.

Johnson, A. 1986. *Breaking the Banks.* Toronto: Lester & Orpen Dennys.

Kryzanowski, L. and G. S. Roberts. 1993. "Canadian Banking Solvency, 1922–1940." *Journal of Money, Credit and Banking* 25 (3): 361–76.

Longworth, David. 2010. "Bank of Canada Liquidity Facilities: Past, Present, and Future." Paper presented at the C. D. Howe Institute, Toronto, February 17.

Lynch, K. 2010. "Avoiding the Financial Crisis: Lessons from Canada." *Options Politiques*, May 2.

Macdonald, David. 2012. "The Big Banks' Big Secret: Estimating Government Support for Canadian Banks during the Financial Crisis." Ottawa: Canadian Centre for Policy Alternatives.

Macmillan, Lord. 1933. *Report of the Royal Commission on Banking and Currency in Canada.* Ottawa: King's Printer.

Neufeld, E. P. 1972. *The Financial System of Canada.* Toronto: Macmillan.

Pauly, Louis W. 1988. *Opening Financial Markets: Banking Politics on the Pacific Rim.* Ithaca: Cornell University Press.

Porter, T. 2010. "Canadian Banks in the Financial and Economic Crisis." Paper for a conference at the North-South Institute, Ottawa, June 8-9.

Pozsar, Z., Tobias Adrian, Adam Ashcraft and Hayley Boesky. 2010. "Shadow Banking." Federal Reserve Bank of New York Staff Report No. 458, July. www.newyorkfed.org/research/staff_reports/sr458.pdf.

Ratnovski, L. and R. Huang. 2009. "Why Are Canadian Banks More Resilient?" IMF Working Paper WP/09/152.

The Globe and Mail. 2011. "Move to Have More Power over Banks' 'Prudential': Flaherty." *The Globe and Mail*, November 25.

Turley-Ewart, J. 2000. "Gentlemen Bankers, Politicians and Bureaucrats: The History of the Canadian Bankers Association, 1891–1924." Ph.D. dissertation NQ53761, University of Toronto, Canada.

———. 2004. "The Bank That Went Bust." *The Beaver: Exploring Canada's History*. August.

9

The Finance-Trade Crossover

John M. Curtis

● ● ● ● ● ● ● ● ● ● ● ● ● ● ● ● ● ● ●

INTRODUCTION

Although finance and trade seem to occupy two different worlds, in fact, throughout history they have been intertwined with each other. The exchange of goods, services, capital, technology, ideas and even people across international borders has always required some means of payment. In earlier times, such exchange usually involved largely goods-for-goods (barter) exchange; by the late medieval period, trade credits, bills of lading or other forms of trade-related finance were well in place over large parts of Europe and, to a lesser extent, elsewhere. Families such as the Medicis in Italy and the Rothschilds and the Fuggers in Germany rose to prominence during this rapidly expanding era of international trade, financing this international commercial activity — their contribution to what became known as the Renaissance and the Reformation was an important by-product of their economic success at that time.

With the expanding reach of international trade activity from Europe westward to the Americas and eastward to the Spice Islands (the Moluccan chain of islands in today's Indonesia), China and Japan, the financing of trade became even more important. Fortunes were made and lost by financial institutions, governments and individuals. What we now define as an international financial regime also began to take shape during this period:

gold, silver, thalers, ducats, as well as other Genoese and Venetian currency became the international means of cross-border commercial transactions — while gold, in particular, became a kind of store-of-value and a reserve currency. In this context, countries attempted to manage their international finance by maximizing their exports and minimizing their imports in order to preserve, if not to expand, their holdings of gold and other precious metals. This practice became known as mercantilism, an international trade practice, indeed policy, which governments maintain, at least superficially and in their press releases, to this day.

With the development of joint stock companies during the late seventeenth and eighteenth centuries and particularly in the nineteenth century — the century of relative peace following the Napoleonic wars — international trade grew rapidly in the latter century, due largely to major innovations in transportation and communication; London became the world's financial centre and the pound sterling became the international currency of choice (Auboin 2012). This was the period that many refer to as the first wave of globalization, an era that by its end in 1913-1914 saw the percentage of goods, services, capital and people crossing international borders higher than ever in history. That high-water mark remains the case even now, a century later.

Following World War I and the impact of that war on the victors and vanquished alike, the underlying economic strength of the United States became increasingly clear. The pound sterling — and to a lesser extent the French franc — came under continued pressure in terms of their external value, and by the 1930s were used less and less in international transactions. The US dollar gradually replaced these and all other currencies (the exception being the German reichmark for quite different reasons); the dollar's central role in the international monetary system was then institutionalized by international agreement towards the end of World War II as part of the 1944 Bretton Woods Agreement. By the 1970s, over 80 percent of world trade was conducted in dollars; the prices of all natural resources, most services and large elements of manufactured goods trade were denominated in US dollars, even if the United States was not involved in the particular transaction.

During the Bretton Woods era, the US dollar served as a stable anchor for the global system of prices. In part, this reflected the fact that the US economy was large relative to the global economy, and international trade and finance was small relative to global economic activity. Equally as important, the value of the US dollar was anchored by gold convertibility.

International trade and finance during this period constituted essentially a secondary, derivative system tacked onto a foundation of largely national systems of production and exchange. The contribution of trade and finance to economic welfare was twofold: dampening fluctuations in national economies' growth paths by allowing the disposal of domestic surpluses and providing supply to offset domestic shortages, and, by encouraging as well as accommodating international exchange, promoting growth through various mechanisms, such as enabling the exploitation of economies of scale and scope, and facilitating the transmission of technology.

In this context, international finance served as the handmaiden of international commerce. At the domestic level, the role of finance was to increase efficiency in the intermediation of savings into investment and allocating scarce capital to its most rewarding applications. Foreign direct investment (FDI) was layered on this system, providing for flows of capital from capital-abundant developed countries to capital-scarce developing economies where returns to capital, in theory, were higher, thus accelerating the convergence of economic structures that is driven by the spread of technology across borders. Meanwhile, exchange rates, which linked the national systems of monies, adjusted to offset differentials in national inflation rates to keep trade in balance, taking into account net FDI flows.

This post-World War II model changed with the measures announced by US President Richard Nixon on August 15, 1971, which ended gold convertibility. The decades since have featured very different price and financial behaviours compared to that during the pre-1971–1973 Bretton Woods system. The fixed exchange rates of the Bretton Woods era, which were seen at the time as the solution to enabling the expansion of trade, became a problem in the system that followed — which might be labelled the era of the international dollar standard.

In the current world of the international dollar standard, which is now the norm, the system of production became international because of the fragmentation of production chains across borders; global sales of multinational firms, taking into account both cross-border trade and foreign affiliate sales, now dominate global commerce. This transformation took place in part because of the revolutions in transportation and telecommunications, and the reduction of trade barriers, which drove down the cost of doing business internationally; however, arguably it also was encouraged by the volatility of exchange rates that emerged in this more recent era. For a large global firm, global sourcing of its production inputs acts as a natural hedge. Moreover, such firms can shift sourcing to countries with undervalued exchange rates, exploiting the factor cost distortions arising from exchange rate disequilibria. By contrast, small- and medium-sized firms that source locally can be priced out of the market by an extended period of exchange rate overvaluation.

The system of international finance, earlier the handmaiden of international commerce, now dominates it; today, it generates a volume of transactions — US$10 trillion in face value per day — (Bank for International Settlements [BIS] 2010) that in a single business *week* rivals the volume of global trade in goods and services and FDI in a *year*.

Thus, exchange rate movements today are predominantly driven by the flux of transactions in international financial markets in which national monies are commodities with volatile prices, not by the needs of the trading system and the underlying system of production.

In the domestic sphere, the massive flows of capital within and between the equity, bond, money and commodity markets exceed anything that has to do with allocation of capital in the production sector. The flow of capital is now as much from the capital-scarce developing world to the capital-rich industrialized countries as the other way round.

In retrospect, economic history has proved to be episodic, with each episode having unique behaviours and institutional features (Gastle and Ciuriak 2003). The era of the gold standard (1870–1914) witnessed a considerable convergence of industrial structures worldwide in a context of overall price stability. By contrast, the preceding era (from about 1820 to 1870) also witnessed a great increase in globalization, but very little convergence. The Bretton Woods era (1944–1973) was distinctly different from the 1919–1939 interwar era, again featuring widespread convergence. And the current era of the international dollar standard that succeeded Bretton Woods has differed just as sharply from its predecessor — in this case, it featured divergence.

In the world of finance, the US dollar, which has been the linchpin of the global economy for decades, might eventually be superseded by another,[1] although this is still far from an imminent prospect (Auboin 2012). While this preponderance of the US dollar has lessened slightly in recent years — the euro, yen, Swiss franc, the Canadian and Australian dollars, and progressively the renminbi (yuan) are increasingly seen and used as part of a "basket" of important currencies — the US dollar remains the undisputed heavyweight with respect to international trade transactions, notwithstanding ongoing recent concerns about governance and economic management issues in the United States. By the same token, the jitters in the world of finance regarding the soundness of the greenback have sent unsettling tremors through the system of global production.

It is clear that the international monetary system, which evolved over centuries, has been a key underpinning of the international trade regime. Yet, except for export financing at the most microeconomic level, there is still little institutional, policy or academic interface between the two major contemporary international economic regimes. International trade rules — the mutually agreed framework for conducting commercial exchange across borders — barely touch on financial matters to this day, except for the voluntary Organisation for Economic Co-operation and Development guidelines on export credits that have been in place since the 1970s, and two articles in the original General Agreement on Tariffs and Trade (GATT) of 1947 (Articles XII, XVIII.B), plus the 1979 statement by members on the "Understanding on the Balance of Payments Provisions of the General Agreement on Tariffs and Trade 1994."[2] Further, and surprisingly, the monitoring and surveillance activities of the WTO's Trade Policy Review Mechanism (TPRM), in operation since the creation of the global trade organization in 1995, rarely make mention of the influence of international financial developments on trade performance, notwithstanding the concern of politicians and business people about the issue. In addition, current international trade theory, with its

---

1   Note, for example, the statement on the shift to the Special Drawing Right as the pivotal global currency (Zhou 2009).
2   In the "Understanding," members (of the World Trade Organization [WTO]) confirm their commitment to: "announce publicly, as soon as possible, time-schedules for the removal of restrictive import measures taken for balance-of-payments purposes" and to explain why if they do not do so; "give preference to those measures which have the least disruptive effect on trade"; justify why price-based measures are not adequate if they have chosen to impose quantitative restrictions; and not apply more than one type of restrictive trade measure to the same product.

focus on the individual company or firm, rather than the industry as a whole or the country, suggests that without considering the impact of both the level and volatility of exchange rates, an assessment of the volume, direction and composition of trade will be incomplete.

THE THEORY

Modern day macroeconomic theory, dating from the mid-twentieth century, frames international capital flows as accommodating international trade imbalances, which derive from domestic savings-investment imbalances, and smoothing out consumption over the business cycle. This basic macroeconomic analysis derives from the balance-of-payments accounting framework: given that it is an accounting mechanism, the balance of payments must, in the end, balance for each and every country. Capital, which is fungible and relatively free in the contemporary world economy to cross borders, compared especially to the two other major factors of production — labour and land, moves in and out of any given country to balance the current account — the total amount of exports, imports and other, relatively small, international transactions. With a current account surplus, capital tends to flow out of the surplus country to areas of the world where potential gains, or returns on capital, would be greater; the reverse is true in the case of a current account deficit. This is the equilibrating principle, one of the key principles of theoretical economics.

The original GATT measures addressing exchange rates and macroeconomic imbalances were framed with this theoretical understanding in mind — that trade is inherently self-balancing and that exchange rates adjust to equalize prices globally. Obviously, this conceptual framework provides no compass to understand the persistent exchange rate disequilibria and sustained massive trade imbalances observed in today's global economy. For the most part, classical and neoclassical trade theory did not even acknowledge the role of money, let alone many different monies, or the idea that the exchange rates between these various currencies might not reflect the relative efficiency of production across economies in real terms. For the same reason, classical and neoclassical theories were unable to explain the nature, composition and direction of international trade in the contemporary world economy.

Modern trade theory (which has become known as "new new trade theory" and articulates trade theory at the level of the individual company or the firm, recognizing that, in a private sector economy, it is firms that trade, not industries as a whole or countries) also acknowledges the possibility of persistent deviation of the exchange rate from purchasing power parity and, given international debt trading, persistent external imbalances due to net capital inflows. In this theoretical formulation, net capital inflows finance the accelerated entry of firms into economies with relatively more favourable business environments (Ghironi and Melitz 2005). Moreover, exchange rate volatility is now seen to have implications at the microeconomic level.

"New" new trade theory builds on the trade models of Krugman and others in the 1980s and 1990s, which emphasized the importance of increasing returns to scale and scope, and of variety (Helpman and Krugman 1985). It also builds on the earlier theories of trade — classical and neoclassical theory — which emphasized international differences in resource and factor endowments and international differences in the nature and quality of technology as the basis of trade. New new trade theory recognizes that it is at the firm level that decisions are made to trade or not to trade, whether to pursue new markets with new goods or services, to adopt new technology (the "extensive" margin) or to focus primarily on existing markets with existing goods, services or technology (the "intensive" margin) (see Ciuriak et al. 2011). This newest trade theory, with the "learning" and absorptive capacity of the firm so central to its operation in international markets, makes clear how important the international monetary regime is to its functioning (ibid.). The larger and more productive that a firm is, the more it is capable of hedging against exchange rate change and thus risk; on the other hand, the smaller that a firm is, the less it will be able to afford the cost of hedges and, thus, the less likely it will be to participate in international trade (ibid.).

Trade rules have not caught up with trade theory, however, and much of the thinking about trade policy continues to be based on the equilibrium assumption that effectively sweeps under the rug the issues relating to hedging, volatility and the exit and entry of firms out of and into trade — not to mention the costs imposed in terms of writing off sunk assets.

THE RECENT EXPERIENCE

Recent international economic developments bear out this connection between a well-functioning international monetary system and the effective operation of the international trade system.

The post-Bretton Woods era was marked by a sequence of crises — the Latin/African debt crises of the early 1980s, Japan's post-Plaza Accord meltdown of the mid-to-late 1980s, the Asian Crisis that spiralled into an emerging market crisis that culminated in Argentina's 2002 default, the global financial crisis of 2008-2009, and the protracted euro-zone crisis that followed as a knock-on to the global financial crisis.

Each of these crises emanated from the global financial system.

The Latin/African debt crises were the by-product of the monetarist experiment conducted by the US Federal Reserve under Paul Volcker's chairmanship: the Fed adopted the monetarist prescription that reducing the money supply would reduce inflation (implicitly with little or no pain) and allowed interest rates and the US exchange rate to be determined by the market. The direct result was to send interest rates in the United States to the 20 percent level. Global capital was quick to move, and the debt service costs of developing countries that had borrowed heavily to finance development soared. Africa and Latin America were marginalized in global trade and direct investment — although these were far from the worst consequences, which included the failure of states, internecine wars and the resulting humanitarian crises that followed hot on their heels.

Formal economic scholarship and much of the financial press had little trouble in pinning the blame on the bankrupted borrowers in Africa and Latin America, and turned to showering praise on the successful Asian economies — the rising sun of Japan being *primus inter pares*. Japan, however, following the Plaza Accord of 1985, allowed the yen to appreciate steeply. The consequences were profound. Japanese industry relocated labour-intensive production to East and Southeast Asia, sparking the "Asian Miracle" in that region. While the term "global value chain" (GVC) was first coined in 1985 as a reflection of earlier developments, it was Japanese multinationals' creation of Asian production webs that subsequently gave the GVC production framework its initial significance, often referred to in Japan as the "flying geese" phenomenon. At the same time, Japan experienced a hollowing out: first a massive asset price bubble as the soaring exchange rate forced the Bank of Japan to cut interest rates, which in turn induced the flow of funds into stocks and real estate, and second, the follow-on lost decade of growth after the bubble burst as all bubbles eventually do. Again, global finance transfigured the face of global production and direct investment.

As Japan floundered, the global finance system was not called into question, rather, the Western economic model was declared triumphant. The focus on Asia shifted to the new "Asian Miracle" economies. Their success prompted John Williamson (2004) to articulate the "Washington Consensus," a distillation of the policy frameworks followed by these rapidly industrializing East Asian economies. The fact that these economies focused on exports (i.e., mercantilism), routinely practiced industrial policy and "manipulated" their currencies (i.e., managed the so-called "float") was largely ignored. What mattered seemed to be the private sector orientation of public policy, the emphasis on trade, prudent fiscal and monetary policies, and the mobilization of factors of production through business-oriented microeconomic frameworks. But once again crisis intervened, even as the phrase "Asian Miracle" was leaving the lips of then Chair of the US Council of Economic Advisers Joseph Stiglitz.

What became known as the Asian Crisis from mid-1997 onward upset apple carts everywhere, but not within formal economic scholarship. Within weeks of the first manifestations of the symptoms of the crisis and well before the full-blown consequences, the crisis was "explained" in terms of well understood orthodox theory. A villain had to be found and what might be termed the "usual suspects" were quickly rounded up by the profession: premature capital account liberalization and financial market liberalization without the prerequisite "beefing up" of supervisory and regulatory capacity.

The emerging market crisis spread from East Asia to Russia, Brazil, Turkey and Argentina, among others. Although Russia's default on its ruble-denominated debt was a self-inflicted wound that can hardly be laid at the doorstep of global finance, Turkey was bailed out by extraordinary International Monetary Fund (IMF) relief. On the other hand, Argentina was not bailed out, perhaps, among other factors, because offshore oil in the Falkland Islands had already been secured for Western oil companies following the Falklands War.

Argentina had, nonetheless, been a poster child for neoclassical policies. It defaulted in the early months of 2002 at the height of the US dollar's post-1995 appreciation. The US dollar's appreciation had nothing specifically to do with Argentina; it was engineered by a Japan-US decision to ease the tourniquet of yen overvaluation on Japan's economy, and emerged in the form of then Secretary of the Treasury Robert Rubin's "strong dollar" policy. The tourniquet was simply transferred from Japan to Argentina, which had pegged its currency to the dollar to create a credible commitment to non-inflationary monetary policy, an essential element of the neoclassical framework. Formal economic scholarship, which had previously lauded credible commitments to non-inflationary monetary policy and advocated corner solutions for exchange rate policy (free float or ultra-hard pegs), found fault with Argentina for not having an exit strategy from its hard peg. As it turns out, formal economic scholarship had, for its part, no shortage of exit strategies from failed advocacy positions.

These events had massive consequences for global trade and direct investment. In the destabilized emerging markets, imports were compressed and exports grew massively in real terms. Current accounts swung from deficits to surpluses, resulting in the anomaly of emerging markets financing developed-country growth (or, more likely, asset prices). In the developed countries, the gradual reallocation of industrial activity resulted in de-industrialization. When the developed countries (particularly the United States and the European Union) caught up with this fact, they started to re-evaluate their public stance against the practice of industrial policy, a practice that continues.

While the Asian emerging market crisis was unfolding, another financial debacle was shaping up, this time in the world's financial centres — primarily in the United States — the dot-com equity boom and bust. As financial debacles go, this one was almost trivial: it wiped trillions of dollars' worth of ephemeral assets off balance sheets and triggered a johnny-come-lately attempt at financial re-regulation in the form of the Sarbanes-Oxley Act. But otherwise, the dot-com bust served only to set up the next crisis by inducing the Federal Reserve to eliminate real interest rate costs in the US economy for a protracted period to reflate the bubble. The crisis that was set up by the bursting of this new bubble — the global financial crisis — was far from trivial.

The fact that a national housing finance problem could cause a global economic disruption should not fly under the radar of any observer: it highlights the role of global financial volatility. Countries that do not issue reserve currencies typically have to maintain large stores of foreign exchange reserves as an insurance policy against destabilization — there are a handful of exceptions, Canada being one of them. These foreign exchange or "forex" reserves are invested in a limited range of highly liquid assets, the main ones being US Treasury bonds. The low yields on US Treasury bonds during the period of reflation of the early to mid-2000s created incentives to generate alternative US-dollar-denominated financial assets with higher yields to minimize the cost of holding exorbitant amounts of liquid US-dollar-denominated assets. Mortgage-backed securities filled this need. This worked both to expand the scale of the US crisis by giving the market more rope with which to hang itself and to spread the problem globally. The impact on international trade was immense. Trade fell by some 70 percent in 2009 immediately following the crisis; it took until 2012 for 2007 trade values and volumes to be restored.

And the financial crisis of 2008-2009 onward did not really end. Rather, it metastasized into the euro-zone crisis. Some would argue, of course, that the euro zone's problems were mainly due to the fixed exchange rates within the 17-member euro zone, the single currency area. These prevented the less competitive regions of the zone (the Mediterranean fringe in particular) to devalue while the more competitive regions (Germany and the Nordics) revalued. The result of economic strength in the northern regions of the zone led to an overvaluation of the European currency overall, with the resulting devastating trade, employment, economic activity and prosperity outcomes affecting the less competitive, largely southern member states (Greece, Italy, Spain, Portugal, and even France and Hungary) that has been seen in recent years. Many observers thus attribute this crisis to human error — the obdurate decision to maintain fixed parities within the euro zone to promote internal trade against the sounder advice to allow currencies to be determined by market forces (however speculation-driven these might be). However, any traveller in Europe knows that, in purchasing power terms, a dollar is worth about a euro, although the exchange rate is usually at least 30 percent higher. The law of one price does not hold between the two largest economies in the world: the United States and the euro zone. The idea that the global economy efficiently allocates production and consumption when this condition is violated to such an extent is, to put it mildly, questionable. Yet, ironically, commentators have not focused on the international valuation of the euro; rather, they have found fault with the existence of the euro itself.

The holy grail of research, particularly economic research, is to find a unifying explanation for apparently disparate problems. For the problems plaguing the global system of trade and finance, this has been something of a problem. However, it is fair to say that the main culprits have been capital account liberalization, financial deregulation and fixed exchange rates. Yet, Canada's elimination of interest rate regulations in the 1967 Bank Act helped it avoid the US savings and loan debacle that developed in the 1970s, and only belatedly led to the Depository Institutions Deregulation and Monetary Control Act of 1980. Moreover, in 1987, Canada repealed its version of the Glass-Steagall Act, a decade ahead of the United States, to avoid the banking sector disruptions of the shift to direct market finance. Deregulation, and allowing banks to play in securities markets, did not predestine Canada for crisis, but resulted in the highest rated financial system in the world in recent years. Canada did have a market-determined exchange rate during this period; however, this does not appear to have been a factor in these outcomes, one way or the other. The unifying explanation remains elusive.

What is clear, however, is that turbulence emanating from the financial sphere, and particularly from the system of exchange rates, has had major implications for the direction and scale of international trade and direct investment flows, as well as for the optimal policy for countries regarding the management of their external accounts. Countries and firms, rather than importing goods and services, for example, have in the past 15 years or so built up additional foreign exchange reserves to shield themselves from sharp swings in exchange rate values. Moreover, the pervasive role of exchange rate dynamics stands out. This has been brought out most recently with respect to the BRICS (that is, Brazil, Russia, India, China and South Africa) and the resource-intensive exporters that are increasingly so dependent on them (Canada, Australia and South Africa): falling demand and prices for commodities have led to capital outflows and downward pressures on their exchange rates recently, further contributing to the slow economic recovery seen worldwide.

As well, activist monetary policy on the part of the United States, the United Kingdom and Japan to stimulate their domestic economies, particularly through quantitative easing, has led in effect to competitive devaluation by these three large economies, particularly on the part of Japan whose currency has declined almost 25 percent in US dollar terms since mid-2012.

Finally, China, which is quickly becoming the world's largest trader, has proved to be a cautious, careful manager with respect to its exchange rate policy and to its economic policy more generally, permitting the renminbi to appreciate slowly by some 10 percent in terms of the US dollar over the past two years — a steady, incremental managed float within now-expanded boundaries that has, however, been insufficient to remove the strains in the trading system or to reduce public pressure, particularly from several prominent US and European politicians.

Less obvious are the perturbations at the microeconomic level. The new firm-level trade literature shows that large shifts in the real exchange rate can undermine the profitability of exporters that remain in export markets or lead to their exit from export markets altogether — with damaging consequences for their productivity performance. Baldwin and Yan (2010) show that the steep rise of Canada's real exchange rate in the 2000s eradicated the benefits of exporting that Canadian firms had enjoyed in the 1990s. Meanwhile, the sharp increase in the number of Canadian firms that withdrew from the US market in the mid-2000s compared to previous years, documented by Acharya (2010), can also be attributed to the exchange rate shift.

These firm-level costs appear to be largely, if not completely, ignored in current macroeconomic-based analysis of the effects of exchange rate fluctuations (which concludes the effects of such fluctuations are minimal). However, the welfare costs of these firm-level effects might well be the single most important factor to take into account in such evaluations.

THE FUTURE: INSTITUTIONAL AND POLICY PROPOSALS

It seems clear from the foregoing analysis that in the future, the two pillars of the international economy, the international financial system and the international trade regime, will have to be dealt with in a more coordinated, coherent manner by governments than has been the case over the entire postwar era. Ironically, at the most senior levels, heads of state and of governments meeting in fora such as the Group of Twenty (G20) annual summits, appear to be well ahead of their officials and of those working in various universities and think tanks worldwide. Leaders at these meetings, almost in the same breath, have routinely called for stronger, more effective financial regulation and higher capital requirements, and for a more open, less unpredictable trade system, including completing the still-unfinished business in the multilateral Doha Round. These sentiments are often echoed by major international umbrella organizations such as various national and multinational chambers of commerce, which often appear captured to a greater or lesser degree by those sector-specific interest groups that finance them and have their own less integrated view of the overall situation.

Below the leaders, subject-area ministers and even central bank governors tend to focus on their specific areas of responsibility, reflecting the current organization of governments, international institutions, and private sector groups and even non-governmental organizations that follow their activity. Ministers of finance and/or central bank governors, for example, have paid little attention to the impact of the international monetary system on the trade system and its performance (Would a central bank governor ever acknowledge that the policies followed by his institution had induced "Dutch disease"[3]?). Conversely, international trade ministers — whether meeting in a WTO, regional or bilateral context — rarely mention the behaviour of the international monetary system in affecting and shaping the nature, composition or direction of trade and investment. Their officials, at most, refer to GATT Articles XII and XVIII.B as being as far as they feel responsible. They appear, therefore, to be avoiding the very difficult, yet important, possibility that a trading partner, by loosening monetary policies or building up foreign exchange reserves might well be frustrating, if, for example, the intent of WTO provisions that restrict or prohibit subsidies practices that are actionable.

To be sure, the issues outlined above are not being entirely ignored in officialdom. Particularly in the Trade in Services Agreement negotiations, officials are beginning to set out proposals to use the WTO's General Agreement on Trade in Services framework to regulate certain aspects of the

---

3 Dutch disease refers to the currency appreciation that could result from an inflow of capital or a surge in export earnings. This undermines the competitiveness of exports.

financial sector — for example, financial firm capitalization and hedge fund practices. However, to date, little or no concrete progress on these matters has been made.

Another positive development has been increased institutional contact and cooperation at the international institution level over the past 20 years. IMF representatives are now posted in Geneva and regularly attend WTO committees as observers in areas that they consider closest to the IMF's core mandate. WTO representatives follow IMF and related activities in Washington and report back to their headquarters in Geneva. That being said, cross-linkages in the WTO's TPRM reports, which perform the monitoring and surveillance functions created as part of the multilateral Uruguay Round outcome in 1994, are rarely publicly or explicitly drawn in IMF work and could be strengthened. The IMF and the WTO could perhaps work together on this, possibly in conjunction with the Financial Stability Board (FSB), to integrate trade into the Mutual Assessment Program, mandated in 2009 by G20 leaders (Torres 2013). Similarly, the surveillance mechanisms of the IMF and, more recently, of the FSB, focus little on the impact of exchange rate movements and the operation of the international monetary system more generally on the trade system, and in particular on firms that take the day-to-day decisions concerning their involvement in trade and investment. FSB representatives have not asked for accreditation to the WTO, nor have any officials from the BIS.

At a more operational level, the role of trade finance as a facilitator of international transactions has been closely monitored. This issue first arose in a major way during the Asian Crisis, when the drying up of trade finance was found to have been a significant factor exacerbating the liquidity shortage in East Asia, which was the prime reason for the collapse in economic activity in that region during the crisis. During the global financial crisis, tightening in trade finance was not a major driver of the collapse in trade, although it was an important factor (Chauffour and Malouche 2011). Surveys conducted during the crisis and post mortems on the crisis found that trade finance conditions tightened during the crisis with measurable adverse effects on trade flows. At the same time, awareness of this issue from the Asian Crisis experience led to prompt action at the G20 level to address the drying up of private sector trade credit. As usual, the impacts were more severe in developing countries and for small- and medium-sized enterprises than in the developed countries and larger firms. Accordingly, more can be done in this area — and the need for better data to monitor developments has been prominently flagged. This is, however, clearly far from the area needing most urgent attention.

The way ahead is unclear. However, for a relatively open, trade-dependent economy such as that of Canada, with a currency that is characterized by wide fluctuations in its valuation shaped largely by international developments over which it has very little control, it is incumbent to propose fresh ideas to better coordinate the two major pillars of the contemporary international economic system — as it did in the 1944–1947 era.

Canadian economists have historically been in the forefront in identifying features in the economic system that would not naturally occur to someone viewing the world from within the Beltway, for example: Robert Mundell (the implications of the open economy for fiscal policy and the optimal common currency zone), Dick Lipsey (the theory of second best), and James Brander and Barbara Spencer (strategic trade policy) come immediately to mind, not to mention stalwarts of Canadian political economy such as Harold Innis and W. A. Mackintosh, whose "staples" theory anticipated modern "resource curse" and Dutch disease theories. Today, Canadian economists again need to step up to the plate: Canada is today's poster child of an economy distorted by capital flows and exchange rate disequilibria. Arguably, no country studies the global economic centre (the United States) more closely or is better attuned to its conventional wisdoms than Canada. By the same token, no country is better positioned to identify the anomalies in the US-sponsored global system that have led to the myriad dysfunctions of the modern economy.

What is clear is that the agendas of both "sides" — finance and trade — are already overloaded and will continue to be as new issues particular to each are raised and need to be addressed — improved financial regulation and capital requirements on the one hand and climate change, information, standards, state capitalism and innovation on the other. Something must be done.

Although the two international economic systems are functioning, the financial not as well as the trade, the outcomes are not optimal. Perhaps a new Bretton Woods Agreement — Bretton Woods II — is not too much for the world community to ask for and to work toward. With new and evolving communications and technology, as a global society we should be able to do better than we are at present.

The real issue is where do the solutions lie? In fact, it might be asked whether there are solutions. The amount of figurative ink that has been put to figurative paper since the 2008-2009 global financial crisis is nothing if not awe-inspiring. The solutions proposed — from capital controls and international financial transactions taxes to the establishment of a new international numeraire currency — are myriad.

Reflecting on the path of crises past, the common feature that stands out is the role of the US dollar: a national currency that is managed by a central bank that has objectives narrowly circumscribed by US economic developments, but which, nonetheless, serves as the global medium of exchange. As the US economy has shrunk relative to the global economy, the feedback from global demand for the US dollar to developments in the US economy has intensified: the subprime crisis demonstrated this in spades. Although US policy thinking is unlikely to recognize the value of giving up the "exorbitant privilege" that the US dollar holds in the global economy, it is an issue that friends of the United States might wish to take up — for its sake as well as their own.

WORKS CITED

Acharya, Ram. 2010. "Canada's Share of U.S. Product Markets: Dissecting the 1998-2006 Trends." In *Trade Policy Research 2010: Exporter Dynamics and Productivity*, edited by Dan Ciuriak. Ottawa: Foreign Affairs and International Trade Canada.

Auboin, Marc. 2012. "Use Of Currencies in International Trade: Any Changes in the Picture?" Staff Working Paper ERSD-2012-10, May.

Baldwin, John and Beiling Yan. 2010. "Export Market Dynamics and Plant-level Productivity: Impact of Tariff Reductions and Exchange Rate Cycles." In *Trade Policy Research 2010: Exporter Dynamics and Productivity*, edited by Dan Ciuriak, 19–62. Ottawa: Foreign Affairs and International Trade Canada.

BIS. 2010. "Triennial Central Bank Survey: Foreign Exchange and Derivatives Market Activity in April 2010 — Preliminary Results." September.

Chauffour, Jean-Pierre and Mariem Malouche. 2011. "Trade Finance During the 2008–9 Trade Collapse: Key Takeaways." *Economic Premise* 66, September.

Ciuriak, Dan, Beverly Lapham and Robert Wolfe, with Terry Collins-Williams and John M. Curtis. 2011. "New-New Trade Policy." Queen's Economics Department Working Paper. http://ssrn.com/abstract=1814226.

Gastle, Charles M. and Dan Ciuriak. 2003. "The Social Dimensions of Globalization: Some Commentaries on Social Choice and Convergence." In *Trade Policy Research 2003,* edited by John M. Curtis and Dan Ciuriak, 199–279. Ottawa: Department of Foreign Affairs and International Trade.

Ghironi Fabio and Marc J. Melitz. 2005. "International Trade and Macroeconomic Dynamics with Heterogeneous Firms." *Quarterly Journal of Economics* 120 (3): 865–915.

Helpman, Elhanan and Paul R. Krugman. 1985. *Market Structure and Foreign Trade: Increasing Returns, Imperfect Competition and the International Economy.* Cambridge, Mass.: MIT Press.

Torres, Hector Rogelio. 2013. "Exchange Rates: Alien to the WTO?" In *Building on Bali: A Work Program for the WTO,* edited by Simon J. Evenett and Alejandro Jara. www.voxeu.org/content/building-bali-work-programme-wto.

Williamson, John. 2004. "A Short History of the Washington Consensus." Paper prepared for the conference "From the Washington Consensus towards a new Global Governance," Barcelona, September 24-25.

Zhou, Xiaochuan. 2009. Statement on Reforming the International Monetary System. The People's Bank of China, March 23.

10

Europe's Monetary Union in Crisis

Juliet Johnson

• • • • • • • • • • • • • • • • • • • •

> The current crisis of the euro is the biggest test Europe has
> faced...since the Treaty of Rome was signed in 1957....This test
> is existential...if the euro fails, then Europe fails.
> — *German Chancellor Angela Merkel (2010)*

At first, it seemed that Europe might quickly overcome the financial crisis
sparked in 2007-2008 when the United States' immense asset bubble popped
and Lehman Brothers collapsed. The European Central Bank (ECB) rapidly
provided emergency liquidity support to troubled euro-zone countries, the
International Monetary Fund (IMF) arranged funding for the hardest hit non-
euro-zone states (Hungary, Latvia and Romania), European governments
engaged in traditional crisis management policies and the European Union
collectively patted itself on the back for having taken the situation in hand.
Instead of resolving the problem, however, government bank bailouts in euro-
zone countries such as Ireland and Spain transformed private sector bank
debt into sovereign debt, and helped to fuel a second financial crisis within
the euro zone that proved to be far more intractable. By 2010, an initial,
apparently modest European banking crisis had turned into a sovereign debt
crisis within the euro zone that shook the European Union to its core.

The sovereign debt crisis erupted soon after Greece's admission in late
2009 that its annual budget deficit would be over 12 percent of GDP, more

than twice as high as it had estimated earlier. This drove up bond yields sharply. Whereas investors had previously treated euro-zone sovereign bonds as roughly equivalent, ratings agencies immediately began to downgrade sovereign debt in euro-zone states now perceived as "risky," and financial markets demanded increasingly high premiums amid a growing fear of sovereign defaults. To make matters worse, banks across Europe held extensive sovereign debt obligations from a wide range of euro-zone states, such that market concerns about bank viability and sovereign creditworthiness fed on one another. The crisis spread to Ireland and Portugal, and then to Spain, Italy and Cyprus. Governments fell across Europe, European public support for the euro and the European Union more broadly took a beating, the euro's international prestige fell, the European Union's north-south economic divide widened and many began to question the ongoing viability of the euro zone itself. In short, Europe's monetary union found itself in the midst of an existential crisis. Although Canada and other international actors regularly exhorted the European Union and its member states to engage in bolder, more fundamental reforms to deal with the crisis, they have instead taken a mostly reactive, defensive and piecemeal approach. Resolving the crisis sustainably will require greater political integration, cooperation and commitment on the part of euro-zone member states to deal with the four fundamental challenges facing the euro zone.

CHALLENGE ONE: SUPRANATIONAL MONEY, FISCAL SOVEREIGNTY

The euro zone is a supranational monetary union in which member states retain national control over fiscal matters. While all euro-zone states share the ECB's monetary policy, each sets its own budget and generally handles its own fiscal affairs. What this means in practice is that individual euro-zone states may have budget surpluses or deficits, not to mention varying levels of public debt, but monetary policy remains the same for all of them and cannot, for example, simultaneously address overheating and stagnant national economies. Although the European Union's Stability and Growth Pact (SGP), limiting government budget deficits to three percent of GDP and public debt to below 60 percent of GDP, was designed to avoid a clash of monetary and fiscal policies, it proved impossible to enforce, particularly after core euro-zone members France and Germany flouted its provisions in 2003. Moreover, as Barry Eichengreen (2012) notes, the SGP did nothing to avert the kind of private sector imbalances that built up in Ireland, Portugal and Spain before the crisis, as their banks "fuelled debt-financed spending binges" and then had to be bailed out when the bubble burst, producing massive government fiscal imbalances through the back door. With no monetary policy flexibility to help avert or adjust for the imbalances, these states were forced to adopt drastic, unpopular and often counterproductive public spending cuts in order to compensate.

The European Union's initial policy fix for the SGP's failings was the "Six-Pack," a set of six regulations first tabled in 2010 that went into force in December 2011 after over a year of negotiations. Like the SGP, the Six-Pack regulations technically bind all EU member states, not just euro-zone members. The Six-Pack aimed to put teeth into the SGP by increasing budgetary surveillance, sanctioning non-compliant states through the excessive deficit procedure (EDP) and imposing automatic financial penalties in order to make the system more credible and fair. In practice, however, no EU state has yet been hit with financial sanctions under the Six-Pack, although many have exceeded the SGP thresholds.

The Six-Pack also introduced surveillance and "correction" for macroeconomic imbalances, such as credit bubbles, through a Macroeconomic Imbalance Procedure (MIP) that requires non-compliant states to adopt corrective action plans and potentially be subject to heavy fines for continued non-compliance. Like the EDP, however, EU authorities have been reluctant to use the MIP to sanction member states. For example, the European Union did not cite Cyprus for excessive imbalances in 2012, although it exceeded several thresholds set in the macroeconomic imbalance scorecard, a significant issue given the crisis that erupted in Cyprus the following year (Eichengreen 2012).

In tacit acknowledgement of these problems, the European Union followed up with the "Two-Pack" in May 2013, which introduced even more stringent budgetary surveillance for euro-zone member states. Euro-zone states also became bound by a Fiscal Compact that came into force in January 2013, establishing an annual euro-zone summit and requiring member states to introduce a national balanced budget law that allows a maximum structural deficit of 0.5 percent of GDP. The European Union also embedded the budget-cutting mores of the SGP and its successors into its European Stability Mechanism (ESM), an institution created in September 2012 to provide financial assistance to euro-zone states in distress. In order to be eligible for ESM assistance, a state must have ratified the Fiscal Compact and signed a memorandum of understanding outlining its commitments to fiscal consolidation.

To complement these extensions of the SGP, in early 2011, Germany and France proposed a so-called Competitiveness Pact that, after criticism and adjustment, became the Euro Plus Pact, adopted in March 2011. Only 22 of the 27 EU member states (including all of the euro-zone states) agreed to participate in the pact, which aims to reduce labour costs, promote employment and labour productivity, contain government pension expenditures, control private debt and encourage more coordinated tax policy.

All of these reforms, however, still leave ultimate fiscal authority — the power to tax and spend — with the member states. The European Union may only monitor and sanction offenders who miss the agreed-upon targets. The targets themselves, meanwhile, all point in the same direction: balancing public budgets, primarily by reducing government expenditures. As the European bailouts managed by the troika (the European Commission [EC], the ECB and the IMF) have revealed, imposing simple austerity programs on already troubled economies can actually make matters worse. Greece, Portugal, Spain, Ireland and Cyprus experienced rising public debt, high unemployment and low to negative growth under the conditionality programs mandated by the troika's bailout terms.

As Blyth (2013) argues, these European countries "cut their budgets and as their economies shrank, their debt loads got bigger not smaller, and unsurprisingly their interest payments shot up...austerity is clearly not working if 'working' means reducing the debt and promoting growth." Even Ireland, a nominal success story, exited its bailout in December 2013 with a public debt of 125 percent of GDP, compared to 32 percent in 2008 before the crisis. Ireland also has a 2014 budget that includes both tax increases and new government spending cuts of €2.5 billion, on top of the large tax increases and nearly €30 billion in other spending cuts already introduced since 2008. The Greek program proved so problematic that it led to a deep split in the troika between the European authorities and the IMF. A critical IMF report released in June 2013 argued that the initial Greek program was too harsh and should have included debt forgiveness, a report that the EC slammed as "plainly wrong and unfounded" (IMF 2013).

In short, none of the reforms adopted so far represent meaningful correctives to the underlying challenge of supranational money and fiscal sovereignty; in fact, applying the prescribed sanctions through fining member-state governments would exacerbate the deficit and debt problems that trigger the fines in the first place, rendering the sanctions both less credible and potentially counterproductive.

CHALLENGE TWO: THE ROLE OF THE ECB

The ECB was created with a narrower mandate, a more limited set of policy tools and a higher level of independence than was typical for other national central banks. While these are not necessarily problems in and of themselves, they cause difficulties when combined with the euro zone's economic diversity and the ECB's conservative ethos. The ECB's mandate is to maintain price stability in the euro zone, defined as an inflation level at or just below two percent. The ECB also had no formal lender-of-last-resort function or ability to issue debt, meaning that in the absence of a Europe-wide treasury or fiscal authority, the ECB had significant limits in its ability to support troubled euro-zone financial institutions. Nor could it supervise euro-zone financial institutions, constraining its ability to recognize problems early or adopt regulatory policies to support systemic financial stability. The high level of independence, in turn, meant that the ECB — guided by a conservative, German-inspired central-banking mindset — often resisted pressure to move beyond its narrow mandate and traditional policies. In sum, the diverse economies of the euro zone possessed a supranational central bank that was, by design and inclination, the least flexible and accountable among the advanced industrial democracies.

Unlike the US Federal Reserve, the ECB under Jean-Claude Trichet reacted slowly to the evolving crisis. In the face of the sovereign debt crisis, the ECB clearly made a mistake in dragging its feet on cutting interest rates. In addition, when it finally began to buy government bonds through its securities market program in 2010, its insistence on doing so in a limited way and only through the secondary markets diminished the program's effectiveness. Moreover, even that timid action spurred the February 2011 resignation of German Bundesbank president and inflation hawk Axel Weber, who had been expected to succeed Trichet as ECB president. In September 2011, ECB chief economist and Weber's fellow Bundesbank veteran Jürgen Stark also resigned from the ECB in opposition to the bond-buying program.

Mario Draghi's ascension to the ECB presidency at the end of Trichet's term in November 2011 broke a key barrier to more significant innovation and led to bolder and more effective responses to the crisis. With Draghi at the helm, the ECB introduced long-term refinancing operations (LTROs) in December 2011, enabling euro-zone banks to borrow money at low interest rates for three years, often using their own country's sovereign bonds as collateral. The LTROs worked well as a stopgap measure, both propping up European banks and reducing sovereign bond yields. Draghi (2012) followed up the LTROs by signalling an impending move toward more significant bond-purchasing efforts, famously declaring in July 2012 that "the ECB is ready to do whatever it takes to preserve the euro. And believe me, it will be enough." Of course, most neglect to mention the three other words that Draghi uttered at the beginning of that oft-quoted sentence: "*Within our mandate*" (ibid.; emphasis added). How to interpret, and whether or not to expand that mandate rests at the core of the heated debate over the ECB and the euro's post-crisis future.

Draghi's speech upped the ante and the tensions both within and outside the ECB. While markets rebounded and many observers cheered Draghi, Weber's successor at the Bundesbank, Jens Weidmann, threatened to resign over the anticipated new bond-purchasing program. The resulting program, the ECB's so-called Outright Monetary Transactions (OMTs), announced in August 2012, represented a compromise between the ECB president and many of his critics, although Weidmann voted against it, while the German Constitutional Court ruled in February 2014 that the OMT program probably violates German law and referred it to the European Court of Justice for ruling and clarification. The OMT program authorized the ECB to act nearly, but not completely, as the euro zone's lender of last resort, inasmuch as it in principle placed no upper limit on ECB bond purchases (Hodson 2013). The goal of the OMT program was to ensure that euro-zone member states' sovereign bond spreads reflected only domestic economic conditions rather than market fears that a state might exit the euro zone. As such, the OMT framework limited the ECB's purchases to the secondary market and required that states seeking ECB support through the OMT previously commit to an ESM fiscal reform program. The OMT program would also stop short of a true quantitative easing policy, as adopted in the United States and elsewhere, since the ECB insisted that any bond purchases would be fully sterilized; that is, they would not result in additional net liquidity in the financial system.

Draghi and other key ECB board members argued that the OMT program was necessary to stabilize market expectations and fit firmly within the bounds of the ECB's mandate to protect price stability. Critics argued that engaging in OMT would amount to unlawful ECB financing of member states (the basis of the German court case) and that the ECB would be left holding the bag in the event of sovereign default, putting the entire euro system at risk. The OMT announcement did calm markets and the ECB has not had to use this instrument; however, the uproar caused by the announcement signalled reluctance by many to see the ECB extend its mandate. Moreover, this was a tempest in a teapot compared to the next issue: that of the ECB's role in a new pan-European system of bank supervision and resolution.

CHALLENGE THREE: INADEQUATE BANKING SUPERVISION AND RESOLUTION

Not only did the ECB lack financial supervisory authority, but banking supervision and resolution within the euro zone was both nationally based and incapable of preventing overly risky financial activities or dealing with them once the bubble burst. While the crisis revealed inadequacies among supervisory authorities worldwide, these problems had more significance in the euro zone because of the greater potential for contagion and the correspondingly greater difficulty of coordination in addressing the systemic problems caused by national regulatory differences and bank failures. Moreover, instead of acting as a single economic unit in the face of crisis, national supervisory authorities moved to protect their own financial institutions and markets at the expense of other European states. These problems reduced market confidence in the euro, in euro-zone financial institutions and in euro-zone sovereign debt, exacerbating the crisis.

After the global financial crisis hit, the European Union, like the rest of the international community, recognized that its supervisory mechanisms needed a fundamental overhaul. The EC invited Jacques de Larosière — former IMF managing director, president of the European Bank for Reconstruction and Development, and governor of the Banque de France — to convene a high-level commission to recommend improvements to European supervisory arrangements. The February 2009 de Larosière report suggested that Europe create new, EU-level institutions to supervise individual financial institutions (microprudential supervision) and monitor systemic financial stability (macroprudential supervision).

In response, the European Union created the European System of Financial Supervision (ESFS). While the EC presented its initial proposals in September 2009, the ESFS only came into existence in January 2011. The ESFS's microprudential wing consisted of the European Banking Authority, the European Insurance and Occupational Pensions Authority, the European Securities and Markets Authority, a joint committee of these three authorities to facilitate cooperation, plus the supervisory authorities of the member states. The European Systemic Risk Board, with the ECB president serving as chair, formed the ESFS's macroprudential wing.

Although an improvement over the old system, the ESFS was still a far cry from a banking union and could do little more than strengthen coordination among national supervisory authorities. Therefore, in September 2012, the EC proposed a new, unified financial supervisor under the auspices of the ECB. The European Union's December 2012 report suggested that a single supervisory mechanism (SSM) be put into place by the end of 2013 as the first in a three-stage plan towards a full banking union (Van Rompuy et al. 2012).

While Draghi agreed with the creation of the SSM under the ECB, the German financial community blew up, arguing that the de Larosière report explicitly stated that microprudential supervision should *not* be placed within the ECB because of the risk of diluting the ECB's price stability mandate, creating conflicts of interest and undermining its independence. Some also suspected that southern euro-zone states supported the SSM as a covert means of facilitating fiscal transfers from the north to the south. While the ECB insisted that it would maintain a "Chinese wall" between monetary policy and banking supervision, international experience called into question both the possibility and desirability of doing so.

The European Parliament approved the SSM in September 2013 and the EC signed off on it in October. The ECB sees the SSM as a key precondition to allow the ESM to recapitalize struggling banks, and thus break the troublesome bank-sovereign link that helped turn the European Union's initial banking crisis into a sovereign debt crisis. In another positive development, the European Parliament approved a necessary complement to the SSM — the single resolution mechanism (SRM) — in April 2014. The laws, which come into force in 2015, provide for the creation of a bank recovery and resolution system and a single resolution fund to be built up over eight years. Accompanying legislation requires all EU member states to build up deposit guarantee funds to protect individual deposits up to €100,000, although it stopped short of requiring cross-national deposit guarantees. To the extent that these efforts are successful, they will moderate a key generator of the crisis and move the euro zone far closer towards a banking union.

CHALLENGE FOUR: INCOMPATIBLE GROWTH MODELS

The euro zone is a monetary union of economically diverse states without a mutual adjustment mechanism. Put simply, the euro zone has an export-led north and a demand-led south. Northern euro-zone countries — particularly Germany — derive their economic dynamism from exporting high-value goods, which generates a persistent current account surplus. In contrast, southern euro-zone states — such as Spain, Italy and Greece — have traditionally had demand-led economies, with consumption financed by government spending and occasional devaluations to balance the books. This is an interdependent system — the north built up surpluses in part by exporting to the south, and the south financed those purchases by borrowing from northern banks and sovereigns. Once in monetary union, however, the traditional adjustment mechanisms for the south disappeared, with no transfer union put in place to replace it. The questionable financial market (and, crucially, ECB) practice of treating all euro-zone sovereign debt as risk-equivalent masked this problem during times of relative international financial stability, but the practice could not withstand the impact of the global financial crisis.

Current EU policies primarily put the burden of adjustment on the south. The troika's bailout programs mandate fiscal austerity, while the Six-Pack punishes current account deficits more than current account surpluses, serving

German interests. The European Union has also attempted to deal with this challenge through the ESM and the "European Semester." Introduced in 2011, the European Semester mandates simultaneous EU-level discussion of national fiscal policies, structural reforms and macroeconomic imbalances as national governments prepare their budgets. Where national interests align, this coordination mechanism may prove helpful, but that is often not the case. Similarly, the ESM will, in the best-case scenario, serve as an improved crisis resolution mechanism — and there are already significant concerns about the adequacy of its funding — but despite the fears of the German government, it seems far-fetched to envision it as a back door towards debt mutualization or a transfer union.

In fact, ongoing concerns about structural imbalances have increasingly led to fingers being pointed in Germany's direction. From US Treasury officials to the Organization for Security and Co-operation in Europe's renowned Canadian economist William White, many international observers have insisted that Germany engage in expansionary policies to address its persistent trade surpluses. In November 2013, the EC started a formal review to investigate whether or not Germany's trade surpluses threatened the future of the euro zone, and Germany's own Council of Economic Experts opined that "the German government should not give the impression that it expects — or even demands — painful adjustment processes from other countries, but shies away from unpopular measures for Germany" (quoted in Ewing, Smale and Kanter 2013). German leaders and Bundesbank officials have, so far, rejected such suggestions; as Bundesbank executive board member Andres Dombret (2013) declared, "We have to accept the structural differences between economies." Given the divergence of opinions and interests within the euro zone, this final challenge remains the most intractable.

CANADA AND THE EURO ZONE

What role has Canada played in the ongoing crisis of Europe's monetary union? Canada has, in several ways, had a constructive influence on the European debate. Canada's deft policy making and remarkably smooth landing in the face of the global financial crisis significantly raised its profile in international financial circles. Canada's prestige was arguably at its height after the Toronto Group of Twenty (G20) Summit, at which Canadian exhortations for world leaders to get their fiscal houses in order were centrally reflected in the agreement emerging from the summit.

Former Bank of Canada (BoC) Governor Mark Carney exemplified Canada's enhanced international profile. Carney became renowned for his bold moves to cut benchmark rates and for being the first to adopt the practice of forward guidance, committing the central bank to pursue a set monetary policy path for a particular period of time. Both the United States and the ECB later adopted forward guidance policies as well, inspired by its effectiveness in Canada. Carney gave strong moral support to the ECB's controversial entry into secondary bond markets in June 2010. He consistently supported other countries' uses of unconventional monetary policies, as well as increased global cooperation in working to solve problems revealed by the crisis. The Bank for International Settlements named Carney the chair of the Committee on the Global Financial System in June 2010, and in November 2011, he was named to succeed Mario Draghi as the chair of the Financial Stability Board. Carney set a bold tone in calling for comprehensive reforms to financial regulation and supervision, first of all in Europe. As he noted in September 2011, "if some institutions feel pressure today, it is because they have done too little for too long, rather than because they are being asked to do too much, too soon" (quoted in Central Banking Newsdesk 2011). Carney's European influence was further confirmed and enhanced in June 2013, when he became governor of the Bank of England.

Carney and others increasingly pressured the European Union and its key member states — particularly Germany — to engage in critical self-reflection and to consider more comprehensive solutions to the euro zone's underlying problems. Through Carney, Canadian models and experiences have played an important role in debates over financial sector reform in Europe. Before leaving the BoC, Carney identified several interlocking reforms that would be required to turn the euro zone into a viable monetary union: a banking union, a fiscal transfer system, sovereign debt mutualization, labour market and competitiveness reforms, and sustained deficit reduction (Carney 2012). Canadian experience on how to run a fiscal transfer union and on methods of cooperation among financial sector regulators in a federation have clear relevance for Europe. So, too, does the lesson that such a monetary union cannot thrive without broad political agreement on its importance and a concomitant willingness to compromise in order to maintain its health.

However, the frustrations of Canadian officials with the pace and tenor of European crisis responses have also expressed themselves in ways that have, at times, undermined Canada's diplomatic role in Europe. The Harper government's decision in June 2011 to support Mexican central banker Agustín Carstens for IMF managing director over France's Christine Lagarde reflected concerns that continued European leadership of the IMF would reinforce the perception of the IMF as unwilling to share governance with developing countries and would represent a conflict of interest, given the IMF's integral role in the ongoing resolution of the European sovereign debt crisis. While a principled argument, Canada's support for Carstens came late in the game when Lagarde's appointment was already a *fait accompli,* and therefore, in practice, was a symbolic gesture that did little to endear the Canadian government to European leaders.

Tensions grew further when Lagarde asked IMF member states to contribute to an IMF stabilization fund for Europe. Canadian officials stood alone with the United States in declining to do so, insisting that Europe was rich enough to bail itself out. Former Canadian Finance Minister Jim Flaherty pointed out in early 2012 that, at minimum, any such IMF funding program should be subject to a special veto power for the non-European countries, given that European countries controlled a plurality of seats on the IMF's board. Canadian Prime Minister Stephen Harper spoke more bluntly before the Los Cabos G20 Summit in June 2012, exhorting Europe to fix its "half-done project" for monetary union instead of asking for handouts (quoted in Canadian Press 2012). Canada's reluctance to financially support the troika's bailout programs met a strong European response, with EU President José Manuel Barroso tersely rejecting Harper's criticisms of EU economic policies and suggesting that it was in Canada's own interest to work with the EU to overcome the crisis (Elliott 2012). The unusually strident and uncooperative Canadian approach had its public domestic detractors, such as federal New Democratic Party leader Thomas Mulcair and former IMF Executive Director and Deputy Finance Minister Scott Clark, but the Harper government stood its ground (Geddes 2012). This decision meant that the Canadian government did not have a place at the IMF's table when discussing how best to resolve the European sovereign debt crisis and reform the euro zone, which many regarded as a missed opportunity.

Does this matter for Canada in practice? Right now, as the worst of the current crisis appears to be abating, probably not. Canada's trade levels with the European Union are low and the two economies are not especially dependent on one another. However, in the medium to long term, a successful and sustainable resolution of the European crisis will likely matter to Canada a great deal. First, the recently signed Comprehensive Economic and Trade Agreement with Europe will bolster the trade relationships between the two sides and potentially encourage the United States to pursue a similar agreement at a more rapid pace (Hancock 2013). Setbacks or stagnation in Europe would put at risk this evolving trade relationship and compromise future Canadian growth prospects. Second, as recent experience has shown, local financial crises can have international repercussions. Such contagion effects can be rapid and devastating. If renewed problems within the European Union affect the international financial system more broadly, this will negatively impact Canada. As the BoC (2010) dryly put it, "While the Canadian financial system has continued to function well in the face of adverse spillovers from Europe, it is vulnerable to renewed stress in the event of a recurrence of severe tensions in global markets" (see Poloz 2013). Despite Canada's resilient financial infrastructure, if faced with a new crisis it may not be quite so lucky as last time.

EUROPEAN MONETARY UNION STAGGERS ON

Sustainably solving the euro zone's problems would require much deeper reform than European leaders currently seem capable of envisioning: it demands eurobills, a banking union, and a fiscal and economic union. The barriers to such reforms are political rather than economic. Deeper financial integration would delegate far more power to supranational EU authorities than is presently the case. The European Union, and especially the ECB, is already widely viewed as having a significant democratic deficit. Ceding more sovereignty to less accountable supranational institutions in the name of better financial management could be a tough sell in any EU member state. Equally problematic, the most powerful state in the euro zone, Germany, will be unwilling to deepen the economic and monetary union in a way that would effectively and fairly deal with the underlying north-south disparities. The German electorate could fatally lose confidence in the euro if it perceived that

Germany would somehow become forever responsible for financing southern "profligacy" while locked together in monetary union.

The worst-case scenarios would be a messy breakup of the euro zone or a euro zone reformed completely on German terms that would further entrench the existing north-south divide in Europe. However, both seem unlikely. Under current conditions, Europe is stuck. Key EU member states' deep political commitment to the euro, but not to supranational governance, leaves no means by which to sustainably resolve fundamental structural issues. As Benjamin J. Cohen (2012) persuasively argues, the euro zone's probable future is one of "muddling through...defective but defended, it will simply endure." So, although the euro zone will survive the crisis, its structural — and ultimately political — limitations will remain an important source of future instability for the euro zone and, by extension, for Canada and the rest of the international financial system.

Acknowledgements

The author would like to thank the organizers and participants in the Canada Among Nations authors' workshop held at CIGI in December 2013 — in particular Rohinton Medhora, Dane Rowlands, Pierre Siklos and Domenico Lombardi — for helpful comments made on an earlier version of this chapter.

WORKS CITED

Blyth, Mark. 2013. *Austerity: The History of a Dangerous Idea*. New York: Oxford University Press.

BoC. 2010. *Financial System Review*. June. www.bankofcanada.ca/wp-content/uploads/2010/09/fsr_0610.pdf.

Canadian Press. 2012. "Harper in Paris Stresses Need for Closer European Union: PM Has Breakfast with New French President Francois Hollande." Canadian Press, June 7. www.cbc.ca/news/world/harper-in-paris-stresses-need-for-closer-european-union-1.1198511.

Carney, Mark. 2012. "Uncertainty and the Global Recovery." Speech given at the Vancouver Island Economic Alliance, Nanaimo, October 15.

Central Banking Newsdesk. 2011. "Carney to Banks: Stop Blaming Each Other." *Central Banking*, September 26.

Cohen, Benjamin J. 2012. "The Future of the Euro: Let's Get Real." *Review of International Political Economy* 19 (4): 689–700.

Dombret, Andreas. 2013. "How to Overcome Fragmentation in the European Financial Market." Speech at the 23rd European Banking Congress, Frankfurt am Main, November 22. www.bundesbank.de/Redaktion/EN/Reden/2013/2013_11_22_dombret.html#doc161452bodyText1.

Draghi, Mario. 2012. Speech given at the Global Investment Conference, London, July 26.

Eichengreen, Barry. 2012. "European Monetary Integration with Benefit of Hindsight." *JCMS: Journal of Common Market Studies* 50: 123–36.

Elliott, Louise. 2012. "Europe to Canada: Don't Lecture Us: Harper Tight-lipped about Canada's Bid to Join Pacific Trade Talks." CBC News, June 18. www.cbc.ca/news/politics/europe-to-canada-don-t-lecture-us-1.1191574.

Ewing, Jack, Alison Smale and James Kanter. 2013. "Germany's Neighbors Admonish It Over Surplus." *The New York Times*, November 13.

Geddes, John. 2012. "It's Harper vs. Europe at the G20: What's Behind Stephen Harper's Refusal to Pay into an European Bailout Fund?" *Macleans*, June 17. www2.macleans.ca/2012/06/17/just-say-non/.

Hancock, John. 2013. "A Lever to Move the World: Why the CETA Is Great News not nly for Canada, but also for the Cause of Global Trade Liberalization." October 19. http://opencanada.org/features/blogs/roundtable/a-lever-to-move-the-world/.

Hodson, Dermot. 2013. "The Eurozone in 2012: 'Whatever It Takes to Preserve the Euro'?" *JCMS: Journal of Common Market Studies* 51: 183–200.

IMF. 2013. "Greece: Ex Post Evaluation of Exceptional Access under the 2010 Stand-By Arrangement." IMF Country Report 13/156. www.imf.org/external/pubs/cat/longres.aspx?sk=40639.0.

Merkel, Angela. 2010. "Crisis-hit Europe Needs 'New Stability Culture.'" Address to the German Parliament, cited in Richard Carter, *Agence France Press*, May 19.

Poloz, Stephen S. 2013. "Opening Statement: Release of the Monetary Policy Report." October 23. www.bankofcanada.ca/2013/10/publications/ speeches/opening-statement-23-10-2013/.

Van Rompuy, Herbert, with José Manuel Barroso, Jean-Claude Juncker and Mario Draghi. 2012. "Towards a Genuine Economic and Monetary Union." December 5. www.consilium.europa.eu/uedocs/cms_Data/ docs/.../en/.../134069.pdf.

11

The Developing Countries and the Great Financial Crisis: Was This Time Different?

Roy Culpeper

• • • • • • • • • • • • • • • • • •

INTRODUCTION

In the past three decades, we have witnessed a series of international financial crises. These have frequently started in developing countries — the periphery of the globalizing economy — often with negative repercussions for the advanced countries.[1] The spillover effects of financial crises from poor to rich countries are clearly of concern since they expose the fragility of the global economy. But what are the spillover effects for poor countries when financial crises erupt in the rich countries? The Great Financial Crisis that originated in the United States and Europe — the centre of the globalizing economy — was in fact the worst in 80 years. Developing countries were certainly not unscathed, but exhibited considerable and perhaps surprising resilience

---

[1] There were, of course, episodes of bank failures and financial crises in industrial countries from the 1970s until the 1990s, including, for example, the Savings and Loan Crisis in the United States from 1984 to 1991, a series of bank failures in Europe in the late 1980s and early 1990s, and the stock market crashes of 1987 and 2000-2001 (the dot-com crash). However, none of these approached the magnitude of the "Great Financial Crisis" of 2007, nor were they as crippling as the debt crises repeatedly afflicting developing countries.

in the face of the ensuing Great Recession in the United States and Europe. There are many explanations for why this time may have been different, to paraphrase the title of a much referenced treatise on the history of the world's financial crises during the last eight centuries, *This Time Is Different: Eight Centuries of Financial Folly*, by Carmen Reinhart and Kenneth Rogoff. These include the recent, frenetic evolution of the financial sectors in the advanced countries, the role played by their macroeconomic policies, longer-run policy and institutional changes in the developing countries, and shifts in the pattern and relationships of global trade and investment. However, what is perhaps more interesting are the policy implications of these shifts for developing countries and advanced countries alike in the future.

This chapter examines some of the evidence and arguments that this time *was* different — that the developing countries were spared the negative spillovers expected from the advanced countries. True, there have been fundamental changes in the policies of many developing countries and the structure of the global economy. Likewise, the relationships prevailing between the advanced and developing countries have changed, and will continue to do so. But the evidence is mixed and the implications uncertain. Some developing countries have gone through a structural transformation to become emerging markets. Others, even among the poorest countries in Africa, may be beginning a similar transition. The advent of China as a major trading and investment partner has provided developing countries with a new market and source of financing. Yet, as encouraging as these trends may be, they are far from universal, and their longevity is questionable.

WHETHER, HOW AND WHY THIS TIME WAS DIFFERENT

A long-term perspective is critical to understanding why and how, and also whether, the developing countries are more resilient to the recent crisis than past crises. It should be noted that there is no consensus on this issue. One more optimistic view, articulated by some experts and the international financial institutions, is that there has been a structural change in the global economy, resulting in a long-term trend toward convergence between developing and advanced economies (International Monetary Fund [IMF] 2012; 2013a). The other, more skeptical view is that the significant improvements in the economic performance of some developing countries since the 1990s must be juxtaposed with setbacks in other countries. Moreover, the better-performing countries enjoyed a favourable mix of circumstances unlikely to persist, putting into question, at least for some countries, the notion of a long-run structural transformation.

In the more optimistic view, since World War II, the global economy has experienced a subtle but profound structural transformation. Beginning in the 1950s with Japan, a number of countries embarked on a path of historically unprecedented rapid industrialization and economic growth. Other emerging market countries in East Asia followed in the 1960s and 1970s, and China joined this group in the 1980s. The speed of their transformation was such that today, it could be said that "after two centuries of high-speed divergence [between the advanced and developing countries], a pattern of convergence has taken over" (Spence 2011, 5; Commission on Growth and Development 2008; Harrison and Sepulveda 2011; Bhattacharya 2013).

The magnitude and pervasiveness of the structural transformation taking place throughout the developing world was not fully apparent until the mid-1990s, when India and several Sub-Saharan African countries also began to enjoy sustained rates of growth higher than in the past, elevating the average growth rate of all emerging market and developing countries (EMDCs) above that of the advanced countries. The case of Sub-Saharan Africa has been perhaps the most surprising in the developing world, since that region has been afflicted by a series of economic shocks, both natural and man-made since 1980, leading to stagnation or decline in many countries. Yet, despite these earlier setbacks, 17 countries in the region realized a growth of 3.2 percent per capita over the period 1996–2008, well above the global average of 1.9 percent (Radelet 2010, chapter 1; World Bank 2013a).[2]

By the mid-2000s, further evidence came to light to support the claim that convergence was taking place, not just between the fastest-growing emerging market countries and the advanced countries, but also between the poorest and the richest countries. Low-income countries as a group, measured by growth

---

2 The 17 countries are: Botswana, Burkina Faso, Cape Verde, Ethiopia, Ghana, Lesotho, Mali, Mauritius, Mozambique, Namibia, Rwanda, São Tomé and Principé, Seychelles, South Africa, Tanzania, Uganda and Zambia. The cumulative increase in average real income over this period was 50 percent for the whole group, ranging between 25 percent (Zambia) and 96 percent (Mozambique). The Commission on Growth and Development (2008) identified 13 countries experiencing high growth for 25 years or more: Botswana, Brazil, China, Hong Kong, Indonesia, Japan, Korea, Malaysia, Malta, Oman, Singapore, Taiwan and Thailand.

in output, have considerably outperformed both the developed countries and the developing countries as a whole since 2006 (with the exception of 2010; see Table 1).

Table 1: Growth of World Output 2006–2014
(Annual Percentage Change, in %)

	2006–2009	2010	2011	2012	2013
World	1.1	4.0	2.7	2.2	2.4
Developed Economies	-0.4	2.6	1.4	1.1	1.1
Developing Economies	5.2	7.7	5.7	4.7	5.1
Low-income countries	5.9	6.6	6.0	5.7	5.9
Lower middle-income countries	5.8	7.4	5.6	4.4	5.5

Sources: Data for 2006–2011 are from the UN's *World Economic Situation and Prospects* (2013). Data for 2012-2013 are the author's projections.

According to this optimistic account, the emerging and developing countries as a group had enjoyed a growth momentum in the years leading up to the Great Financial Crisis. This momentum stretched back at least a decade and, in some cases, as much as four decades, despite occasionally serious setbacks (for example, the debt crises of the 1980s and 1990s). When the crisis struck, their growth rates were adversely impacted, but not as seriously as the advanced countries, while still remaining high by historical standards. In this view of "structural transformation," the developing countries have "decoupled" from their traditional trade and investment links in the North, that is, with the Organisation for Economic Co-operation and Development (OECD) countries, and have been able to benefit from a world with multipolar growth (Harrison and Sepulveda 2011).

There is, however, a more skeptical view of the structural transformation-resilience-decoupling thesis, based on the variation in economic performance of different EMDCs. Critics of the optimistic narrative have also questioned whether the underlying causes of the pre-crisis boom are sustainable in the longer term. Thus, it is true that the slowdown in developing countries as a whole (with an average growth rate of 4.92 percentage points lower in 2009 than in the boom years 2003–2007) was less pronounced than in the advanced countries (6.13 percent lower). However, certain countries and regions have fared much worse — for example, economies in transition in southeastern Europe (with an average growth rate 9.06 percent lower), Mexico and

Central America (10 percent lower), and South America (6.37 percent lower) (Ocampo et al. 2010).

To understand these differing outcomes, it is worth noting that those developing countries that are more specialized in manufactured exports (for example, Mexico and Latin America, more generally) fared worse than countries that are more dependent on commodity exports. This was due to the fact that as the Great Financial Crisis morphed into the Great Recession in the United States and Europe, the chief markets for these countries' manufactured exports contracted significantly. In contrast, low-income commodity exporters were more dependent on the Chinese market. While its growth rate had fallen by 2.59 percentage points from pre-crisis peaks, it was still a vigorous 8.7 percent in 2009 and 9.2 percent in 2010, levels that continued to fuel a high level of commodity imports. Accordingly, the average growth rate of the least-developed countries (more reliant on commodity exports) fell by 3.98 percent compared to 2003–2007 — in other words, almost a full percentage point less than the fall in growth rates for all developing countries (Ocampo et al. 2010).

Whether the pre-crisis surge in growth is a robust, long-term trend (at least among the low-income countries), the issue revolves around explanations of their structural transformation. According to the IMF (2012), three-fifths of the improved growth performance of developing countries is explained by "better policies." These policies, aimed at low inflation, favourable fiscal and external balances, provided "greater policy space" permitting counter-cyclical fiscal policy, unlike in past financial crises (Harrison and Sepulveda 2011).

However, critics (Akyüz 2013) point out that favourable external shocks and buoyant commodity prices (driven primarily by Chinese demand) played an important role, particularly during the period 2002–2007. The favourable external shocks included a surge of capital flows into the EMDCs, as well as remittances, all of which contributed to "greater policy space" rather than the "good policies" enumerated by the IMF. Moreover, these positive external shocks may not be sustainable: Chinese growth is gradually slowing down and becoming less trade intensive, and capital outflows from the principal sources in the North have been driven by the extraordinarily expansive monetary policies (such as the Federal Reserve's quantitative easing [QE] programs, along with other "unconventional monetary policies" conducted by the European Central Bank, the Bank of England and the Bank of Japan) aimed at combatting the Great Recession.

It is true that these policies have helped forestall a possible financial collapse in the advanced economies and to build their recovery, and have, thereby, supported growth in the EMDCs (IMF 2013a); however, they have also resulted in an enormous buildup of liquidity and chronically low interest rates, causing a search for yields that has led many investors with huge capital outflows into the EMDCs. But these policies are also not sustainable. At the slightest hint of "tapering" of the Federal Reserve's QE program (which happened in May 2013), capital pours back out of the emerging markets, putting pressure on their exchange rates and posing challenges for macroeconomic stabilization.

At the time of writing (February 2014), there was considerable currency turmoil among certain emerging market countries due precisely to anticipation of the phasing down of monetary stimulus. In the four months prior to October 1, 2013, the Indian rupee had lost more than 15 percent against the euro, the Brazilian real 12 percent and the Mexican peso 10 percent (*Financial Times* 2013). The investment bank Morgan Stanley has referred to the South African rand, the Brazilian real, the Indian rupee, the Indonesian rupiah and the Turkish lira as the "fragile five" emerging market currencies, because they are most susceptible to depreciation due to current account and fiscal deficits (Bloomberg Personal Finance 2013). Other seriously affected countries included Argentina, Ukraine and Russia. This bout of volatility differs from that experienced in the Asian financial crisis when exchange rates were effectively pegged, and emerging markets (excluding China) now hold US$2.9 trillion in foreign exchange reserves (compared to US$1 trillion in 2000). However, there could still be considerable turmoil occasioned by capital flight and offsetting measures adopted by host countries (particularly by raising interest rates) that will slow down domestic investment and growth.[3] Resilience, even among emerging market economies, is fragile, and — just as in the financial crises of the 1980s and 1990s — prone to being whiplashed by monetary policies in the advanced economies.

---

3   Early indications were that markets expected greater hikes in interest rates than those proffered by monetary authorities. The Turkish lira stalled and the South African rand and Indian rupee continued to fall despite surprise increases in interest rates by central banks (*Financial Times* 2014).

What, therefore, can be said with any confidence about whether or not the developing world has embarked on a structural transformation with significantly higher growth rates than in the past, and the possibility of convergence between poor and rich countries? And, if such a transformation has taken place, can this explain the extent to which developing countries have increased their resilience to global downturns (emanating from the advanced countries) and, indeed, does it indicate that "decoupling" from the advanced countries has taken place? The short answer is that it is impossible and unwise to generalize about the whole group of 170-odd developing countries. A small group of Asian countries on the Pacific Rim, led today by China, has unquestionably experienced historically unprecedented economic growth. Whether India is now a member of this group is less clear. Its growth spurt from 1992 until the crisis was higher than its historical levels, but lower than that of China. As the current crisis has persisted for five years, India has decelerated more than China, due to its openness to capital flows and the increasingly unsettled conditions in capital markets (Gokarn 2013). As noted previously, other emerging markets (South Africa, Brazil, Indonesia and Turkey) are also now experiencing capital outflows and currency turmoil.

As to low-income countries, and Sub-Saharan Africa in particular, acceleration in aggregate growth rates over the past two decades to around six percent is certainly worth celebrating, given their much more dismal performance in the previous decades, and particularly since 1980. However, as Radelet (2010) points out, per capita growth averaged just 3.2 percent in the 17 countries he highlights. Although considerably higher than that of the advanced countries, growth at this pace can only lead to convergence in the very long run. And 3.2 percent is only half or less of the per capita growth rates in excess of six percent in the East Asia and Pacific region.[4]

Moreover, as the World Bank (2013a) has recently pointed out, there is reason to be skeptical about the extent to which growth is widely shared in Sub-Saharan Africa. Rising inequality indicates otherwise: the benefits of growth are being enjoyed largely by upper income deciles. The region, which is the world's poorest, suffers from low growth elasticity of poverty, meaning that growth alone will not suffice to rapidly reduce poverty. To do

---

4 Per capita incomes would double at a sustained 3.2 percent annual rate in 22.5 years, from a base that is one or two percent of per capita income levels in the advanced countries. In contrast, at a sustained growth rate of six percent, per capita incomes would double in about 12 years.

that will require more inclusive growth processes to tackle inequality. From the perspective of the poorest people in the poorest region in the world, notwithstanding a possible "takeoff" in the region's economic growth in the face of the worst global downturn in 80 years, resilience and structural transformation have not yet delivered any benefits for them.

Rising inequality is, in fact, now a global phenomenon, encompassing the advanced and developing countries alike. Ironically, convergence may be taking place, even over a long time horizon, but only between average national incomes. In parallel, because of growing inequality within all countries — the result of the skewed distribution of the benefits of growth — there could be growing divergence between the world's poorest and richest citizens.

In conclusion, sweeping claims that there has been a long-term structural transformation among developing countries should be qualified, along with claims that developing countries have collectively exhibited great resilience to the current crisis. At best, such claims may be supported principally by the performance of several East Asian countries during the past five decades. As to the low-income countries, and Sub-Saharan Africa in particular, it may be true that there has been a turnaround in economic performance in the last 20 years among many countries in the region. However, it is too soon to tell if this is the harbinger of a longer-term trend rather than the consequence of unusual circumstances that may not persist, and if it is a trend that will encompass all 42 countries in this group. Finally, claims of a universal convergence between rich and poor countries seem exaggerated, even more so if such claims imply convergence between the world's poorest and richest individuals and households.

Thus, it is crucial to differentiate among a very diverse group of EMDCs. Some Asian countries have clearly performed much better, both in coping with the current crisis and over several decades, leading to convergence (at least in national averages) with the advanced countries. Latin American countries are still too firmly coupled to North American and European markets to have escaped the fallout from the crisis. For some poorer developing countries, improved performance suggests that it is possible to begin to rise out of the "low-income trap," even if not dramatically, while others must still demonstrate that they too are able to take these first steps.

POLICY IMPLICATIONS AND LESSONS

For EMDCs: Strengthened Regulation, More Caution about External Debt, Macroeconomic Policy Responses and the Need for International Reforms

For the EMDCs as a group, one policy lesson stands out: they have benefited from policy shifts oriented to strengthening financial regulation and supervision, and against the accumulation of possibly unsustainable debt — and, in some cases, from a concerted reduction in existing debt. Also, many of the more seriously affected countries have suffered through similar episodes in previous financial crises, which led to the demand for reforms in global financial governance — in addition to debt restructuring, reforms in IMF conditionality and the need for a better international financial safety net. The current crisis further strengthens the rationale for such reforms.

Financial and debt crises in the recent past have led almost all countries to exercise greater caution toward financial sector liberalization, capital account openness and the accumulation of unsustainable external debt. In particular, the Asian financial crisis in the late 1990s resulted in the recognition that financial sector supervision and regulation are critically important as developing countries become increasingly open to globalization. That crisis led to the formation of the Group of Twenty (G20) Finance Ministers and the Financial Stability Forum, as well as initiatives by the World Bank and IMF aimed at strengthening institutions, policies, norms and standards meant to ensure the stability of the financial sector in member countries. Even advocates of financial liberalization warned that these measures were crucial to prevent crises. Otherwise, currency, interest rate and maturity mismatches, along with undercapitalized or over-leveraged banks — which were commonplace in the lead up to the Asian crisis — could again lead to volatility and financial turmoil with sudden stops or shifts in market sentiments (Mishkin 2006, chapter 9).

The Asian financial crisis also interrupted the policy momentum toward capital account liberalization that culminated in an initiative to amend the IMF's Articles of Agreement in 1997. This proposal was shelved because of the deepening crisis. At the same time, capital account liberalization was not completely abandoned by the IMF or its advocates among the advanced economies. Instead, it was made a longer-term policy objective that was promoted, for example, through IMF programs in selected countries and via regional trade and bilateral investment agreements. Some emerging market countries — for example, India — have sought greater capital account openness as part of a wider process of liberalization.

Finally, in responding to the crisis, Asian emerging markets' robust macroeconomic policy responses, through counter-cyclical monetary and fiscal measures, increased their resilience to the shock emanating from the United States and Europe. Although these measures could not completely insulate the Asian economies from the shock, as noted above, they helped prevent a worse downturn (Gokarn 2013).

For Emerging Markets: Shift toward Self-insurance

One unforeseen consequence of the Asian financial crisis was that Asian countries, in particular, positioned themselves to reduce their vulnerability to the vagaries of international capital flows. These had led to currency appreciation followed by speculative attacks in the Asian financial crisis, which then led to IMF borrowing and mostly unwelcome policy conditionality. Accordingly, they pursued strategies of generating trade and current account surpluses, and the accumulation of foreign exchange reserves, in order to provide "self-insurance" against the contingency of sudden outflows or future speculative currency attacks (Akyüz 2010).

As a result, many EMDCs began the twenty-first century with a policy stance aimed at strengthening financial sector regulation, cautiousness toward capital account liberalization and defensive measures against future instability that did not involve recourse to the IMF. In addition, the financial sector of most EMDCs is largely bank-based rather than market-based, since local bond and equity markets are typically thin and less susceptible to the excesses of innovation and speculation that were becoming common in the advanced economies.

These EMDC policy stances seem particularly wise now, when we look at how the advanced economies addressed regulation in the years leading up to the crisis. In the advanced economies, as we now know, financial sector deregulation was gathering speed, spurring the growth of increasingly risky and opaque financial instruments. The growth of asset bubbles was financed through the accumulation of household and financial sector debt that, by

2007, proved unsustainable, leading to the ensuing crisis. Thus, it is not surprising that the Great Financial Crisis erupted in the advanced countries, where the regulatory and supervisory infrastructure had become totally inadequate to ensure the safety and stability of the financial system. While some emerging markets (such as India) were also, to some degree, embarking on the road to "increased financialization," their financial markets lacked the depth and sophistication that led to the buildup of debt and asset bubbles in the advanced economies.

Finally, in the low-income countries, there had been concerted international efforts to significantly reduce the debt overhang via the Heavily Indebted Poor Country (HIPC) initiative and the Multilateral Debt Reduction Initiative (MDRI), which effectively left most countries in this group at low or moderate risk of debt distress.[5] This group of countries, predominantly reliant on official lending rather than private capital flows, was not as vulnerable to the contagion characteristic of the emerging market countries more integrated into the international capital markets.

For EMDCs: More Reliance on Domestic Savings and Domestic Resource Mobilization

There is another, more paradoxical lesson to be learned from the experience of the EMDCs, which is reflected in the decision of some countries to pursue a strategy of generating current account surpluses, reserve accumulation and self-insurance. Essentially, such a strategy entails becoming a capital *exporter*, contrary to what one traditionally expects of developing countries. But that is precisely where countries pursuing this strategy (China being the most conspicuous example) have ended up. Foreign exchange reserves typically represent claims on other countries — whether they are in the form of currency, treasury bills or other financial instruments.[6] Upending the

---

5   The HIPC initiative emerged from discussions among the Group of Seven (G7) countries during the 1990s. Implementation was spearheaded by the World Bank and the IMF, and involved the reduction of bilateral debts owed primarily to creditor governments. However, the HIPC initiative did not include the reduction of large debts to the multilateral agencies, primarily the World Bank and the IMF, which is why the MDRI emerged subsequently.

6   Such a strategy, it should be noted, also substitutes one risk — that of potentially troublesome external liabilities — with another — that of potentially volatile external assets, such as US Treasuries, which may represent a "safe haven," but one subject to low returns and a depreciating dollar.

traditional pattern of capital flows from advanced to developing countries has been likened to "water flowing uphill" (Prasad, Rajan and Subramanian 2007).

There is, however, more at issue here than a paradoxical upending of the traditional North to South pattern of capital flows. Rather, this goes to the heart of the debate about the role of cross-border finance for investment and development. The rationale of the traditional pattern of capital flows is based on the notion that developing countries are savings-constrained and, therefore, that foreign savings will help fill the gap. But evidence suggests that countries relying less on foreign capital have grown faster in the long run, and countries with high investment ratios and low current account deficits have grown faster than those with low ratios and high deficits. Moreover, developing countries with a higher level of savings for a given level of investment enjoy higher growth (Prasad, Rajan and Subramanian 2007).

There are also other reasons for "why financial globalization has disappointed" (Rodrik and Subramaniam 2008). Notably, foreign inflows have a perverse effect on investment in the tradables sector because they lead to upward pressure on the exchange rate (due to the phenomenon of "Dutch disease").[7] Conversely, higher domestic savings and a reduction in foreign inflows induce a real depreciation. The former scenario leads to lower investment and growth, while the latter leads to higher (ibid.).

Thus, another policy implication for developing countries of international financial crises (including the present one) is that increased reliance on domestic savings is preferable to foreign savings in supporting domestic investment and growth (Commission on Growth and Development 2008). It is no accident that the high-growth economies are precisely those with high investment[8] and high domestic savings rates — so high, in the case of savings rates, that they are capital exporters, China being the pre-eminent but not sole example. However, the evidence seems to indicate a long-term trend toward increased levels of savings in East Asia and the Pacific, South Asia, and the Middle East and North Africa (see Figure 1).

---

7 Dutch disease refers to the currency appreciation that can result from an inflow of capital, or a surge in export earnings, undermining the competitiveness of exports and the tradeables sector more generally.

8 The Commission on Growth and Development's benchmark for 13 high-growth countries was an investment to GDP ratio of at least 25 percent.

Figure 1: Trends in Long-term Savings in EMDCs

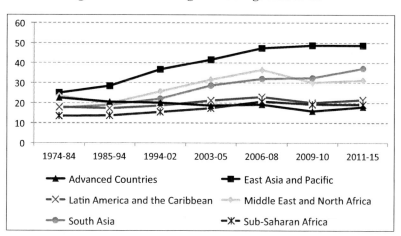

Source: Bhattacharya (2013). Data sourced from Kraay et al. (2000), IMF (2013b) and World Bank (2013b).

In practical terms, the upshot of mobilizing more domestic savings for EMDCs has been twofold: first, the development and deepening of local-currency bond markets; second, greater attention to tax mobilization. With regard to the former, developing country governments around the world have increasingly borrowed from domestic treasury bill and bond markets, initially with short-term maturities, but, over time, gradually lengthening terms to 10 years or more. By 2005, domestic local-currency debt already accounted for 69 percent of the total public sector debt of developing countries (Panizza 2008).

Efforts to increase tax mobilization have, likewise, increased among many developing countries and regions. Higher tax revenues decrease the need for external borrowing (typically with increasing risk of debt distress) and for grants provided by aid donors (typically with policy conditionality and a measure of unpredictability). The scope for increased taxes, even in the poorest countries, is greater than has previously been acknowledged, and is seen as an essential ingredient in state building (Bräutigam, Fjelstadt and Moore 2008). But an area of greatest potential — taxing the wealthy and foreign corporations — tends to be politically sensitive. This issue has global ramifications, since one of the challenges faced by developing countries is the competition to attract and retain transnational enterprises, via tax incentives that can deeply erode revenue streams. In addition, tax avoidance and evasion takes place through practices such as transfer pricing. A recent report prepared for the G20 estimates that between 2008 and 2010, transfer mispricing cost Africa US\$38.4 billion each year, an amount greater than its inflows from either international aid or foreign direct investment (Annan 2013).

Low-income Countries: New Sources of Vulnerability

The current crisis has also revealed new sources of vulnerability, particularly for some low-income countries. First, in the run-up to the crisis, the increasing use of commodity derivatives contributed to volatility in food prices, negatively impacting food-importing countries (see, for example, Clapp 2013a). Second, some countries that are dependent on trade finance were adversely affected by the drying up of this particular segment of the financial sector at the height of the crisis. This led the G20 in 2009 to endorse efforts through the international financial institutions and bilateral export credit and investment agencies to ensure the availability of at least US\$250 billion in trade finance over the next two years. Third, the crisis also exposed the dependence of some countries on workers' remittances from the advanced economies, where the downturn threatened the employment of those workers; however, remittances have proved to be more resilient to these threats than feared (Sirkeci, Cohen and Ratha 2012). Fourth, also in the run-up to the crisis, land in developing countries had become an object of financial speculation, thereby exerting additional pressure, particularly in regions experiencing food insecurity (Clapp 2013b).

CONCLUSIONS: LESSONS FOR CANADA

This chapter has argued that while the most successful (fast-growing) EMDCs have succeeded in escaping the worst fallouts of the Great Financial Crisis and the ensuing Great Recession, other developing countries have been less fortunate. A more complete picture can, therefore, only arise by disaggregating the EMDCs. Latin American countries, with their close international trading ties to North America, have most clearly suffered the effects of the downturn. And while some low-income countries have also registered, on average, surprisingly high growth rates over the past 15 years, this experience is far from being shared, for example, throughout Sub-Saharan Africa. It is true that the emergence of China as a key trading and investment partner has provided a welcome alternative to the OECD countries as a source of demand and investment financing. Nevertheless, there remain some crucial differences between the performance of the low-income countries and the fast-growth Asian countries, both in terms of the pace of growth and its composition. Unlike the Asian countries, the low-income countries do not, as yet, seem inclined toward promoting industrialization as a key part of their development strategies.

It is clear that the most relevant comparators from which to draw lessons for Canada are not the EMDCs, but other advanced economies — namely, the United States, Europe and Japan — as well as countries such as Australia, with which Canada has many more similarities than with the EMDCs. That said, it might be worth considering possible lessons for Canada drawn from the impact of the crisis on the EMDCs. First, and most obviously, the emerging markets' more cautious approach to financial sector regulation and their greater caution regarding "financialization" (i.e., the aggressive financial sector innovations and risk-taking that was evident in the United States and Europe) resonate with Canada's policies. Although it could be said that this is a lesson that Canada did not "need" to learn from the high-growth emerging market countries, it is also perhaps worth noting that the latter did not "need" the degree of financialization common in advanced economies in order to achieve their high-growth performance.

Second, and equally uncontroversially, the Government of Canada already relies primarily on borrowing in its own currency, thereby reducing its exposure to currency risk, exchange rate volatility and the fiscal impact of fluctuating public debt liabilities. Of course, the Canadian economy is exposed to currency risk and exchange rate volatility by virtue of its high degree of integration with private international financial markets.

The prospect of achieving a Canadian version of the emerging markets' policy of "self-insurance" is, however, highly unlikely, given Canada's traditional stance on exchange rate management (namely, that the exchange rate of the Canadian dollar should be determined by market forces). Nonetheless, it could be argued that Canada should actively intervene in currency markets and accumulate foreign exchange reserves in order to prevent Dutch disease, thereby maintaining the international competitiveness of its non-resource sectors.[9]

With regard to lessons from the low-income countries, the discussion above points in the direction of possible policy implications for Canada — particularly for its aid program. First, there is considerable scope for supporting aid recipients in their efforts to mobilize taxes, particularly from foreign corporations operating in developing countries. This was an issue that came before the G20 in its 2013 summit held at St. Petersburg. As mentioned previously,[10] as a result of tax evasion and avoidance strategies, African countries are foregoing tax revenues that amount to more than their aid receipts. Closing tax loopholes and limiting these tax-avoidance strategies could thus have a significant impact on the resources available for development purposes. However, such measures would be helped by the active cooperation of the home countries where foreign corporations are domiciled. Canada is headquarters for a great majority of mining multinationals with operations in developing countries. There have also been discussions in the OECD and the G7 aimed at limiting tax avoidance measures by transnationals. Canada's advocacy of these initiatives, which has hitherto not been evident, would be significant.

Second, Canada and other aid donors can capitalize on the latitude provided by the HIPC initiative and MDRI to move away from the policy conditionality that has characterized aid programs in the past (Radelet 2010). New modalities of aid delivery, such as "cash on delivery" (COD), permit donors to support innovative initiatives by aid recipients that deliver results, without the need for policy conditionality. Although the COD approach was conceived for concrete deliverables through specific aid projects, there is no reason why it could not also be applied to program aid and budget support, if the "deliverable" included job creation, lower levels of inequality or higher levels of growth (Birdsall et al. 2011). Among other things, this would enable donors to support industrial policies or strategies adopted by aid recipients.

---

9   Using Norway as a model, it could also be argued that Canada should develop a sovereign wealth fund based on its oil and natural resource income. Some emerging market countries (Chile, for example) have also established similar resource funds to ensure that the proceeds of depleting natural assets can be available for future generations and to have an extra-budgetary instrument for counter-cyclical fiscal policy. However, this idea goes considerably beyond that of "self-insurance."

10 See footnote 6.

Finally, other chapters in this volume (see chapters 4, 5 and 6) address Canada's active role in developing the regulatory and institutional reforms needed to respond to the current crisis. Some of the initiatives that were undertaken through the G20 — for example, increasing the resources of the IMF and multilateral banks, and assuring an adequate flow of trade credits — were of obvious importance to EMDCs. This chapter highlights the crucial importance for the EMDCs of a system of global financial governance that meets their needs, which are different from the advanced economies. Since the developing country debt crises beginning in the 1980s, there have been a series of initiatives to reform the international financial architecture and to provide options for debt restructuring and reduction. Canada has been an enthusiastic participant in these initiatives, in particular through the IMF, World Bank and Paris Club (the forum in which bilateral debts are restructured). It has been an advocate of debt relief for the poorest countries, leading to the HIPC initiative in the 1990s and the MDRI in 2005. It has been an active player in the G7, and was a prime mover in the creation of the G20 Finance Ministers in the wake of the Asian financial crisis (see chapter 4 in this volume), an initiative that was explicitly aimed at bringing the leading emerging market countries to the table along with the advanced economies of the G7.

Canada has also been vocal about the need to make the Bretton Woods institutions more representative at the highest levels. In particular, Canada has endorsed merit-based appointments to the chief executive positions at the IMF and World Bank, in place of the established tradition whereby the managing director of the IMF is drawn from a European country while the president of the World Bank is nominated by the United States. Although recent appointments to these positions have not broken that mould, Canada's continuing advocacy of a more representative governance structure — going beyond the issue of how the chief executives are appointed — is crucial to help preserve the legitimacy of the international financial institutions. Modest increases in the quota and voting shares of the BRICS countries (Brazil, Russia, India, China and South Africa) in the IMF and World Bank, respectively, have reduced the degree of overrepresentation of advanced European countries and the United States, but have, nevertheless, resulted in the BRICS continuing to be significantly underrepresented, in view of their larger share of global GDP.[11]

Acknowledgements

I am grateful to several individuals for their comments on an earlier draft, including Gerry Helleiner, Eric Helleiner and participants in the Canada Among Nations authors' workshop held in Waterloo, Ontario in December 2013.

WORKS CITED

Akyüz, Yilmaz. 2010. "The Management of Capital Flows and Financial Vulnerability in Asia." In *Time for a Visible Hand: Lessons from the 2008 World Financial Crisis*, edited by Stephany Griffith-Jones, José Antonio Ocampo and Joseph E. Stiglitz, Chapter 12. Oxford: Oxford University Press.

———. 2013. "Waving or Drowning? Developing Countries after the Financial Crisis." South Centre Research Paper 48. Geneva, June.

Annan, Kofi. 2013. "G20: How Global Tax Reform Could Transform Africa's Fortunes." *The Guardian,* September 5. www.africaprogresspanel.org/g20-how-global-tax-reform-could-transform-africas-fortunes/.

Bhattacharya, Amar. 2013. "Challenges and Opportunities in the Emergence of the BRICS." Presentation to the G78 Annual Policy Conference, Ottawa, September 27.

Birdsall, Nancy and William Savedoff, with Ayah Mahgoub and Katherine Vyborny. 2011. *Cash on Delivery: A New Approach to Foreign Aid.* Washington, DC: Center for Global Development.

Bloomberg Personal Finance. 2013. "Emerging Nations Save $2.9 Trillion Reserves in Rou." *Bloomberg Personal Finance,* September 4. www.bloomberg.com/news/2013-09-04/emerging-nations-save-2-9-trillion-reserves-in-rout-currencies.html.

---

11 There is, for example, the distinct prospect of the establishment of the BRICS Development Bank. While there is enough "room" for another international financial institution, given the enormous financing needs of the EMDCs, the advent of this new entity may heighten the concerns about the legitimacy of the existing international financial institutions.

Bräutigam, Deborah, Odd-Helge Fjelstadt and Mick Moore, eds. 2008. *Taxation and State-Building in Developing Countries: Capacity and Consent.* Cambridge: Cambridge University Press.

Clapp, Jennifer. 2013a. "Banks on the Counter-attack in the Food and Finance Debate." February 15. http://triplecrisis.com/banks-on-the-counter-attack-in-the-food-and-finance-debate/.

———. 2013b. "Financialization, Distance and Global Food Politics." Paper presented at Food Sovereignty: A Critical Dialogue conference, Yale University, September 14-15. www.yale.edu/agrarianstudies/foodsovereignty/pprs/5_Clapp_2013.pdf.

Commission on Growth and Development. 2008. *The Growth Report: Strategies for Sustained Growth and Inclusive Development.* Washington, DC: World Bank.

Financial Times. 2013. "European Groups Buffeted by Emerging Market Currency Volatility." *Financial Times*, October 1.

———. 2014. "Rate Rises Fail to Staunch EM Currency Sell-off." *Financial Times*, January 29.

Gokarn, Subir. 2013. "Strengthening Macroeconomic Frameworks: The Indian Experience." In *New Paradigms for Financial Regulation: Emerging Market Perspectives,* edited by Masahiro Kawai and Eswar S. Prasad. Tokyo: Asian Development Bank Institute, and Washington, DC: Brookings Institution Press.

Harrison, Ann and Claudia Sepulveda. 2011. "Learning from Developing Country Experience: Growth and Economic Thought Before and After the 2008-9 Crisis." Policy Research Paper 5752, August. Washington, DC: World Bank.

IMF. 2012. *World Economic Outlook: Coping with High Debt and Sluggish Growth.* October. Washington, DC: IMF.

———. 2013a. "Global Impact and Challenges of Unconventional Monetary Policies." IMF Policy Paper, October.

————. 2013b. *World Economic Outlook: Hopes, Realities, and Risks.* April. Washington, DC: IMF.

Kraay, Aart, Norman Loayza, Luis Servén and Jaume Ventura. 2000. "Country Portfolios." Economics Working Papers 913. Universitat Pompeu Fabra: Department of Economics and Business.

Mishkin, Frederic M. 2006. *The Next Great Globalization: How Disadvantaged Nations Can Harness Their Financial Systems to Get Rich.* Princeton and Oxford: Princeton University Press.

Ocampo, José Antonio, Stephany Griffith-Jones, Akbar Noman, Ariane Ortiz, Juliana Vallejo and Judith Tyson. 2010. "The Great Recession and the Developing World." Paper for a conference on Development Cooperation in Times of Crisis and on Achieving the MDGs, Madrid, June 9-10.

Panizza, Ugo. 2008. "Domestic and External Public Debt in Developing Countries." UNCTAD Discussion Papers No. 188, March.

Prasad, Eswar, Raghuram Rajan and Arvind Subramaniam. 2007. "The Paradox of Capital." *Finance and Development* 44 (1).

Radelet, Steven. 2010. *Emerging Africa: How 17 Countries are Leading the Way.* Washington, DC: Center for Global Development.

Rodrik, Dani and Arvind Subramaniam. 2008. "Why Did Financial Globalization Disappoint?" *IMF Staff Papers* 56: 112–38. doi:10.1057/imfsp.2008.29.

Sirkeci, Ibrahim, Jeffrey H. Cohen and Dilip Ratha. 2012. *Migration and Remittances in the Global Financial Crisis and Beyond.* World Bank e-library.

Spence, Michael. 2011. *The Next Convergence: The Future of Economic Growth in a Multispeed World.* New York: Farrar, Straus and Giroux.

United Nations. 2013. *World Economic Situation and Prospects 2013.* New York: United Nations.

World Bank. 2013a. *Africa's Pulse.* Vol. 8. October.

————. 2013b. *World Development Indicators.*

12

The Contours of the Post-financial Crisis Global Political Economy

Randall Germain

• • • • • • • • • • • • • • • • •

INTRODUCTION: FINANCIAL GLOBALIZATION AFTER THE CRISIS

A strange thing has happened since 2007: the world economy has become less connected and seemingly less economically integrated on a global basis. Many of the principal measurements of economic globalization, such as international trade and capital flows, are either lower today than prior to the financial crisis or no higher in absolute terms, and thus lower as an overall proportion of economic activity (DHL 2012).[1] These developments suggest that, as a global phenomenon, further increases in economic integration, and

---

1   The DHL report examines global connectedness along four dimensions of cross-border activity categorized in terms of depth (how much) and breadth (where): trade flows, capital flows, information flows and people flows. Its main finding is that nearly all measures of global connectedness have fallen since 2007 and now stand at the same level as 2005. A recent review in *The Economist* (2013c) of the world economy comes to the same conclusion. For example, total global trade (merchandise and services) has fallen from 30 percent of world GDP in 2007 to 25 percent in 2012, while world foreign direct investment flows as a percentage of world GDP have fallen by 50 percent in just over a decade, peaking at almost 4.5 percent in 2000, but now standing at just under two percent. Similarly, total world capital flows stood at nearly US$12 trillion in 2007, but were just over US$3 trillion in 2012.

especially financial globalization of the kind we have experienced over the past half century, may be at an end.

After more than five decades, the global political economy has become much less hospitable to the trends of increasing liberalization and globalization. Led by the recalibration of relations between the state and global finance in the advanced industrialized economies, an enlarged regulatory footprint for the state, and by the determination of states in key emerging market economies (EMEs) to keep their financial institutions on a shorter regulatory and political leash than is the norm in the industrialized North, we are moving toward a reformulation of the parameters of financial globalization. A central tenet of this development is the pursuit of a "constrained finance" model of financial institutions, which is distinguished from the "finance unleashed" model of the previous era. We are now entering an era of constrained and/or reduced levels of globalization and liberalization, and this will influence the content of political debates over the next decade.

POLITICAL ECONOMY AND GLOBAL FINANCE

A complex phenomenon such as the global financial crisis of 2008-2009 contains many different dimensions worthy of analysis. There are two conjunctural developments which, in effect, bookend the crisis. The first is at work in advanced industrial economies and involves the changing relationship between state and market in the specific form of the regulatory footprint of the state. Here, the key focus is on the particular ways in which state regulatory agencies oversee and regulate financial markets and institutions at the national level. It is at this level where the strongest and clearest relationship exists between the resources available to regulatory agencies and the statutory authority they possess in relation to the activities they carry out. The international level is not unimportant to this relationship, but in many respects it follows from and helps to reinforce national level activities. The political economy of financial globalization cannot be considered apart from its national base and the state-market relations that constitute that base in large, industrialized economies. How those relations are changing has a marked bearing on the scope of financial globalization.

The second conjuncture is at work in EMEs and concerns their changing reach or leverage within the world economy, as exemplified most significantly by the BRICS (Brazil, Russia, India, China and South Africa) nations. As these emerging economies grow in relation to industrialized northern economies, they are shifting the major currents of economic transactions from a long-established North-North or North-South flow, to a South-North or even South-South flow. Thus, China has become the largest trading partner for a number of emerging (and industrialized) economies, which generates enhanced leverage over economic bargaining in bilateral and multilateral fora for the Chinese state. Given the form of capitalism and market economies practised in these countries, what is at stake now is whether the existing liberal international order will continue to be multilateral in form or evolve in ways that more closely approximate the political economy models of the BRICS economies and their analogues, which reflect a much heavier presence of the state.

Both of these conjunctures are at work today, making their intersection and its consequences a potent source of change in the global political economy. For example, post-2007 regulatory changes among key financial powers, such as the United States and United Kingdom, are recasting the weight of financial systems in their economies, which are smaller today than prior to the financial crisis. Similarly, the growing prominence of BRICS economies in the global economy has taken off since 2000, when their growth trajectories suddenly became elevated compared to Group of Seven (G7) economies. In terms of both established and rising economic powers, a recalibrated regulatory capacity of the state has become a central dynamic driving the global political economy forward.

This dynamic is clearly visible in the advance of the constrained finance model of financial institutions, as distinct from the finance unleashed model that prevailed over the past three plus decades. The constrained finance model is a depiction of financial institutions that see their activities much more closely monitored and even controlled by state regulators or authorities. Whether this refers to how much capital these institutions must hold, how they are to structure themselves and their various units, or even what kinds of activities they can perform, this model of finance allows regulatory agencies a much greater say over what institutions do within financial systems and how they are organized, including how they structure their international operations. In some formulations, it is also about direct state control or ownership of financial institutions, although this is more pronounced in developing economies and EMEs than in advanced industrialized economies. The main point in identifying a constrained finance model is to recognize not only that states are adding capacity to their regulatory activities, but that these activities are reaching into and having an impact upon the institutional fabric of financial systems.

The constrained finance model may be contrasted with the finance unleashed model, which was at the heart of the progressively liberalized financial systems of the pre-2007 era. Finance unleashed required less capital to be held by institutions, it gave greater reign to innovation in financial instruments and, above all, it provided for a larger degree of self-surveillance in the application of regulatory rules and codes of conduct, including in the implementation of risk management systems. Today, among both industrialized and emerging economies, this model has been eclipsed, albeit in different and uneven ways. By contrasting finance unleashed with constrained finance, global political developments can be linked up with regulatory efforts in particular nation-states that are making the world less hospitable to further advances in financial globalization. Though these developments are not free of tensions and problems, they do suggest a future marked out by lowered global connectedness levels.

THE GLOBAL POLITICAL ECONOMY OF THE FINANCIAL CRISIS: FROM THE G7 TO THE BRICS COUNTRIES

The financial crisis prompted a sustained response across industrialized economies that have redrawn the relations between financial institutions and states. These responses have resulted in an enlarged and deepened regulatory footprint that places more constraints on what financial institutions can do and how they are run.

In the United States, the legislative core of its response to the financial crisis is contained in the 2010 Dodd-Frank Wall Street Reform and Consumer Protection Act, which has two major components (US Securities and Exchange Commission 2010). The first streamlines and brings more coherence to a relatively fragmented system of financial oversight by making the Federal Reserve Board the principal agency responsible for systemic risk, giving it enhanced supervisory functions and establishing a national council of regulators to close supervisory gaps. Second, Dodd-Frank brings all systemically significant financial institutions under the purview of the Fed, and gives it increased power to regulate what kinds of activities banks can undertake. This includes the application of the "Volcker rule," which now guides how banks are able to undertake proprietary trades, capitalize their special investment vehicles, and invest in hedge funds and private equity firms.[2] The Volcker rule is having a significant effect on banks, a number of which have already wound down their proprietary trading desks and released large numbers of employees.[3] With the vetting powers that the new consumer protection agency will have for financial instruments, the Dodd-Frank legislation is enabling regulators to pay more attention to what banks actually do in those areas that formerly received less scrutiny.

In the United Kingdom and European Union, similar regulatory trajectories are underway. Both jurisdictions are moving to unify or harmonize financial regulation, albeit in different ways. In the United Kingdom, this involves stripping bank supervision from the Financial Services Authority and returning it to the Bank of England. In the European Union, this involves creating new regulatory institutions and EU-wide systemic councils to oversee banking supervision and risk management. In both cases, these developments emerged out of reviews of how regulatory authorities came up short in the run-up and in their responses to the financial crisis (Turner 2009; de Larosière 2009). The United Kingdom is also moving toward ring-fencing the domestic retail operations of UK-based banks, which will impose considerable costs on how British banks are organized, as compared to their international competitors (Her Majesty's Treasury 2012; Jenkins et al. 2011; Jenkins and Wilson 2013), while pressure has mounted over the past two years within the European Union to establish a euro-zone-wide banking union, limits on how much bankers are paid, restrictions on how credit ratings agencies operate and a financial transaction tax (Barker and Spiegel

---

2   The so-called Volcker rule is the stipulation in the Dodd-Frank Act that details how banks are to organize and run their proprietary trading operations. Its main thrust is to significantly reduce that subset of proprietary trading not directly linked to the needs of a bank's customers or a bank's market-making activities.

3   See US Treasury (2011) for the preliminary report. Reaction from major banks has been detailed in *The New York Times* and *The Wall Street Journal* (see McGrane and Lucchetti 2011; Norris 2011). Tett (2009) provides a lively account of the industry and regulatory environment within which financial innovation occurred during the lead-up to the crisis.

2012; McManus 2013; Davenport 2013).[4] Although the exact trajectory of these developments has not yet been completely settled, they suggest that the liberalizing trend of recent decades, marked out by a progressive unshackling of financial institutions from excessive regulatory oversight, is now at an end.

The extent of an enlarged regulatory footprint across northern industrialized countries is matched by its deepening imprint. While transitory in nature, the equity stakes that the US Treasury took in major US banks made visible the direct connections between government and the financial industry, and underlined a critical way in which the financial system is different from most other goods- and service-producing sectors of the US economy. The effective nationalization of Fannie Mae and Freddie Mac has further highlighted this connection (Thompson 2012). This is not a new theme in political economy analyses of the US economy and state (see Helleiner 1994; Panitch and Gindin 2012), but it clarifies how this interconnection has become more pronounced over time.

The state's footprint is also deeper in a second way: by becoming more involved in vetting or influencing what financial institutions actually do, public authorities are having a stronger material effect on the organization of financial systems. This is most evident in the United States with the effects of the Volcker rule. As this rule is being developed and refined in terms of its application, there have been across-the-board reductions in staffing levels at investment banks in the United States (and around the world), including the decision by many banks to get out of the business of proprietary trading altogether (Rappaport and Tudor 2011; Braithwaite 2012).[5] What of the sustainability of this development in light of a resumption of global economic growth? The key points here are the regulatory capacity being built and the international context within which this capacity is emerging. The increased regulatory capacity being constructed in the United States and the United Kingdom looks durable, in terms of the political coalition pushing it along

---

4   Interestingly, the *Global Connectedness Index* notes that 10 of the 12 most globalized economies were European, reflecting the growing integration among EU economies (DHL 2012). It is quite possible that European integration is continuing to grow even as global integration stagnates. This points to the fluidity of the evidence and suggests that political decisions by governments remain at the heart of the process of financial globalization.

5   *The Economist* (2013b, 15-16) has recently estimated that the number of people employed in the banking industry in London and New York is at its lowest point in decades: banking employment in London is down 33 percent from 2007, while in New York it is down nearly 25 percent from a peak in 2000.

and the growing consensus around macroprudential regulation that seems to support it (Baker 2013). It could be claimed that in relation to the organization of finance, the balance of authority between state and private actors has been recast in favour of public authority as a result of the financial crisis.

Looking beyond industrialized states, this claim receives further support. Among EMEs, and especially the BRICS economies, there has been a re-evaluation of the commitment to an international economic order organized around the principles of liberalization (Subacchi 2008). For example, since the financial crisis, many emerging economies have erected barriers to the inflow of foreign capital, halted or reversed liberalization strategies and turned to upgrading the domestic consumption elements of their economies to help wean themselves from an unhealthy reliance on exports.[6] In effect, these countries appear to be moving to embrace a world of shallower globalization, and this will add to the already-stalled program of liberalization signalled initially by the failure of the Multilateral Agreement on Investment in 1995 and followed by the subsequent failure of the International Monetary Fund in 1997 to amend its Articles of Agreement to include full capital account liberalization as a core mandate (Abdelal 2007). What is especially important is that the BRICS and others have begun to erect sturdier defences against the capital mobility that has come to define globalization today, pointing the way toward a global political economy that is more asymmetrically connected than in the past.

We can see this trajectory at work in EMEs such as China, Russia and India. In China, the most important EME, reform of the financial system has been underway since 2000; however, it would be a mistake to characterize this reform as Western-style liberalization. In fact, as China has moved its financial system toward one that more fully reflects market signals, the role of the state in guiding the allocation of credit has remained paramount and

---

6 Since the advent of the financial crisis, Brazil, Chile, Indonesia, Turkey and Korea (among others) have imposed new controls on inflows of capital, but not on outflows. China, India and Russia have slowed or halted movements toward financial liberalization, including efforts to liberalize their currencies (*The Wall Street Journal* 2011; Gallagher 2011; *The Economist* 2013b). From a different direction, a recent legal ruling by the European Free-Trade Association Court that denied the British government's demand for Iceland's government to make good the British deposits of the failed Icelandic bank Landsbanki is another blow to the continued liberalization of global financial markets, with significant potential global ramifications (*The Economist* 2013a). Finally, import restrictions are once again popping up in otherwise trade-reliant economies, such as Argentina (*The Economist* 2011).

foreign competition has remained minimal. The result, as Gruin (2013) notes, is a financial system still characterized by a strong and sustainable degree of financial repression. Similarly, in Russia, despite ongoing official announcements promoting economic liberalization, there are many barriers that remain to developing a genuinely liberal form of state-market relations, and it is unclear at what point these barriers will erode (Yakovlev 2013). Finally, as an economy with a large and persistent current account deficit, Indian regulators view the full convertibility of their currency and full liberalization as some way off into the future, despite the small steps taken over the past few years to introduce more liberal market reforms into India's financial system. As the Reserve Bank of India's Executive Director Shri G. Padmanabham (2013) stated in remarks during the summer of 2013, India can only move at the pace of its Asian trading partners, and that pace is itself constrained by many infrastructural deficits that will not soon be overcome. Similar to key industrialized economies, EMEs are no longer moving to advance liberalization efforts.

Thus, the global financial system should be viewed today as marked by an unstable and precarious balance of forces. On one hand, the centrality of the nation-state and its institutions to the "global" organization of finance appears more clearly delineated than at any point during the past 40 years. One manifestation of this is the United States' continued role as anchor, and a small cohort of financial great powers as the locational site of global regulatory authority. This is the milieu out of which all significant regulatory initiatives arise. Yet, on the other hand, a handful of large emerging market states, less beholden to the precepts of liberalized capitalism and intent on reducing their vulnerability to economic dislocations from industrialized countries, no longer provide a receptive audience to these initiatives.[7] It is the combination of these two features of financial governance that makes the current situation relatively precarious, and therefore well suited to the emergence of a constrained finance model of the relationship between the state and finance.

---

7 This claim dovetails with and supports those arguments that point to the practice of what Walter (2008) calls "mock compliance" in financial regulatory matters among EMEs (see also Mosley 2010).

WHITHER FINANCIAL GLOBALIZATION?

How plausible is the movement from a deep to a more shallow form of financial globalization, and how sustained might this development be? At one level, of course, it should not be surprising that both liberalization and financial openness have come under strain since the financial crisis. Economic growth among advanced industrialized economies has been sluggish at best since 2007, and between the impact of a sovereign debt crisis in Europe and its concomitant policies of austerity, together with a widespread deleveraging among financial institutions from rich countries, it is no wonder that cross-border credit flows have taken a hit. Perhaps we are simply witnessing a pause in the long-term secular rise of financial globalization.

Unlike in the late nineteenth and twentieth centuries, however, today the embrace of liberalization among EMEs is muted at best. Among the BRICS, for example, capital accounts and currencies are actively managed to reduce their economies' vulnerabilities to disruptions in credit flows and, critically, their financial systems are not open to vigorous foreign competition. Financial institutions in these countries and many other EMEs are more strictly subject to the strictures of their governments. Indeed, in all of the BRICS, the largest banks are government owned and financial institutions are not free to allocate capital according to their own criteria, just as their citizens are not allowed to buy and sell their own currencies as they need or want to (except in Brazil). Financial institutions are highly constrained in these countries, and this is where the primary economic drivers of global growth have been since 2007. Thus the model of constrained finance has global resonance.

In a different but equally significant way, advanced industrialized states are upgrading regulatory pressure on their financial institutions and actively shaping them in a way that has not occurred since the early 1980s, when G7 governments pressured their leading international banks to continue to lend to developing countries in the teeth of a severe debt crisis. Through legislation in the United States — and, albeit not quite so forcefully, in the United Kingdom and European Union — state regulators are demanding that banks hold more Tier 1 capital than under previous regulatory regimes, and they are making it much less profitable for these institutions to undertake proprietary trading on their own accounts. None of this means that banks and other financial institutions are closing up shop, but it does suggest that they have less room to manoeuvre under today's regulatory regime, and that the more constricted space that is the financial system in these countries is becoming less hospitable to financial innovation. We may not be returning to an era when finance was the servant, but we seem to have retreated quite significantly from the period when the "masters of the universe" bestrode the economy. A version of constrained finance seems to have become the norm, rather than finance unleashed.

None of this means that globalization is finished or that state regulators have solved all of the problems that capitalism and financial globalization might generate. It simply means that we have turned a corner on one long-established trajectory — increasing financial liberalization and openness leading to a growing degree of financial globalization — and embarked on a new direction that will witness an increase in the explicit politicization of financial institutions and the imposition of further constraints on their activities, size and, ultimately, global reach. This may or may not have a detrimental impact on trade and the continuing development of global production supply chains. As Susan Strange (1985) long ago suggested, and as current trade negotiations appear to bear out, increases in levels of trade can proceed with or without financial globalization, and are driven as much by bilateral bargains as by multilateral agreements.

The development of a constrained finance model is not without tensions. Among both industrialized economies and EMEs, constrained finance can, paradoxically, encourage the parallel development of a shadow banking system — financial institutions that are not formal banks (and therefore not regulated as such), but which nevertheless provide credit to the economy. Dynamics associated with the shadow banking system in the United States were heavily involved in the subprime mortgage crisis, and this continues to be a concern in EMEs such as China. How state regulators move to subject the shadow banking system to formal regulation will be one important test of the constrained finance model (Financial Stability Board [FSB] 2012). It is also the case that in China, in particular, the actual soundness of many financial institutions is not certain (Gruin 2013). Although all of the largest and most active banks are effectively backed by the state, it is unclear how a system-wide liquidity crisis would affect growth prospects for the Chinese economy (and, by extension, the many other economies now more tightly tied to exports to China). All that can be granted is that if such a crisis occurs, it is unlikely that its resolution would include dollops of more financial liberalization.

While this chapter argues that we have turned a corner toward what might be identified as an increasingly *deliberalized* and somewhat *deglobalized* global political economy, there are important barriers to how far this process itself can travel. Key advanced industrialized states, including the United States and the United Kingdom, still have a large set of political and economic stakes in a certain degree of internal liberalization alongside a given level of globalization. Moreover, Europe and North America are so regionally integrated and maintain such a level of trans-Atlantic exchange, that whatever happens globally, they will remain highly interdependent as an economic space.[8] Beyond this, the overlap among the managerial class at the heart of the interlocked trans-Atlantic corporate structure is also a key barrier to the dissolution of globalization within these economies. There is a substructure of class relations that will not dissolve simply because state actors are becoming more interventionist. In a world awash in credit, the result of six years of extraordinary monetary stimulus, the raw fuel of financial globalization, which is credit, will ensure that ample opportunities for its deployment will continue to exist. This chapter does not challenge the continuation of the mode of capitalist accumulation that has driven the global political economy since at least the end of World War II. Rather, capitalism is simply becoming less liberal in its character.

Finally, as financial globalization comes under strain and is even rolled back a bit in the coming decade, we may ask what the implications are for Canada. Most likely, the Canadian economy and Canadian financial institutions will be affected only on the margins. Although Canada is a trading nation, its financial system is relatively small in relation to its economy (by advanced economy standards); thus, innovation and change in how global finance operates has a muted impact in Canada. Its economy continues to be heavily oriented toward that of the United States, thereby ensuring that the degree of liberalization at work in the United States will have a strong spillover effect in Canada. In many respects, Canada's financial institutions already cleave to the constrained finance model, most clearly in relation to the trade-off they have long accepted between heavy prudential regulation and near-certain

---

8 This is an important finding of the *Global Connectedness Index*, namely that regional rather than global integration is on the rise (DHL 2012).

market dominance. Canadian banks have, for almost their entire histories, been content to exchange a heavier regulatory footprint for the guarantee of a captured domestic market, where competition is strictly confined among a select number of favoured institutions. In its financial system, Canada already practises constrained finance, and its history of relative financial stability is perhaps a further clue as to why this model may well resonate in the future among a wider number of states looking to reduce their vulnerability to the crisis-prone effects of a volatile global financial system.

Acknowledgements

I would like to thank the editors of this volume, the participants at the authors' workshop in Waterloo, Ontario, where all of the contributions to this volume were discussed, and especially Juliet Johnson, for providing constructive comments on an earlier draft. All remaining errors of omission and commission are mine.

WORKS CITED

Abdelal, Rawi. 2007. *Capital Rules: Constructing Global Finance.* Cambridge: Harvard University Press.

Baker, Andrew. 2013. "The New Political Economy of the Macroprudential Ideational Shift." *New Political Economy* 18 (1): 112–39.

Barker, Alex and Peter Spiegel. 2012. "Berlin Gives Ground on Banking Union." *Financial Times*, December 13.

Braithwaite, Tom. 2012. "Leaner and Meaner: The New Wall Street." *Financial Times,* October 1.

Davenport, Claire. 2013. "EU Lawmakers Approve Limited Rules for Rating Agencies." *Reuters*, January 16. www.reuters.com/article/2013/01/16/eu-credit-rules-idUSL6N0AKHJ020130116.

De Larosière, Jacques. 2009. "The High-Level Group on Financial Supervision in the EU." http://ec.europa.eu/internal_market/finances/docs/de_larosiere_report_en.pdf.

DHL. 2012. *Global Connectedness Index.* December. www.dhl.com/en/about_us/logistics_insights/studies_research/global_connectedness_index/global_connectedness_index_2012/gci_results.html.

FSB. 2012. *Global Shadow Banking Monitoring Report, 2012.* Basel: FSB. November 18. www.financialstabilityboard.org/publications/r_121118c.pdf.

Gallagher, Kevin. 2011. "Regaining Control? Capital Controls and the Global Financial Crisis." Political Economy Research Institute Working Paper Series No. 250.

Gruin, Julian. 2013. "Asset or Liability? The Role of the Financial System in the Political Economy of China's Rebalancing." *Journal of Current Chinese Affairs* 42 (4): 73–104.

Helleiner, Eric. 1994. *States and the Re-emergence of Global Finance.* Ithaca: Cornell University Press.

Her Majesty's Treasury. 2012. "Banking Reform: Delivering Stability and Supporting a Sustainable Economy." June. The Stationery Office: London. www.hm-treasury.gov.uk/d/whitepaper_banking_reform_140512.pdf.

Jenkins, Patrick, Brooke Masters, Tracy Alloway, Sharlene Goff and George Parker. 2011. "Volcker Plan Shakes up City." *Financial Times,* September 12. www.ft.com/intl/cms/s/0/68870a5c-dd03-11e0-b4f2-00144feabdc0.html#axzz1ZeI7ALZS.

Jenkins, Patrick and James Wilson. 2013. "UK Urges EU to Adopt Banking Reform." *Financial Times,* February 20. www.lexisnexis.com.proxy.library.carleton.ca/hottopics/lnacademic/?shr=t&sfi=AC00NBGenSrch&csi=293847.

McGrane, Victoria and Aaron Lucchetti. 2011. "Volcker Rule Delay Is Likely." *The Wall Street Journal.* http://online.wsj.com/article/SB10001424053111904265504576564623589787108.html.

McManus, Bryan. 2013. "11 EU States to Adopt Global Financial Transactions Tax." *The Globe and Mail*, February 14. www.theglobeandmail.com/report-on-business/international-business/european-business/11-eu-states-to-adopt-global-financial-transactions-tax/article8687026.

Mosley, Layna. 2010. "Regulating Globally, Implementing Locally: The Financial Codes and Standards Effort." *Review of International Political Economy* 17 (4): 724–61.

Norris, Floyd. 2011. "Volcker Rules May Work, Even if Vague." *The New York Times*, January 20. www.nytimes.com/2011/01/21/business/21norris.html?pagewanted=all.

Padmanabham, Shri G. 2013. "Internationalisation and Integration of Asian Capital Markets." Remarks made at the Lee Kuan School of Public Policy, National University of Singapore, July 12. www.indiainfoline.com/Markets/News/INR-is-not-fully-convertible-at-this-stage-RBI/5729938060.

Panitch, Leo and Sam Gindin. 2012. *The Making of Global Capitalism: The Political Economy of American Empire*. London: Verso.

Rappaport, Liz and Alison Tudor. 2011. "Banks Spell Out Deep Cost Cuts." *The Wall Street Journal*, November 2. http://online.wsj.com/article/SB10001424052970204394804577011981981737346.html.

Strange, Susan. 1985. "Protectionism and World Politics." *International Organization* 39 (2): 233–59.

Subacchi, Paola. 2008. "New Power Centres and New Power Brokers: Are They Shaping a New Economic Order?" *International Affairs* 84 (3): 485–98.

Tett, Gillian. 2009. *Fool's Gold*. New York: Freedom Press.

The Economist. 2011. "Protectionism in Argentina: Keep Out." *The Economist*, September 24. www.economist.com/node/21530136.

―――. 2013a. "The Icesave Ruling: In the Cooler." *The Economist,* February 2. www.economist.com/news/finance-and-economics/21571184-court-ruling-over-icelandic-bank-blow-global-banking-cooler.

―――. 2013b. "Twilight of the Gods: Special Report on International Banking. *The Economist,* May 11.

―――. 2013c. "The Gated Globe." *The Economist,* October 12.

The New York Times. 2011. "Adding Up the Government's Total Bailout Tab." *The New York Times,* July 24. www.nytimes.com/interactive/2009/02/04/business/20090205-bailout-totals-graphic.html.

The Wall Street Journal. 2011. "Update on Recent Capital Control Measures." *The Wall Street Journal,* January 7. http://online.wsj.com/public/resources/documents/capital_contro0107011.pdf.

Thompson, Helen. 2012. "The Limits of Blaming Neo-Liberalism: Fannie Mae and Freddie Mac, the American State and the Financial Crisis." *New Political Economy* 17 (4): 399–419.

Turner, Adair. 2009. "The Turner Review: A Regulatory Response to the Global Banking Crisis." London: Financial Services Authority. www.fsa.gov.uk/pubs/other/turner_review.pdf.

US Securities and Exchange Commission. 2010. "Dodd-Frank Wall Street Reform and Consumer Protection Act." Washington, DC: USGPO. www.sec.gov/about/laws/wallstreetreform-cpa.pdf.

US Treasury. 2011. "Study and Recommendations on Prohibitions on Proprietary Trading and Certain Relationships with Hedge Funds and Private Equity Funds." Financial Stability Oversight Council. www.treasury.gov/initiatives/Documents/Volcker%20sec%20%20619%20study%20final%201%2018%2011%20rg.pdf.

Walter, Andrew. 2008. *Governing Finance: East Asia's Adoption of International Standards.* Ithaca: Cornell University Press.

Yakovlev, Andrei. 2013. "Is There a 'New Deal' in State-business Relations in Russia?" *BOFIT Online* 7, May 20. www.suomenpankki.fi/bofit_en/tutkimus/tutkimusjulkaisut/online/Documents/2013/bon0713.pdf.

Canada in the
Global Financial System

James M. Boughton

• • • • • • • • • • • • • • • • • • •

The preceding chapters in this book have explored two main themes: Canada's role in the international financial system (IFS) and the implications for Canada of the global financial crisis that began in 2007. This concluding chapter steps back from the many specific issues to better examine the big picture: what is Canada's role and how is it likely to evolve in the wake of the global crisis?

One point that emerges strongly from these chapters is that the IFS is a complex set of institutions and relationships. Too often, one thinks of it as equivalent to the exchange rate system, which evolved through the twentieth century from the classical gold standard, through the chaos of the interwar period to the dollar-based Bretton Woods system of 1946–1973 and finally to the oft-called "non-system" of the past four decades. Today's system is a far richer complex of institutions, procedures and relationships. In broadest terms, the IFS has three parts.

Part one is the nexus of oversight and support for the formulation of national economic policies: not just exchange rate policies, but monetary, fiscal and even some structural policies as well. Surveillance by the International Monetary Fund (IMF) is the core element. Through usually annual consultations with each member country, the preparation and publication of global and regional assessments, and other activities, the IMF seeks to encourage consistency and sustainability of policies both within each country and among countries and regions. It centres on the consistency between exchange rate and macroeconomic policies, but especially since the 1990s it has been clear that longer-term sustainability requires coverage of a much broader range of policies and conditions. IMF surveillance has expanded accordingly.

The IMF does not act in a vacuum. Beginning in 1961 with the formation of the Group of Ten (G10) as a group of central banks and culminating in 1999 with the formation of the Group of Twenty (G20) as a group of finance ministers, national authorities have acted together to oversee the Fund and ensure that their own interests are promoted. Although such self-selected groups lack the legitimacy of a formally established institution, they have come to be an integral part of the system. Separately, and to some extent in competition with the ad hoc groups, the full 188-country membership of the IMF acts through the 24-member constituency structure of the International Monetary and Financial Committee (IMFC). Meeting semi-annually, the IMFC guides the policies and work program of the IMF and thereby guides the evolution of the system.

On a smaller institutional level, the Bank for International Settlements (BIS) (with 60 central banks as members) and the Organisation for Economic Co-operation and Development (OECD) (with 34 member countries) also offer forums and guidance for financial policies. Regional groups, such as the Association of Southeast Asian Nations and the European Union, hold regular meetings of finance ministers that complement and feed into the work of the global institutions.

Part two of the IFS is the oversight and regulation of national financial sectors. As a main component of the system, this activity is fairly recent. Until the late 1990s, regulation of financial sectors was mostly left to national authorities. The combination of an explosion of financial globalization and the onset of a wave of crises, triggered in part by weak regulatory oversight, rendered international neglect obsolete. The establishment of the Financial Stability Forum in 1999 and its expansion and conversion into the Financial Stability Board (FSB) in 2009 are the key developments in this sphere.

Part three is the handling of sovereign debt problems. The informal Paris Club of official creditors was formed in 1956 to restructure sovereign debts, mostly those of developing countries. The London Club of commercial bank creditors has been meeting as needed since 1976 to restructure sovereign bank debts, often alongside the work of the Paris Club. Other creditor groups, such as the Washington-based Institute of International Finance and the Tokyo-based Japan Center for International Finance, have sprung up to provide ongoing assessments of possible problems. None of these groups is comprehensive. The Paris Club's informal membership has usually covered the great bulk of developing-country debt, but the rise of China and other non-member sovereign creditors has weakened the club to some extent.

The linkage between debt restructuring and policy improvements is of critical importance, and the IMF is again at the heart of the issue. Both official and private creditors depend heavily on the IMF to negotiate policy conditions with indebted countries, with the dual aim of enabling the debtor to service and repay the restructured debt and putting the country on a more secure economic footing so as to reduce the risk of future problems. Beginning in 1982 with the debt crises in Mexico and Argentina, the IMF has been thrust more actively into the role of coordinating the overall management of international financial crises, often including arrangements involving private creditors in the workout through negotiated "haircuts" or other debt service adjustments.

To call this structure a "non-system" is clearly a misnomer, and yet it would be just as wrong to pretend that it is a complete and integrated system. The main difficulty is that each institution tends to be ensiled in its own area of concern and expertise. Procedures exist for information sharing and other forms of informal cooperation between institutions, but each one ultimately has to take responsibility for its own decisions and actions. There is no institution with a mandate to oversee, much less guide, the IFS. By default, the G20 today comes as close as any group to playing this role, but it has neither the legitimacy nor the expertise to do so effectively.

The absence of oversight and coordination is even more striking when one views the IFS as one component of global governance. Finance is, or perhaps should be, the handmaiden of trade; trade is, or at least can be, a powerful engine for economic growth. And sustaining growth and prosperity requires vigilance over broader issues including energy, education, distributional equity, sanitation and health, public safety, peace and the natural environment. Multilateral institutions exist for each of these areas, but without any real connective tissue. As John Curtis explains in chapter 9, the World Trade Organization is largely isolated from discussions of financial regulatory issues, even when those issues have major implications for trade. Again, in today's world, the G20, for all its limitations, is the only body capable of tying the pieces together.

Where does Canada fit into this scheme?

Canada is not and never has been a major power. Throughout most of the second half of the twentieth century, economic and political power was wielded primarily by the United States and the Soviet Union. The economic strength of Germany and the gradual financial and economic integration of Europe eventually put the European Union on a similar footing.[1] The collapse of the Soviet Union and its economic system left a void that has not yet been filled, but the rise of China, India and other large emerging markets has begun to reshape that space. Canada does not have the resources to alter any of those relationships.

The key to understanding Canada's place is that it sits just below the major-power level and just above the United States on the map. It might not be able to demand a seat at the table, but it usually will be invited in because the larger countries will find it useful to do so. Consider the origins of the Group of Seven (G7) as an outgrowth of the Group of Five (G5). The earlier group (France, Germany, Japan, the United Kingdom and the United States) was the only club of advanced countries from which Canada was excluded. It began meeting at the level of finance ministers in 1973, to develop responses to the sudden increase in oil prices and the associated Arab oil embargo. When leaders of the same countries decided to meet at the summit level at Rambouillet, France, in 1975, the host country decided to invite the prime minister of Italy as well. The leaders agreed to meet again in Puerto Rico the following year, and the United States used its prerogative as host to invite the Prime Minister of Canada, Pierre Trudeau. Thus, a group that otherwise would have been very Eurocentric (four of six members) was rebalanced through the inclusion of a second member from North America.

The G7 summit configuration endured for more than two decades, until Russia was added in 1998 to form the Group of Eight (G8). Meanwhile, the finance ministers of the G5, without Canada or Italy, continued to meet through the mid-1980s. When the G5 initiated a series of coordinated interventions in

1 Japan had the second-largest economy in the world from 1968 until 2010, when it was overtaken by China. Throughout that period, however, Japan's international influence was primarily through trade rather than finance.

exchange markets in 1985, Italy was called upon to participate as a member of the Exchange Rate Mechanism of the European Monetary System. That gave Italy some leverage to insist on inclusion in subsequent meetings of the G5. When the ministers began planning for a critically important meeting on exchange rates at the Palais du Louvre in Paris in 1987, US officials agreed to include Italy, but on the condition that Canada be invited as well. That agreement solidified the G7 as the primary forum for discussion of financial policies as well as broader issues of political economy.

Being a mid-level rather than a major power gives Canada a surprising measure of credibility and influence. The major powers often find that their national interests — at least in the short term that is critically important politically — conflict with the global interest, which tends to depend more on longer-term economic stability and strength. Mid-level powers such as Canada are more dependent on the smooth functioning of the global system, and hence their national interests tend to coincide more naturally with the global. As David Longworth puts it in chapter 5 of this book, "Canada's narrow parochial interests...are less visible than those of larger countries." That synergy gives mid-level powers a credibility in international fora that is difficult for larger countries to achieve. Canada seems to have understood and exploited this advantage better than any other mid-level power over a long period.

The only other mid-level country in a position roughly comparable to Canada is Australia. None of the mid-sized European countries (the Netherlands, Spain, Sweden or Switzerland) is a member of the G20. South Korea and Mexico are relative newcomers in the ranks of advanced economies, and the BRICS (Brazil, Russia, India, China and South Africa) are still emerging markets. The other non-major G20 members (Argentina, Indonesia, Saudi Arabia, South Africa and Turkey) have much smaller economies.

Australia's economy is only slightly smaller than Canada's, and it is an advanced economy of long standing. Like Canada, it is a highly active and influential participant in the G20. It does not, however, have an international standing commensurate with Canada's. Historically, Australia participated in the Bretton Woods conference of 1944, but then waited until 1947 to join the institutions that were founded there (the IMF and the World Bank). Canada joined as an original member in 1945, and became the second creditor country in the IMF in 1956, nine years before Australia. Canada has always had a seat on the executive board of the IMF, whereas Australia has shared its seat with South Korea since 2004. Canada was an original member of the OECD when it was established in 1961; Australia joined 10 years later. Unlike Canada, Australia has not been a member of the G7, the G8 or the G10.

Canada thus has a unique position in international financial governance. The key questions are: How well has Canada exploited that position? And what are Canada's prospects for preserving its influence in the years to come?

On many occasions, Canada has made substantial contributions to global financial governance. First, as Eric Helleiner discusses in chapter 1, Canada had a prominent role in the preparations for the 1944 Bretton Woods conference because it took a multilateralist stance and its delegates were bold enough to present a fully articulated proposal as an alternative to those put forward by the United Kingdom and the United States. As the two main protagonists battled for supremacy in the negotiations, Canada offered paths toward compromise that proved to be helpful.[2]

Second, as a contrasting example, Canada almost inadvertently had a major influence on the evolution of the IFS when it insisted on allowing its exchange rate to float from 1950 to 1962 and again from 1970, at a time when IMF rules prohibited floating. Canada acted out of necessity and in response to idiosyncratic circumstances, but its actions demonstrated the general viability of floating long before it became accepted practice (see Helleiner 2008; Bordo, Gomes and Schembri 2010).

Third, in the late 1980s, Canada was instrumental in breaking up a logjam over the resolution of a crisis in excess sovereign debts of low-income countries. Major creditor countries, abetted by senior officials in the IMF and other multilateral financial agencies, insisted for years that forgiving even a small part of such debts would be unfair to other countries that were continuing to service their debts fully, and it would set a dangerous precedent that would give rise to moral hazard. As time went on, however, it became increasingly clear that such a policy was counterproductive and was making it impossible for many indebted countries to escape the shackles of overhanging debts. When it was Canada's turn to host the annual G7 summit meeting in 1988, its delegation made the adoption of a more lenient standard

---

2   For fuller discussions, see Helleiner (2006; 2008) and Boughton (2014).

a central element of the agenda. The resulting "Toronto Terms"[3] called on the Paris Club to arrange for the reduction in present value (not just a lengthening of payment schedules) of qualifying debts of low-income countries.[4] Over time, the Toronto Terms were gradually liberalized to reduce further, and in some cases even eliminate, outstanding debts.

Fourth, in 1999, Canada helped establish momentum for the Financial Sector Assessment Program, which was devised by the IMF and the World Bank with G20 support in response to a wave of financial crises that had been precipitated, in part, by weaknesses in domestic financial systems in East Asia and elsewhere. The major advanced countries envisaged the program as a way to assess and ward off potential problems in emerging market countries, whereas the latter resented being singled out for such scrutiny. Canada's willingness to be the first G7 member to volunteer for an assessment made the program more palatable, and eventually all G7 countries agreed to let the Fund and the Bank assess their systems and publish the findings. When shortcomings in oversight of the US financial system triggered a global crisis in 2007, the relevance and importance of universal participation became all the more evident.

At other junctures, Canada has failed to take advantage of opportunities to take the lead in financial governance. In one little-known but telling episode, Canada repeatedly missed the chance to have a Canadian elected to head the IMF. The first three times that a managing director was to be chosen (1946, 1951 and 1956), Canadian officials were the first choices of either the US or UK authorities, but the government apparently made no effort either to generate broader support or even to persuade the candidates to step forth and campaign. Each time, a European was chosen instead. By the third time, Europe had established a lock hold on the job, and every managing director since then has been a European almost by default.[5] Canada's reluctance to assert itself in this matter not only weakened its own standing, it also

---

3   Paris Club creditors responded to the request from the G7 by agreeing to reduce the present value of the debts of qualifying countries by one-third. Twenty countries benefited from the new policy through 1991, at which time the Paris Club adopted the London Terms with a larger percentage reduction.

4   Canada was not alone within the G7. In 1988, the French and British governments put forward proposals that became known as the Mitterrand and Lawson plans, respectively. Canada's role, as it was at Bretton Woods, was to meld features of the competing plans into a broadly acceptable proposal.

5   This history is explored more fully in Boughton (2014).

contributed to an unfortunate mythology that each managing director *had* to be a European. That tradition, although it has led, on the whole, to a succession of highly qualified and successful leaders at the IMF, has led more generally to a damaging deficit in legitimacy and relevance for the institution, which it is now struggling to overcome.

Canada's failure to obtain leadership at the IMF should not obscure the fact that Canadians have more recently been chosen to head other major multilateral financial institutions. Malcolm D. Knight, former deputy governor of the Bank of Canada (BoC), served as general manager of the BIS from 2003 to 2008. Mark Carney, former governor of the BoC and the current governor of the Bank of England, has been chairman of the FSB since 2011.[6] Moreover, Canadians have often taken the lead in proposing innovations in international financial governance, including most notably the crucial role that Paul Martin played, first as finance minister and then as prime minister, in promoting the establishment of the G20 and its subsequent elevation to the summit level.

A more general and ongoing example of the limitations to Canada's leadership concerns the country's financial contributions to global financial stability. Canada has been a fairly generous contributor to economic development through its official development assistance (ODA) programs. In the latest year of available data, 2012, Canada placed sixth out of 45 donor countries covered by the OECD Development Assistance Committee. Ranked by percentage of gross national income devoted to ODA, Canada placed in the top half (19 of 45 countries). On the financial side, however, it has been no better than average among advanced economies.

As a creditor member of the IMF, Canada contributes proportionally to its quota, along with all other creditors, to each ordinary IMF lending operation. Occasionally, however, the IMF has to borrow from governments or central banks to supplement its ordinary quota-based resources so that it can make large loans to countries facing financial crises. Such lending to the IMF is voluntary and is not structured by quota size. Canada's record is mixed. It has responded to most IMF calls for loans over the years, but the size of its loans has been modest. Notably, in the primary ongoing vehicles for lending to the IMF — the General Arrangements to Borrow and its successor, the New

---

6 In a related, but not financial, position, Donald J. Johnston served as secretary general of the OECD from 1996 to 2006.

Arrangements to Borrow — Canada's participation has been well below its quota share among all contributors. Canada has passed up this opportunity for leadership in an important multilateral arena.

Looking forward, one must anticipate that large changes will occur in the world economy and that those changes will have substantial consequences for international financial governance.

The biggest changes will not be financial, but will have serious financial effects. The growth of the world's population is continuing and is unlikely to end as soon as had been projected even a few years ago. From 7.2 billion today, the United Nations estimates that the number of people in the world is likely to exceed 9.5 billion by 2050 and might not top out until it reaches 11 billion in the next century. The ranks of the elderly will also rise dramatically, and nearly all of the overall increase will take place in developing countries, including the poorest. These demographic trends will overwhelm the current levels of ODA and severely strain the finances of many national governments. As one consequence, international finance is likely to be further destabilized as governments and central banks struggle to keep up with rising demands on limited resources. Similar challenges may be expected from increasing pressures on energy markets, the need for better sanitation and greater access to clean water supplies, and the globalization of health concerns.

One effect of these expected developments is that the bureaucratic inertia that inevitably infects international governance will become even more of a problem. Since the end of World War II, the number of creditor countries in the IMF has risen from one to nearly 50. As that number continues to grow, the notion that a small number of countries can serve as a steering committee for global finance will become ever harder to sustain. The G20 will not expand to keep pace, because it would soon become (if it is not already) too unwieldy and too diverse in the interests it encompasses to be effective.

Pressures on the continued role and even existence of the G20 will have profound consequences for global financial governance. The establishment of the G20 finance ministers in 1999 fundamentally transformed the IFS in an unanticipated and unsustainable way. Previously, various groups would caucus prior to the plenary IMF meetings, and differences in their positions would be resolved through consensus building at the general meetings. In the 1990s, the G7 and the Group of Twenty-Four (G24) developing countries were the primary configurations, although other groups such as the British-led Commonwealth of Nations also regularly developed common positions on issues of particular interest.

The G7 was by far the most cohesive and powerful of these pre-G20 groups, but it still had to take the views of the rest of the world into account if it needed collective action to achieve a goal. The clearest example of this need occurred at a meeting of the Interim Committee (the predecessor of the IMFC) in Madrid in September 1994. The G7 wanted the committee to approve a special allocation of special drawing rights for the benefit of countries that had recently become IMF members, primarily those that had emerged from the ashes of the Soviet Union or were making a transition from central planning to market economics. The G24 insisted that any such allocation keep open the option for a subsequent general allocation for all countries. The G7 refused, and the proposal was abandoned.[7]

In a G20-dominated world, if a compromise proposal could have been developed within the G20, approval by the IMFC would have been virtually assured, because the G20 alone controls more than 75 percent of the total voting power.[8] Today, the IMFC has been reduced to little more than an echo chamber in which the G20 agenda is ratified and translated into an IMF work program. This relationship is neither desirable nor sustainable.

As Barry Carin notes in chapter 3, the G20 is likely to contract over time so that it can represent the shared interests of advanced economies more effectively. As that happens, new competing groups should arise to represent the shared interests of emerging markets, low-income countries and limited geographic regions. In that scenario, the global multilateral financial institutions, with their advantageous constituency structure and their disadvantageous reliance on bureaucracy and formal rules, will have to adapt so as to regain enough credibility and effectiveness to retake the reins from the ad hoc country groups.

A second consequence is that the absence of a comprehensive structure for global financial governance will become even more of a hindrance than it is

---

7 The special allocation was finally approved in 1997 as part of a large general allocation, in line with G24 demands. Ratification was not completed until 2009. See Boughton (2012, 764–73).

8 As of the end of 2013, the 19 countries that are G20 members held 63.4 percent of the voting power in the IMF board of governors. The other members of the European Union — the final member of the G20 — held 13.6 percent, for a total of 77 percent.

today. If issues ranging from climate change to income inequality to security all have major effects on international financial flows, institutions such as the IMF and the World Bank cannot be expected to assume responsibility for preserving stability and ensuring good governance. The United Nations and the G20 are the only bodies that can even pretend to oversee the system in its entirety, but the inadequacies of each are abundantly clear. Whether it is reasonable to envisage an overarching global institution that is both legitimate and effective enough to overcome the insularity of today's multilateral institutions remains to be seen. What these projections mean for Canada is that opportunities will arise to guide the IFS toward greater stability and effectiveness, but those opportunities will become harder to seize. Canada's voice could become increasingly diluted as more countries gain seats at the table. For G8 summit meetings, Canada serves as host country once every eight years. Such opportunities come far less frequently in the G20. Nonetheless, as discussed above, Canada has historical, cultural and geographic advantages that still exceed those of any other country except for the five major powers. As the BRICS and other fast-growing countries find and assert their own voices in discussions of the future of the IFS, the quiet and self-effacing approach that Canada has always favoured may no longer be sufficient if it wishes to continue to be a positive force for the global good.

One avenue for Canada to make a positive contribution to the future evolution of the system, consistent with its national character and experience, is through promoting the voice and representation of smaller and poorer countries. That voice and representation ("chairs and shares," in the evocative phrase popularized by Ted Truman [2006]) has long been sidetracked for a variety of reasons, ranging from ineffectiveness and lack of coordination by the affected countries to indifference and hostility on the part of larger and richer countries. This shortcoming in the IFS, always a serious one, has been severely aggravated by the rise of the G20 as a powerful voice for the large and the rich. Canada is well positioned to speak up for the disadvantaged and to help find solutions, given its history of active concern and its long experience in the IMF and the World Bank as the head of a constituency that includes a number of very small Caribbean nations.

More generally, Canada can help restore systemic balance by promoting a return to the caucusing procedures that prevailed before the rise of the G20. It is important for the IMFC to regain a measure of independence so that the informal rule of the large countries can be tempered by more global considerations and so that policy decisions can be validated by the legitimacy of the formal institutions. That outcome depends, in part, on actions by the IMFC to increase its own effectiveness, but it also depends on having a range of views and concerns presented to the committee — not just those of the G20 — so that it can do its job properly. In the coming years, as discussed above, the G20 will come under internal pressure to contract. That will create opportunities for Canada, as a mid-level but influential player within the corridors of power, to help close some of the gaps in the IFS.

WORKS CITED

Bordo, Michael, Tamara Gomes and Lawrence Schembri. 2010. "Canada and the IMF: Trailblazer or Prodigal Son?" *Open Economics Review* 21 (2): 309–33.

Boughton, James M. 2012. *Tearing Down Walls: The International Monetary Fund 1990–1999.* Washington: IMF.

———. 2014. *Boxing with Elephants: Can Canada Punch above Its Weight in Global Financial Governance?* CIGI Papers No. 28.

Helleiner, Eric. 2006. *Towards North American Monetary Union? The Politics and History of Canada's Exchange Rate Regime.* Montreal & Kingston: McGill-Queens University Press.

———. 2008. "Ambiguous Aspects of Bretton Woods: Canadian Exchange Rate Policy in the Marshall System, 1950-62." In *Orderly Change: International Monetary Relations since Bretton Woods,* edited by David M. Edwards. Ithaca: Cornell University Press.

Truman, Edwin M. 2006. "Rearranging IMF Chairs and Shares: The Sine Qua Non of IMF Reform." In *Reforming the IMF for the 21st Century,* edited by Edwin M. Truman, 201–32. Washington, DC: Peterson Institute for International Finance.

Contributors

• •

James Boughton, a Centre for International Governance Innovation (CIGI) senior fellow, is a former historian with the International Monetary Fund (IMF), a role he held from 1992 to 2012. From 2001 to 2010, he also served as assistant director in the Strategy, Policy, and Review Department at the IMF. From 1981 until he was appointed historian, he held various positions in the IMF's Research Department. Before joining the IMF, James was professor of economics at Indiana University and worked as an economist in the Monetary Division at the Organisation for Economic Co-operation and Development (OECD) in Paris.

Barry Carin has served in a number of senior official positions in the Government of Canada and played an instrumental role in developing the initial arguments for the Group of Twenty (G20) and a leaders' level G20. A senior fellow at CIGI, Barry brings institutional knowledge and experience to his research on the G20, international development, energy and climate change.

Roy Culpeper is a distinguished research fellow of The North-South Institute (NSI), senior fellow of the University of Ottawa's School of International Development and Global Studies, adjunct professor at the Norman Paterson School of International Affairs (NPSIA) at Carleton University and a fellow of the Broadbent Institute. He was previously president and CEO of the NSI. Earlier in his career, he was an official at the World Bank in Washington, DC, the Departments of Finance and External Affairs in Ottawa, and the Planning Secretariat of the Government of Manitoba. Roy obtained his Ph.D. in economics at the University of Toronto.

He has published widely on the issues of international development, finance and global governance.

John Curtis is currently a senior fellow at the C. D. Howe Institute and at the International Centre for Trade and Sustainable Development, an adjunct professor at Queen's University, and teaches international economic policy at NPSIA. John has worked in the public service of Canada for 35 years, as the founding chief economist of the Department of Foreign Affairs and International Trade, and earlier in a number of economic policy positions in several departments. With a strong interest in Asia over the years, he spent two years with the IMF on Asian economic matters and some years later played a major role in the development of the Asia-Pacific Economic Cooperation forum, serving as the founding chair of its Economic Committee. John has an undergraduate degree from the University of British Columbia and holds a Ph.D. in economics from Harvard University.

Randall Germain is professor of political science at Carleton University. His research examines the political economy of global finance and theoretical developments in international political economy. Among his publications are *The International Organization of Credit* (Cambridge, 1997) and *Global Politics and Financial Governance* (Palgrave, 2010).

James A. Haley is the executive director for Canada at the Inter-American Development Bank, in Washington, DC. Prior to his appointment in September 2012, he was director of the Global Economy Program at CIGI. James moved to CIGI from the Department of Finance in Ottawa, where he held a series of increasingly senior positions with responsibilities for the budget and international trade and financial affairs. As Director General of the International Trade and Finance Branch, he represented Canada in numerous Group of Seven (G7), G20 and OECD working groups. In addition to his tenure with the Government of Canada, he has served as research director for the International Department of the Bank of Canada (BoC), staff member of the IMF, and as a lecturer at NPSIA.

Eric Helleiner is Faculty of Arts Chair in International Political Economy and professor of political science at the University of Waterloo. He received his Ph.D. from the London School of Economics and has taught there and at Trent and York Universities. He is author of *Forgotten Foundations of Bretton Woods: International Development and the Making of the Postwar Order* (Cornell, 2014), *The Status Quo Crisis: Global Financial Governance* *after the 2008 Meltdown* (Oxford University Press, 2014), *Towards North American Monetary Union?* (McGill-Queen's, 2006), *The Making of National Money* (Cornell, 2003) and *States and the Reemergence of Global Finance: From Bretton Woods to the 1990s* (Cornell, 1994). He has won the Trudeau Foundation Fellows Prize, the Donner Book Prize, Marvin Gelber Essay Prize in International Relations and the Symons Award for Excellence in Teaching. He has also been a Canada Research Chair, a CIGI chair and is presently co-editor of the book series Cornell Studies in Money.

Juliet Johnson is associate professor of political science at McGill University, the McGill director of the European Union Centre of Excellence — Montreal, co-editor of the *Review of International Political Economy*, and an elected member of McGill's board of governors. Her research focuses primarily on money and banking in post-communist Europe, as well as on post-communist memory politics. She is the author of *A Fistful of Rubles: The Rise and Fall of the Russian Banking System* (Cornell, 2000) and of numerous scholarly and policy-oriented articles, including in the *Journal of Common Market Studies*, *Comparative Politics*, the *Journal of European Public Policy*, the *Annals of the Association of American Geographers*, *Social and Cultural Geography*, *Post-Soviet Affairs*, *Central Banking*, and *Review of International Political Economy*, among others. She received her Ph.D. and M.A. in politics from Princeton University and her A.B. in international relations from Stanford University.

Domenico Lombardi is director of CIGI's Global Economy Program, overseeing its research direction and related activities. He also serves as chair of The Oxford Institute for Economic Policy and sits on the advisory boards of the Bretton Woods Committee in Washington, DC, the G20 Research Group and the Group of Eight Research Group at the University of Toronto, and the Istituto Affari Internazionali in Rome. Domenico is a member of the *Financial Times Forum of Economists* and editor of the *World Economics Journal*. He has an undergraduate degree (summa cum laude) in banking and finance from Bocconi University, Milan, and a Ph.D. in economics from Nuffield College, Oxford.

David Longworth is deputy director of the Graduate Diploma in Risk Policy and Regulation program in the Department of Economics at Queen's University. Since 2010, he has also been an adjunct research professor in the Department of Economics at Carleton University in Ottawa. Before that, he had a 36-year career at the BoC, including being a deputy governor from 2003 to 2010. In this capacity, David was one of two deputy governors responsible for issues related to financial stability and financial markets. He received a B.Sc. in mathematical statistics in 1973 and an M.A. in economics in 1974, both from the University of Alberta. He also studied at the Massachusetts Institute of Technology (MIT), where he graduated with a Ph.D. in economics in 1979. His most recent publication is "Combatting the Dangers Lurking in the Shadows: The Macroprudential Regulation of Shadow Banking," a C. D. Howe Institute Commentary.

Tiff Macklem will be the dean of the Rotman School of Management at the University of Toronto beginning July 2014. From 2010–2014, he was the senior deputy governor of the BoC. As a member of the BoC's Governing Council, he shared responsibility for the conduct of monetary policy and fulfilling the bank's role in promoting financial stability. As the BoC's chief operating officer, he oversaw strategic planning and coordinated the bank's operations. He was the first chair of the Financial Stability Board's Standing Committee for Standards Implementation from 2009 to 2013. Prior to his appointment as senior deputy governor, Tiff served as associate deputy minister of the federal Department of Finance and Canada's G7 and G20 deputy.

Rohinton Medhora joined CIGI as president in 2012 after having served on CIGI's International Board of Governors since 2009. Previously, he was vice president of programs at the International Development Research Centre. He received his Ph.D. in economics in 1988 from the University of Toronto, where he also subsequently taught for a number of years. Rohinton's fields of expertise are monetary and trade policy, international economic relations and aid effectiveness. He has published extensively on these issues, and in addition to his association with the Canada Among Nations series, co-edited (with Bruce Currie-Alder, Ravi Kanbur and David Malone) a history of development thought and practice published by Oxford University Press in early 2014.

Louis W. Pauly is chair and professor of political science at the University of Toronto, where he also holds the Canada Research Chair in Globalization and Governance. Recent publications include *Power in a Complex Global System*, edited with Bruce Jentleson (Routledge, 2014). He is a fellow of the Royal Society of Canada and currently holds the Karl W. Deutsch Guest Professorship at the Berlin Social Science Centre.

Tony Porter is professor of political science at McMaster University. His books include *Private Authority in International Affairs* (SUNY Press, 1999), co-edited with A. Claire Cutler and Virginia Haufler; *Technology, Governance and Political Conflict in International Industries* (Routledge, 2002); *Globalization and Finance* (Polity Press, 2005); *The Challenges of Global Business Authority: Democratic Renewal, Stalemate, or Decay?* (SUNY Press, 2010), co-edited with Karsten Ronit; *Transnational Financial Associations and the Governance of Global Finance: Assembling Power and Wealth* (RIPE/Routledge, 2013), co-authored with Heather McKeen-Edwards; and *Transnational Financial Regulation after the Financial Crisis* (RIPE/Routledge 2014), edited. His research has focused on institutional changes in transnational governance, with particular emphasis on global finance and on private standards and technical systems.

Dane Rowlands received his Ph.D. in economics from the University of Toronto, and has since been teaching at NPSIA, where he currently serves as director. His primary research interests are in multilateral financial institutions, official development assistance, economic development, migration and conflict intervention.

Eric Santor is chief of the International Economic Analysis Department (INT) for the BoC, responsible for the management and strategic direction of the department, which includes analyzing current and prospective developments in foreign countries and commodity prices, as well as providing analysis and policy advice on global economic and financial issues. His research has focused on issues relating to the international monetary system and global financial architecture, the role and governance of the IMF, and the incidence and effects of unconventional monetary policy. Eric's previous roles with the BoC include economist in the Monetary and Financial Analysis Department, and in increasingly senior positions in INT. He completed his undergraduate degree at Huron College, University of Western Ontario, and his Ph.D. in economics at the University of Toronto.

Lawrence Schembri was appointed deputy governor of the BoC in February 2013. In this capacity, he is one of two deputy governors responsible for overseeing the BoC's analysis and activities in promoting a stable and efficient financial system. As a member of the bank's Governing Council, he shares responsibility for decisions with respect to monetary policy and financial system stability, and for setting the strategic direction of the BoC. Lawrence has previously been assistant professor and associate professor of economics at Carleton University, and visiting research adviser, research director and chief of the INT for the BoC. He received a B.Comm. from the University of Toronto in 1979, an M.Sc. in economics from the London School of Economics and Political Science in 1980, and a Ph.D. in economics from MIT in 1984.

Pierre Siklos is a CIGI senior fellow. At Wilfrid Laurier University, he teaches macroeconomics with an emphasis on the study of inflation, central banks and financial markets. He is the director of the Viessmann European Research Centre. Pierre is a former chairholder of the Bundesbank Foundation of International Monetary Economics at the Freie Universität in Berlin, and has been a consultant to a number of central banks. Pierre is also a research associate at Australian National University's Centre for Macroeconomic Analysis in Canberra, a senior fellow at the Rimini Centre for Economic Analysis in Italy and a member of C. D. Howe's Monetary Policy Council. In 2009, Pierre was appointed to a three-year term as a member of the Czech National Bank's Research Advisory Committee.